Good Reading Material, Mostly Bound and New

Good Reading Material, Mostly Bound and New
The Hudson Library
1884–1994

Randolph P. Shaffner

A Hudson Library Book
The Hudson Library of Highlands, N.C., Inc.
Highlands, N.C.   1994

The Hudson Library of Highlands, N.C., Inc.

Copyright © 1994 by Randolph P. Shaffner
All rights reserved. Published May, 1994
Printed in the United States of America
First edition

Cover photo by Gil Leebrick

Library of Congress Cataloging-in-Publication Data

Shaffner, Randolph P., 1940–
  Good reading material, mostly bound and new : the Hudson Library, 1884–1994 / by Randolph P. Shaffner. — 1st ed.
     p.   cm.
  Includes bibliographical references and index.
  ISBN 0-9640078-3-5 : $13.95
  1. Hudson Library of Highlands, N.C.—History.
2. Public libraries—North Carolina—Highlands—History.
I. Title.
Z733.H932S48 1994   94-6962
027.4756 ' 982—dc20   CIP

∞ The paper used in this publication meets the minimum requirements
  of the American National Standard for Information Sciences—Permanence of Paper for Printed Library Materials, ANSI Z39.48-1984.

*All profits from the sale of this book go to
the Hudson Library.*

To

Miss Gertrude and Miss Dolly

The only good book is an open book.

Contents

List of Illustrations	viii
Preface	ix
In the Beginning: 2500 B.C.	1
Ella Hudson: 1880	3
From Boxes to Bookcase: 1881–83	11
Official Recognition: 1884–94	18
Incorporation: 1895–99	30
Trials and Tribulations: 1900–1914	38
A Home of Its Own: 1915–25	50
Gertrude Harbison: 1926–30	68
Summer Guests: 1931–39	88
Honored Losses: 1940–53	109
A Free Spirit: 1954–72	132
The End of an Era: 1973–74	140
Transition: 1975–79	148
Growing Pains: 1980–84	160
Twins: 1985–93	172
Automation: 1994	190
Appendix I: Librarians of the Hudson Library	202
Appendix II: Presidents of the Board of Trustees	203
Appendix III: Mayors of the Town of Highlands	205
Appendix IV: Members of the Board of Trustees	207
Appendix V: First Books of the Hudson Library	214
Appendix VI: Works by Louise Bascom Barratt	222
Appendix VII: Bascom-Louise Gallery Collection	225
Bibliography	226
Index	246

Illustrations

Main Street, ca. 1890	*Facing page* 1
Whiteside Mountain	2
Short Off Mountain	2
H. M. Bascom	10
The Davis House	10
Samuel Truman Kelsey, Sr.	16
T. Baxter and Eleanor C. White	16
Professor Thomas G. Harbison	17
The First Schoolhouse	17
Albertina Staub	29
J. Jay and Mary Chapin Smith	29
The Smiths on the Bridge	37
H. M. Bascom and Daughter Louise	37
The Hudson Library, 1915	47
The Town-Clock School	48
Lucy P. Elliott	49
Christina A. Rice	49
Gertrude and Dolly Harbison	67
Satulah Road	87
Highlands Inn and the Water Fountain	87
Fourth Street on the "Hill"	108
The Alexander P. Anderson House	108
G. Watson and Louise Bascom Barratt	131
The Bascom-Louise Hotel	131
The Hudson Library with Additions	139
The Hudson Library and Its Patrons	139
Gert McIntosh	147
Betty Service	147
The Hudson Library and Bascom-Louise Gallery	171
The Harbison Home	189
Highlands from Biscuit Rock, ca. 1893	200
Highlands from Sunset Rock, 1993	200

Preface

This book is meant to serve both as a comprehensive history of the Hudson Library for anyone associated with or interested in the past 110 years of its existence and as a readable story for the general public. This twofold purpose has led to conflicts of presentation, because for the former I should have preferred to include the hundreds of volunteers and staff who have escaped mention even by name, whereas the interests of the latter seemed to call for minimal attention to people and issues important to the library but less significant to the public. I trust that the compromise achieved between these two aims of comprehensiveness and readability will prove satisfactory.

This book has grown beyond the scope I first envisioned. Mary Chapin Smith's history of the first fifty years amounted to twelve pages. To keep this history to a practical use, therefore, I have provided a third of it with convenient appendixes, a complete bibliography, and a sizable index for quick reference.

I am grateful to the trustees of the Hudson Library and Bascom-Louise Gallery, to the Highlands Chamber of Commerce, and to several generous patrons for their funding of this book. I also owe my thanks to Jan Chmar, Harriet van Houten, Professor Thomas B. Crumpler, Richard Melvin, and Winnie Hertzberg, who have made a number of useful suggestions. Dr. Barbara Reitt undertook to edit the entire manuscript with extraordinary care. The book has benefited incalculably from her professional familiarity with *The Chicago Manual of Style*, my own bible of composition, and her scrupulous attention to essential details of content and form.

I am indebted to the Hudson Library archives, Harry Wright of the Highlands Historical Preservation Society, Inc., Ralph Morris at the *Highlander*, Lucile Reese, Herbert Rice, Esther Shay, and Earl Young for the photographs and two unpublished poems that appear in the book. Gil Leebrick prepared the photographs with professional expertise for publication. I have had access to the full resources of the Hudson Library, the Town Hall, and the Chamber of Commerce in Highlands, the Macon County Library in Franklin, and the Western Carolina University Library in Cullowhee. At the Hudson Library Carolyn Strader, Annette Herstek, and Virginia Talbot have been of great assistance in locating pertinent materials. I am grateful to Elaine Christian of the State Library of North Carolina for her help in documenting the Hudson Library as the first public library in the state. The following poets have generously given permission to use extended quotations from copyrighted works: Virginia Fleming, Butler Harkins from his own poems and from those of the late Bess Hines Harkins, Dee McCollum, and Jonathan Williams. To my dear wife, Margaret Rhodes Shaffner, I owe a great debt for her fortitude and her unfailing cheerfulness as I did and sometimes did again the most laborious of the tasks needed to publish this book.

In dedicating this history to the Misses Gertrude and Dolly Harbison, I am mindful not only of the values that they have contributed to the library. I am thinking even more of their unyielding integrity in the face of changing times and their endeavors never to lose sight of human values and of the enduring worth of "good reading material," whether new or old. They have proved the truth of the idea that dedication is a word until it takes on human form and becomes a person, and then no word can describe it.

*Good Reading Material,
Mostly Bound and New*

Main Street, ca. 1890

Looking east. T. Baxter White's post office and general store on the right. Notice the telephone pole carrying the line to his store from Seneca, S.C. Taken by R. Henry Scadin. Courtesy of the *Highlander*.

In the Beginning: 2500 B.C.

To hold, as it were,
a mirror up to the big world;
to show the very growth of the little world
in all its forms and pressures
from its beginning to the present;
though it make arrant knaves laugh to scorn,
cannot but make the wise and good
discover their own souls.

*For exploring human nature,
one household is enough.*
—*Quintilian*

The world's first library was established in the third millennium B.C. in Egypt. The first library in Highlands was established four or five thousand years later. The greatest library of ancient times was the Library of Alexandria. The greatest library of Highlands is the Hudson Library. The Library of Alexandria was founded by Ptolemy I shortly after Alexander the Great captured Egypt; it was alleged to have contained seven hundred thousand rolls of papyri. The Hudson Library of Highlands was founded under much more modest circumstances and contains today 19,800 volumes, far fewer than its Alexandrian predecessor. The Library of Alexandria, however, was damaged when Caesar captured the city and was burned to the ground during the great civil war under Aurelian. The Hudson Library of Highlands is still very much alive and can be visited today.

Whiteside Mountain
Viewed from Colonel John H. Alley's house.
Taken by R. Henry Scadin ca. 1890. Courtesy of the *Highlander*.

Short Off Mountain
Altitude 5,054 feet. Taken by R. Henry Scadin ca. 1890.
Courtesy of the Bascom–Barratt estate.

Ella Hudson: 1880

I am only one,
But still I am one.
I cannot do everything,
But still I can do something;
And because I cannot do everything
I will not refuse to do the something that I can do.[1]

The history of the Hudson Library can be said to begin in 1880, the year that Joseph Halleck built Highlands House (later Smith House, now Highlands Inn). In the big world Thomas Edison and Sir Joseph W. Swan were independently producing the first incandescent lamp, and New York's streets were being lit by electricity. Joel Chandler Harris was publishing his now famous tales of *Uncle Remus*[2] in the South, and Dostoevsky's *Brothers Karamazov* was appearing in Russia. Rodin had just completed his *Thinker*, an appropriate beginning to any discussion of a library, since books, as the proverb claims, are the children of the brain.

In this year, 1880, in Worcester, Massachusetts, Mrs. Ella Emmons Hudson, who was suffering from a slight bronchial disorder, decided to visit her elder sister, Mrs. Louise Emmons Wells, in the South to restore her health. In the prime of life yet threatened by her fragile condition, she wished to regain her vitality and experience the joys of a richly unselfish life. She and

---

[1] Guiding principle of Dr. Edward Everett Hale's Lend-a-Hand Society, Boston, Massachusetts.
[2] A century later his great-grandson, Lucien Harris, a well-known painter and library-gallery trustee from Vero Beach, Florida, would establish a second home in Highlands.

many of her closest friends belonged to the Lend–a–Hand Society, a philanthropic organization under the leadership of Dr. Edward Everett Hale of Boston. Dr. Hale was the great-nephew of the famous revolutionary Nathan Hale, who had courageously claimed to have but one life to lose for his country.

A graduate of Harvard, Dr. Hale had founded the Unitarian Church in Worcester and written the now-famous short story, "The Man Without a Country." In Boston he was highly respected for civic improvement and philanthropic projects. It is understandable then that Ella Hudson, with her altruistic turn of mind, was intensely interested in contributing to the work of his Society in Worcester. However, first she sought to regain her health.

Calling the office of Tillman Gaines in New York, she arranged for a train ticket south. Then she took leave of her many dear friends at the society and the Unitarian Church, where she worshipped in Worcester. They wished her a quick recovery; indeed, they fully expected her safe return home.

Traveling to Richmond, Virginia, she boarded the Atlanta & Richmond Air–Line Railroad to Seneca City, South Carolina, where she spent the night. After breakfast she hired a hack for eight dollars at A. W. Thompson's livery stable and began the first leg of a two-day journey to Highlands.

It was an hour's ride to Walhalla, a village surrounded like an amphitheater by towering mountains. While the horses watered, she lunched and climbed to the gallery of the hotel, from where she caught an enticing glimpse of the granite face of Whiteside, the vast back of Terrapin, the shaggy mantle of Stooley,[3] and the bristling head of

---

[3]Stooley, also Stooly, is an early name for Satulah Mountain. These two early forms of the name are used in the minutes of the Board of Supervisors

Rabun before they vanished behind clouds threatening rain. When the journey resumed, the horses strained in the abrupt climb through a tunnel of oaks, hemlocks, and chestnuts overhanging the deeply scarred road. A light rain mixed with water from crystal springs puddled in the ruts, overflowing and cascading down the steep shoulder of the mountain into the gorge. Below roared the torrent of a river.

Descending into a wooded glen, the carriage splashed through a rocky stream and began the long, steady climb over the summits of Stump House, Kadis, and Billings, eighteen hundred, two thousand, twenty-five hundred feet, leveling off at last just under the gray dome of the sky.

The horses stopping to quench their thirst in an ice-cold spring, Ella enjoyed a good home-cooked meal and overnight lodging at the Russell House, a well-known and popular traveler's rest.[4] The ride had been rough and, though breathtaking, exhausting! She was having second thoughts about the wisdom of undertaking such an arduous journey for the sake of health. She fell asleep, however, in the instant that she closed her eyes to rest them, oblivious to the night rain.

The next morning the storm had passed. The driver hitched up the horses, and they forded the Chatooga

---

for the Blue Ridge Township (see District No. 7) in 1880 and following. By 1886 the mountain is called Satooly (District No. 9); and by 1891, Satula (see District No. 4). In an article entitled "In the Mountains," published on April 2, 1880, by the *Franklin Western Reporter*, the mountain is called Stooley.

[4]The Russell House, built by Ganaway Russell as a small house in 1867 and enlarged three times over the next forty years as its popularity increased, was thirteen years old in this year, 1880. It burned to the ground over a century later in the spring of 1988. See the historic plaque erected on site by the Andrew Pickens Rangers of Sumter National Forest. See also "History Buffs, Family Mourn Loss of Russell House," *Highlander*, May 20, 1988.

River. There were times when travelers stayed two or three days at the Russell House after a good rain, waiting for the flooded river to subside. However, Ella was fortunate in that the current was low enough to cross. Almost immediately the road arched into a steep climb, leveled, and fell into a creek crossing. Then began the torturous ascent up a thousand feet in two miles, the carriage twisting and turning and pitching from side to side over the slick sides of boulders in the wet red clay, still slimy from the night's downpour.

At one point near the Georgian turnoff into what is now known as Thompson's Lane or Walking Stick Road, a fallen hemlock blocked the path, and the driver had to wield his ax to remove it. Fording Big Creek several times at the shallows between the falls, the driver faltered only once as the buggy plunged down a steep, wet grade. He had to lock the hind wheels, after which it was still necessary for the horses to hold back. Ella had never imagined travel this arduous.

At long last they reached the narrow pass between Chestnut and Rich mountains. Ella turned to see Big Creek, at an altitude of twenty-nine hundred feet, breaking from its cradle in the first of many falls that descended in frothy leaps to its ultimate escape in a large pool two miles back and four hundred feet below. The clamor of the falls faded as the driver led the horses around the short turn ahead, arriving at dusk in the valley of the river's birth: Horse Cove. Flanked by Sedgy and Stooley, Ella stared immediately opposite into the dark looming face of Black Rock. Its massive shoulders held the gray clouds at bay a thousand feet above her. All at once she experienced the indescribable thrill and chill that such a scene impresses on the minds of newcomers and that time never obliterates.

The climb up the final thousand feet to the little village of Highlands concluded her two-day ordeal. Founded only five years earlier on the roof of the world, Highlands was being promoted by an 1876 brochure as ideally suited to give "health and vigor" and to restore persons suffering from bronchitis, pleurisy, pneumonia, and consumption to a state of complete recovery.[5] Unfortunately for Ella, however, the long, rough ride over the rocks and potholes in the ill-kept mountain road proved too much for her weakened lungs. She had caught cold and, arriving at her sister's home in Short Off community, was hustled off to bed.[6]

Ella had counted on the tonic effects of the higher altitude—the pure light atmosphere—to generate in her a cure, but she arrived worse off than when she had left home. For two months[7] she convalesced, hoping to shake off her affliction, which grew increasingly serious with each passing day. Trying to keep up her spirits, she attended several informal sings at the homes of Mrs. Samuel Kelsey and Mrs. G. A. Jacobs. The town's first piano was causing great excitement in Highlands.

Also the debating society was attracting visitors and townspeople of every age to enjoy or participate in the lively exchange of ideas on Friday evenings. All around her flourished vocal and instrumental entertainment: music, readings, recitations, speeches. Nonetheless, Ella's health constrained her at these popular affairs. She wasn't her usual effervescent self.

---

[5]*The Blue Ridge Highlands in Western North Carolina* (Greenville, S.C., 1876), pp. 2-3. A pamphlet distributed by Samuel T. Kelsey the year after he arrived in Highlands.
[6]Originally known as Short Off, the community's name in 1890 was spelled as a single word: Shortoff.
[7]T. W. Reynolds, *High Lands* (Highlands, 1964), p. 70.

For a time she and her sister found some solace, even excitement, in a plan to provide "good reading material"[8] for the little communities surrounding Highlands. Before their dream could be realized, however, their worst fears became nightmare: Ella Hudson died. For Louise Wells the pain of her sister's swift demise was every bit as intense as that expressed almost a century later by Highlands poet Bess Hines Harkins:

If you know heart-break in these mountains
You will never leave the past,
Whether you go or stay
The hills will hold it fast:

It will float with the mist in the valleys,
It will fall with the falling rain,
It will cry with the birds in the twilight
With the old undying pain.

You will turn from the clouds of the sunset
To brush the tears from your eyes—
The evening star will pierce you,
The frogs and the fireflies . . .

If you know heart-break in these mountains
You will never leave the past,
For the Blue Ridge Hills will hold it
As long as life shall last.[9]

Ella Hudson, age thirty-one, was buried in Mount Hope Cemetery.[10] Hers was the first adult grave near the

---

[8]Mary Chapin Smith, *History of the Hudson Library Association* (Highlands, 1931), p. 1.
[9]Bess Hines Harkins, "Deep Certainty," *Earth Songs* (San Benito, Texas, 1975), p. 24.
[10]The Mount Hope Cemetery Association, founded on November 15, 1880, changed its name on July 25, 1887, to Highlands Cemetery Co., its name

entrance, her headstone bathed each evening in the shimmering golden haze of the setting sun.[11] Her friends in the North, members of Dr. Hale's Lend–a–Hand Society, in their heartfelt anguish donated in her loving memory several boxes of "mostly bound and new" books as a start toward fulfilling her final dream.

These books her sister, Louise Wells, then gave to the town of Highlands in memory of Ella Hudson. They were intended, like everything else proposed by the Lend–a–Hand Society, to put into practice its binding principle:

> *To look up and not down,*
> *To look forward and not back,*
> *To look out and not in, and*
> *To lend a hand.*[12]

---

today, also known as Highlands Memorial Park. Interview with Louis "Bud" Potts, October 17, 1993. See the minutes of the company.

[11]The first death in Highlands was that of Fremont White, the ten-year-old son of T. Baxter and Eleanor C. White on October 16, 1875, only three months after their arrival. He was buried in the forest that covered the hill where Davis House (Lee's Inn) would later be constructed. See Elias D. White, "Early Highlands Days, An Historical Sketch," *Franklin Press & Highlands Maconian,* June 5, 1941. It was in 1881 that his grave was moved to the present Highlands Cemetery and marked by a stone in the southwest corner down the hill from where Ella Hudson rests. His mother's name is misspelled Elinor on his gravestone.

[12]Dr. Edward Everett Hale expressed this rule of the Lend-a-Hand Society in "Ten Times One Is Ten," a poem published in 1870, ten years before the Society's offer of a helping hand to Mrs. Hudson's friends.

H. M. Bascom
Upon his retirement in 1920. Courtesy of the Bascom–Barratt estate.

The Davis House ca. 1900
Louise Bascom plays tennis. Courtesy of the Bascom–Barratt estate.

From Boxes to Bookcase: 1881–83

*These blue mountains are eternity...
Who stays an hour will lose and gain his soul,*

Be greater ever after.[1]

From these several boxes of books grew the first public library in North Carolina.[2] One of the myths that has persisted from the day that the boxes arrived in 1880 has been that the Hudson Library was born from a single box of books. The library still has in its possession seventy of these books in two enclosed sectional bookcases, and they fill six shelves. The original collection would have required a very big box indeed.[3] Although Helen Hill Norris mistakes Mrs. Hudson's older

---

[1] Bess Hines Harkins, "Soliloquy," *Sequoia Bound* (n.p., 1978), p. 27.
[2] The first religious library in North Carolina was a parish library founded in 1700 in Bath. Several university and college libraries existed in the state in the early and mid-nineteenth century, beginning in 1795 with the Louis Round Wilson Library at the University of North Carolina at Chapel Hill. The State Library of North Carolina in Raleigh was the state's first government library, founded in 1812. But North Carolina's oldest, and hence first, public library was the Hudson Library of Highlands. See *American Library Directory, 1993–94*, 46th ed. (New Providence, N.J., 1993), vol. 2, p. 1425. The Macon County Public Library in Franklin and the Lanier Library Association, Inc., in Tryon were the next public libraries to be founded, both in 1890. See also Robert E. Phay, "The Origins of the Public Library in North Carolina," in *The Public Library: A Guidebook for North Carolina Trustees*, 2nd ed. (Chapel Hill, N.C., 1984), pp. 1–2, and Elizabeth House Hughey, "Public Libraries in North Carolina," in *North Carolina Libraries*, vol. 13 (November, 1954), pp. 11–16. Lighthouse service libraries existed along the coast as early as 1876, but their targeted audiences were lighthouse keepers and their families rather than the general public. See Margaretta J. Yarborough, "Library Service to the Strands: North Carolina's Lighthouse Libraries," ibid., vol. 50, no. 1, pp. 27–30.
[3] Conceivably there may have been eighty books in the original collection since a few of the current editions are numbered volumes of an incomplete pair or series.

sister for a daughter she never had,[4] she may not have been too far from the truth when in the same article she narrates her own mother's memory of the library's beginning from, not one, but "several boxes of very fine books."[5]

She describes how Joey Lovingood, a picturesque team driver, was selected to bring the big boxes by covered wagon or "freighter" up over the muddy, rocky road from the express office in Seneca. He was given dire and sundry warnings, Mrs. Norris tells us, as to "what would happen to him if anything should happen to the Library books." Nonetheless, whether slowed by his imbibing a bit too much or by the fact that the back axle "broke plumb in two coming up Pine Mountain," the boxes arrived a day or two late, sent out with loving care from Boston but arriving "a pretty sorry looking mess."[6] Despite the probable accuracy of Mrs. Norris' article, written in 1962, the myth of the single box has persisted to this day.[7] Understandably, of course. But the Lend–a–Hand Society was more generous than that.

As early as 1883, when H. M. Bascom was beginning construction on Davis House (later Lee's Inn)[8] and Is-

---

[4]See "Looking Backward," *Highlander*, July 13, 1962: "The Hudson Library had its beginning through a benevolent-minded, cultured woman from Boston, a Mrs. Hudson, mother of Mrs. Wells . . . ."
[5]Ibid.
[6]Ibid.
[7]See "Box of Books Became the Hudson Library." *Highlander*, April 17, 1964. See also "Journey Begins at Hudson Library," *Highlander*, November 5, 1993: The Hudson Library "started with a single box of donated books."
[8]Davis House was completed in 1890 (see T. Baxter White, "Highlands," *Franklin Press*, May 27, 1890) and named after the adopted mother, Mrs. M. A. Davis, of Mr. Bascom's second wife, Florence Coffin. Mrs. Davis operated it until 1902, when it became the Martin House. In 1937 Mr. and Mrs. Harvey Trice named it Tricemont Terrace. It was the Bascom-Louise under Watson Barratt in 1951. For a short while it was King's Inn II, an annex of King's Inn. Finally, in 1956 it was purchased by Richard Lee, who

lington House (King's Inn after 1925) was being built, the Hudson Library operated from an enclosed bookcase or cupboard of six shelves.[9] It sat in a corner of the main room of the first schoolhouse near the present town hall.[10] Its holdings were approximately seventy volumes, which are still in the library's possession.[11] The public had access to these books only twice a week: on Friday evening during the meeting recess of the Literary Society and from two to three Saturday afternoon. Miss Laura G. Kibbee was the Hudson Library's first librarian.[12]

Laura Kibbee was the nineteen-year-old daughter of Highlands' first physician, Dr. George Washington

---

operated it as Lee's Inn until it burned to the ground in a spectacular fire on December 8, 1982. Eleven years later, on February 21, 1994, King's Inn also was destroyed by an early Sunday morning fire.

[9]Mrs. Hudson's son, on his return to Highlands for a visit in 1939, referred to "the old cupboard, with its six shelves" as containing the original books. See "Mr. and Mrs. A. W. Hudson Visit Highlands," *Franklin Press & Highlands Maconian*, April 20, 1939.

[10]The schoolhouse had been built five years earlier in 1878 at a cost of $300.50. See illustration at the end of this chapter.

[11]For a list of the volumes still held by the library, see Appendix V.

[12]The first librarian of record was Mrs. L. G. Kibbee in the schoolhouse in 1883. See *Blue Ridge Enterprise*, April 19, 1883. Helen Hill Norris claims to the contrary that the records show "that the beginnings of Highlands' present Hudson Free Library had its beginnings in an humble little log house [the Law House] by the side of the road. For in the records, it is noted, Mrs. Kelsey was mentioned as librarian, and books collected, and sent as a nucleus for the library was by no less person than Edward Everett Hale of Boston." See Helen Hill Norris, "First Sunday School 1876," *Looking Backward* (Highlands, c. 1960), p. 47. If this were so, then the librarian would have existed four years prior to the library. The document that Mrs. Norris cites as her source is reprinted verbatim in the *Highlander*, November 19, 1930. In this document, however, it is not *Mrs.* Kelsey but *Mr.* Kelsey who is elected "Secretary and Librarian" not of a *library* but of the newly formed *Sunday school*. Naturally, the document makes no reference to any books collected by Edward Everett Hale of Boston, because it was after Mrs. Hudson's arrival and death four years later that the books were assembled. These facts notwithstanding, Mrs. Norris, like her father and her grandfather before her (Highlands' first elected mayor), spins a fascinating yarn.

Kibbee. It was five years earlier, in 1878, that Dr. Kibbee had moved from New Orleans with his family to Highlands. In the same year his family lost him. Feeling that his hometown needed his help in finding a cure for the yellow fever epidemic that assaulted New Orleans, he had departed and given his life to eradicating the last scourge of the disease as it swept the town.[13]

After his death, his daughter Laura taught at Franklin School, where she married a fellow teacher, Thomas Clingman Reese. Shortly after they moved out West, Tom Reese died. So she returned to Highlands to teach. It was then in 1883 that she also served in the schoolhouse as the Hudson Library's first librarian.

Known affectionately by Highlanders as "Kittie," she was popular as a pantomime at her house, the George Kibbee home (later Chestnut Burr Cottage of James A. Hines, now Nick's Calico Cottage). Twice a month the Glee Club would meet at her home, and a variety of exciting pastimes included an amateur string band, a group of young men debating national issues, prose and poetry recitations, and Kittie Kibbee acting out amusing themes in pantomime.[14]

Leaving Highlands again for the last time, she studied elocution and taught courses in English and expression for a while at Martha Washington College in Arlington, Virginia. In 1922 she was teaching again in the Franklin High School,[15] but sometime thereafter she returned to the West, living first in Idaho, then Washington, and finally California, where a number of early settlers of

---

[13]Dr. Kibbee's death is reported by A. H. Hutchinson, son of Clinton C. Hutchinson, co-founder of Highlands, in "Pioneer's Son Visits Macon," *Franklin Press & Highlands Maconian*, August 31, 1939.
[14]See Helen Hill Norris, "Looking Backward," *Highlander*, July 13, 1962.
[15]See "News of Week of Highlands," *Franklin Press*, April 14, 1922.

Highlands would retire and where in her eighty-third year she passed away.[16]

The library, when Miss Kittie ran it, was a tenant of another organization, in this case the schoolhouse, a situation not uncommon to libraries at the time. One of the greatest libraries in the world, the Library of Congress, was in this year, thirteen years before acquiring its own building, still quartered in the Capitol.

Nevertheless, the little library of Highlands, while newly born, was not yet christened. It existed without official recognition.

---

[16]"Mrs. Kibbee, Ex-Highlands Resident, Dies," *Franklin Press & Highlands Maconian*, February 20, 1947.

Samuel Truman Kelsey, Sr.
Taken ca. 1893. Courtesy of the Bascom–Barratt estate.

T. Baxter and Eleanor C. White
Portraits made ca. 1910. Courtesy of the Bascom–Barratt estate.

Professor Thomas G. Harbison
Taken by Claude Hart in early 1930s. Courtesy of Dolly Harbison.

The First Schoolhouse
Built in 1878. Library room on the left. Courtesy of the *Highlander*.

Official Recognition: 1884–94

I am a millionaire—I own
The starry skies, from pole to pole—
countless gleaming coins
In the treasury of my soul.[1]

In June of 1884, to legitimize the Hudson Library bookcase and promote its future growth and development, a number of prominent citizens met at the schoolhouse to form an official association.[2] Mark Twain would have appreciated the humor of the situation, having just published his *Huckleberry Finn*. We do not know whether the citizens moved the bookcase to a cleared spot in the center of the schoolroom or left it in its accustomed corner as they shifted about in their seats, especially T. Baxter White, who must have found the clumsy, handmade wooden desks intended for school children to be most uncomfortable. We are told, however, that they elected officers and trustees and began to frame for the cupboard a constitution and by-laws.

Mr. Samuel Truman Kelsey, Sr., a co-founder of Highlands, was elected the first president of the Hudson Free Library Association, which today is the oldest civic adult association in Highlands.[3] Elected vice president was Mr. T. Baxter White, Highlands' first settler[4] and first post-

---

[1] Bess Hines Harkins, "Wealth," *Singing of the Heart* (Atlanta, 1943), p. 36.
[2] The month of this meeting is given by Gertrude Harbison in "A Brief History—The Hudson Library," *Highlander*, August 14, 1964.
[3] Minutes of the Annual Meeting of the Hudson Free Library Association, August 5, 1954.
[4] The first settler after S. T. Kelsey and A. H. Hutchinson was T. Baxter White, who "moved into a house without doors and windows" on July 10,

master, a portly gentleman with beard and mustache who operated a general merchandise store and sold insurance on the south side of Main Street, where later the Town House Motel, now Town Square, would be located. Mr. Guy F. Wheeler was chosen secretary, and Mr. W. C. Trowbridge, who ran a sash and door factory, treasurer.

The librarian was Miss Mary L. Sheldon,[5] sister of Frank Sheldon, the architect of Davis House (later Lee's Inn).[6] The first trustees of the library were Samuel T. Kelsey; Reverend James E. Fogartie, pastor of the Presbyterian Church; Charles A. Boynton, Sr., sawmill owner and building contractor; A. S. Esty; and last but far from least, H. M. Bascom.[7] For the next forty years Mr. Bascom, "Town Builder and Merchant Prince of Highlands,"[8] would run the town's hardware and drugstore (currently a service station) on the northwest corner of Fourth and Main, in addition to serving several terms as mayor.

This was in 1884, the year that Grover Cleveland was elected United States President, that Harry Truman was born, and that Captain S. Prioleau and Margaretta A. Ravenel, Sr., of Charleston built the "cream-colored church," as the children knew it, in Highlands, where the bell called them every Sunday to T. Baxter White's

---

1875. See Elias D. White, "Early Highlands Days, An Historical Sketch," *Franklin Press & Highlands Maconian*, June 5, 1941.
[5] Miss Mary L. Sheldon was the second librarian of record, in 1884 and early 1885. *Blue Ridge Enterprise*, January 22, 1885.
[6] Frank S. Sheldon was the architect and builder of Davis House, begun in 1883 and completed in 1890. See "Frank S. Sheldon," *Franklin Press & Highlands Maconian*, February 3, 1944.
[7] Henry M. Bascom was always called "H. M." See "H. M. Bascom Final Rites: Prominent Highlands Resident Dies at Home of Daughter in N. Y.," *Franklin Press & Highlands Maconian*, March 5, 1942.
[8] "Bascom—Town Builder and Merchant Prince of Highlands, Retires," *New York Tribune*, October 21, 1920.

Christian Endeavor.[9] The population of the town at this time stood at three hundred permanent residents hailing from twenty-two states, a truly cosmopolitan mixture.

In 1885, after the now-famous Moccasin War that saw the Billingsley brothers and kin of Moccasin, Georgia, put to rout in their attempt to rescue a fellow moonshiner from the Smith House (now Highlands Inn), the reins of the Hudson Library changed hands. Miss Sheldon left Highlands to become a missionary in India. She was succeeded by Miss Ellison at the library.[10]

During the next few years Samuel Kelsey was engaged in lavishly promoting the little community, enhanced by the Hudson Library, as a delightful summer retreat for "the people of the Eastern States of America." He employed such lures as "the highest incorporated town east of the Rocky Mountains" and a "Paradise of Rest" and touted the temperature as having only once risen to eighty-seven degrees in "forty years of official recording." He waxed poetic in his descriptions, picturing a "mountain Garden bordered by majestic peaks clad in evergreens and far reaches of valleys below stretching to the horizon of foot hills that meet the canopy of azure skies with ever changing panoramas enfolding colors of

---

[9]Interview with Dolly Harbison, September 22, 1993. This was the first denominational church in Highlands; the Presbyterian Church, on the corner of Fifth and Main, was constructed as a memorial to the sister of Mrs. Ravenel. It was begun in 1884 and completed in 1886, two months after the Methodists moved into their completed building in 1885. The first nondenominational services had been held in the Law House and then the schoolhouse from 1876 until denominations were established. See "First Sunday school Record Kept in Highlands Discovered," *Highlands Maconian*, November 19, 1930; see also Elias D. White, "Early Highlands Days, An Historical Sketch," *Franklin Press & Highlands Maconian*, June 5, 1941.

[10]Miss Ellison was the third librarian of record, in mid-1885. See *Highlander*, August 14, 1885, where she is mentioned only by her last name. For Mary Sheldon's foreign mission work, see "Death of Mrs. Olive M. Sheldon," *Franklin Press*, May 31, 1928.

every hue." In other words, living in Highlands was the joy of living. It was life as "God intended it should be."[11]

The years 1886 and 1887 were pivotal in the history of Highlands and its library. Professor Thomas G. Harbison arrived in the spring of 1886, followed the next year by Jessie M. Cobb. Between these two years was the winter of the "deep snow."

The white-winged snow falls down most silently
And softly in large flakes, like many small
White birds that fly to earth; the snowbirds come
With fluttering wings, alighting on the tree,
The little tree that is their resting place,
Their fluffy feathers white like heaps of snow
Upon the limbs; they come in endless flight,
Blown through the air and dropping down to earth,
As swift and silent as the falling snow.[12]

Mr. James Rideout, who was "famous for statements free of exaggeration," reported that he measured thirty-two inches at several locations on level ground. Mr. Bascom reported thirty-six inches. Professor Harbison said that a single, continuous fall of snow covered the ground that winter to a depth of three feet.[13] Harbison

---

[11]*"In the Heart of the Mountains" Lies Highlands, Western North Carolina* (Clinton, S.C.), an 1890 pamphlet of photographs of Highlands.
[12]Mary Chapin Smith, *Earth Songs* (Boston, 1910), p. 16.
[13]See "This Winter At Highlands Mild, Old Paper Suggests," *Franklin Press & Highlands Maconian*, February 7, 1946. For other accounts of the "deep snow" of December, 1886, see "Site of Highlands Was Carved from Mountain Wilderness," *Highlands Maconian,* July 29, 1931; "Romance of Highlands," *Greenwood (S.C.) Index-Journal*, August 24, 1929; "Highlands Site of Beautiful Estates," *Franklin Press*, Teacher Training ed., April 10, 1930; and "Charm of Highlands Mountains Lured Professor Harbison, Botanist," *Franklin Press*, Highlands ed., July 5, 1928. At variance with the above measurements, however, the *Highlander* on December 10, 1886, concluded that it was only "two feet or perhaps nearly 25 inches" of snow that fell on December 3 and 5, 1886. This was also the year of the coldest weather, the snow arriving at the end, the cold having come at the

closed the school for two days so that his students could pack the snow and ice in an old barn to keep it frozen and sell it during the summer as Highlands' first ice cream. The proceeds from the sale paid for a new wing of the school.

It was not long after the "deep snow" that Jessie M. Cobb arrived with her family from Beloit, Wisconsin. It had been a long, hard day in the hack ride from Russell House up the steep, deeply rutted Walhalla road to Buck Horn Gap on Satulah.[14] The horses and Jersey cattle that they had brought with them on the train to Walhalla would probably arrive in Highlands the next day. The sun had already set, the stars sparkling in the black silence of the moonless sky.

Jessie's parents, Judson and Lucy Cobb, stepped out of the carriage to stretch and assess the lay of the land where they would live. Her older sister Gertrude, seeing one flickering light way off to the left, another up on a mountain to the right, and only one or two on the plateau between Satulah and the horizon, stood for a moment pensive and speechless and then piped up, "What kind of place have you brought us to?"[15] For this young teenager brimming with life, Highlands seemed really remote!

The family boarded that night at the Staub House (formerly the Stanhope W. Hill House) on what is now the Horse Cove Road.[16] It was the next night, as the family

---

beginning. On January 11, 1886, the thermometer had dropped to "a point hitherto unapproached during the history of Highlands—19 degrees below zero." *Highlander*, January 15, 1886.

[14] By 1887 the Walhalla Road had replaced the Glades Road and Thompson's Lane as the route after the ford over the Chatooga River to reach Highlands.

[15] Interview (October 14, 1993) with Richard "Bill" Holt, grandson of Judson M. Cobb and son of A. C. Holt, who married Jessie's elder sister Gertrude.

[16] The Staub House was the white Victorian frame house originally built around 1878 for Squire Stanhope W. Hill of Horse Cove by his son. Squire

descended for supper, that Jessie Cobb was introduced to the twenty-five-year-old Thomas Grant Harbison.[17] Little did Miss Cobb realize at this critical moment in her life that she would spend the rest of her days in this "kind of place" to which her parents had brought her, as the wife of its most revered teacher and the mother of its most valued librarians. In the interim, however, between her meeting Tom Harbison and their marriage nine years later, she would live at Altadona, the Cobb house on the property that today is the Highlands Country Club.

It was the year before, the year that the Statue of Liberty was dedicated and Frances Hodgson Burnett published *Little Lord Fauntleroy*, that Professor Harbison had arrived on foot from Pennsylvania searching for the plant lost for a hundred years, the elusive *Shortia galacifolia*.[18] Before this year ended, he had decided to his own surprise to settle in this "kind of place" that fate had selected for him.

It was never his intention to stay. Samuel Kelsey had asked him shortly after his arrival to take charge of the

---

Hill would later become Highlands' first elected mayor. The house is located on the southeast corner of Horse Cove Road at Sixth Street. It was sold around 1880 to a Swiss immigrant, Albert Staub, when Squire Hill moved back into Horse Cove.

[17]Lawrence E. Wood, "Mountain Memories: A Tribute to Miss Gertrude," *Highlander*, August 22, 1974.

[18]André Michaux, the French botanist and explorer, had mentioned seeing this plant "in the high mountains of Carolina" in his journal in 1788 and brought back a single specimen for display in the Jardin des Plantes in Paris. But *Shortia galacifolia* was not discovered again in its original locality "in the high mountains of Carolina" until almost a century later in 1886 (the year of Harbison's arrival in Highlands) by Dr. Charles Sprague Sargent, who found but then lost it. It was in 1887 that two Highlanders, Frank E. Boynton and his brother, Charles A. Boynton, Jr., found it near Bear Camp Creek and brought it home. Nancy Turner and Jim Horton, "Diapensia Family: *Shortia galacifolia* Torrey & Gray," *The Summer Times* (Tampa, 1979), p. 94. See also Bill Sharpe, *A New Geography of North Carolina* (Raleigh, 1961), vol. 3, p. 1435.

school at $160 for a four-month term. Professor Harbison had retorted facetiously that he'd take the job at $600 for a ten-month term. Little thinking that he'd ever see Highlands again, he then left for Pennsylvania, having completed a two-month stay.

Not to be deterred, however, Mr. Kelsey raised his bluff. Informing the professor by mail that $480 had been raised through private subscription, he added that he was expecting the professor to report to school the first Monday in August. Professor Harbison's fate was sealed. He himself admitted, "This is how I happened to be initiated into the order of 'Hopeful Highlanders.'"[19]

Moreover, this is how the Highlands Academy was born.[20] In its early stages it was a cesarean birth. "I arrived," Mr. Harbison reported, "and my troubles began." He described the situation confronting him in these doleful terms:

> A crowded one-room building with poor furniture was filled to overflowing with pupils and students from six to twenty years of age, ungraded in subjects from the primary to algebra—nearly 100 of them. Mr. Kelsey gave me to understand that I might have the honor and the glory, but that I might likewise take the cussing.[21]

He served as principal of the new Highlands Academy for seven years, from 1886 to 1893. For one of these years he also edited the *Mountain Eagle,* the fourth newspaper in Highlands. Then in 1894, even as Rudyard Kipling was publishing his *Jungle Book*, Anthony Hope, his *Prisoner*

---

[19]"Romance of Highlands," *Greenwood (S.C.) Index-Journal,* August 24, 1929.
[20]Professor Harbison founded Highlands Normal College in 1886, which he reorganized as the Highlands Academy in 1888.
[21]"Romance of Highlands," *Greenwood (S.C.) Index-Journal,* August 24, 1929.

of Zenda, and the Episcopal Church was being constructed in Highlands, Professor Harbison was invited by a lifelong friend at Waynesville High School to become its principal and convert it from a private institution to the first public graded school in North Carolina.

Professor Harbison's retirement as principal of the Highlands Academy dealt a painful blow to the little community that had begun to discover itself so completely through his intellectual talents and extensive influence. Perhaps he felt and with all modesty appreciated the town's loss, for he donated to the Hudson Library the annex that he had built for his own library.[22] The enclosed bookcase that until then had constituted the Hudson Library in its entirety was now moved into this small room, still a part of, but apart from, the school.

Like a conch that has outgrown its shell, the library suddenly found room to expand. Almost immediately there was a renewal of interest, and many books were donated to a fast-growing collection. Indeed, gifts came from all sectors of the populace. In a meeting filled with much laughter, jesting, and good fellowship, Mary Chapin Smith relates in her *History of the Hudson Library Association* that the school committee officially donated the small annex for the library's use. "Mr. Harbison loaned the stove, which was cracked a little on one side, so Mr. Boynton had it repaired and set up, Mr. White helping to move it; Mr. J. Jay Smith gave a cord of wood and Mr. Selleck hauled it to the schoolhouse. So on with the rest, the lamp, the table, etc."[23] In the end the library

---

[22]This annex to the school had been built in 1888–89 (Elias D. White, "Early Highlands Days, An Historical Sketch," *Franklin Press & Highlands Maconian,* June 5, 1941).

[23]Mary Chapin Smith, *History of the Hudson Library Association* (Highlands, 1931), p. 2.

was assured of a comfortable setting in its new environment.

Professor Harbison spent only one year in Waynesville and, after a year's study-tour of European schools and forests, returned to Highlands in 1896. He married Jessie Cobb, who by then had definitely decided to stay in this "kind of place." Their marriage set the stage for the future of Highlands but especially for the future of its library. Like a child that is born before its parents, the fledgling library would have to wait another thirty years before two Harbison sisters would guide and nourish it though half of its existence, would care for and tend to its soul.

Professor Harbison, through his interests outside the school proper, became the first president of the Highlands Scientific Society. In his relationship with the Hudson Free Library, he served for one year as its fourth librarian.[24] Books had always been Thomas Harbison's first enduring love. Although devoted to teaching since age seventeen, he was essentially a self-educated man. He attended school during vacations from teaching and studied under professors at Bucknell University concurrent with lecturing. Mostly he read, not narrowly but widely and not at random but with definite intent. Through correspondence courses as outlined by the City University of New York and the National University in California, he earned his bachelor's, master's, and doctoral degrees in botany, completing also a course in landscape architecture and gardening.

---

[24]"Highlands Directory," *Highlands, North Carolina: The Greatest Health and Pleasure Resort in the United States. The Most Perfect Climatic Sanitarium in the World* (Rising Sun, Md., 1887), p. 2. This promotional pamphlet, distributed by Samuel T. Kelsey, lists Professor T. G. Harbison as librarian of the Hudson Free Library in 1887.

Of prime importance to Thomas Harbison during the years that he taught himself and others was the growth of his own personal library. His collection of books in 1893, when he was but thirty-one, was being extolled outside Highlands as "the best school library in Western North Carolina."[25] Ten years earlier, when he was only twenty-one, he had already accumulated over a thousand volumes, which he continued to augment throughout his life.[26] At his own expense he had built the small annex onto the south side of the school to house his collection. This was the wing inherited by the Hudson Library.

A stern but cordial man, with a Prussian's military posture and a Vandyke beard, Professor Harbison had a keen eye for observation and a remarkably retentive memory. He was respected and loved by his students at the Academy, to whom he gave a penny for the first flower of each species found in the new season and five cents for rare finds if they told him, not just the common name of each find, but the Latin name as well, and what the Latin name meant. "He was rough as hell," says Shine Potts, one of his later students. "He didn't take any baloney from anybody. Nobody acted up."[27]

Professor Harbison was in high demand, not only in Highlands as town clerk, commissioner, and twice mayor,[28] but also in educated circles well beyond the two-and-a-half-square-mile limits of the town.[29] "He had a

---

[25]"Carolina Mountain Towns: Highlands," *Asheville Carolina Mountains,* June, 1893.
[26]"Dr. Thomas Grant Harbison," *Journal of the Elisha Mitchell Scientific Society,* vol. 52 (1936), p. 141.
[27]Arthur B. "Shine" Potts, as quoted by Bill Holt, October 14, 1993.
[28]Thomas Harbison served as mayor on at least two occasions: 1892–1893 and 1909. Records are missing for the years 1902 through 1908.
[29]When Highlands was incorporated on March 5, 1879, the corporate limits were as follows: "Beginning at the Post Office known as Baxter White's store, running each way from there so as to make one square mile."

way of relating things that happened to him," says Bill Holt, a nephew. "He was a good storyteller and could make dull things sound interesting. He should have been a Zane Grey."[30] Joe Reese recalls how he'd sit in Gus Holt's Soda Shop and listen spellbound to Professor Harbison and Gus talk about what they'd read or experienced. Gus Holt was well read himself. Indeed, he read all the time. They'd talk all night, about such bizarre topics as the taste of wild game, like hawk or buzzard, but mostly about what they'd read.[31] It was fitting that the Hudson Library should be cradled in its infancy in the room that had housed Professor Harbison's own collection of books.

From 1889 until 1895 the custodian of this growing library was the daughter of trustee president T. Baxter White, Miss Jessie E. White. As the first librarian to serve for more than a token one or two years, she helped assure the institution's passage from local to state recognition.

Evangeline McLennan Davis, *The Lure of Highlands* (Highlands, 1981), p. 11. They were altered in 1883 to one and a half square miles, and in 1889 to two and a half square miles, remaining thus until July, 1980. See "Bill Would Extend Highlands' Limits," *Franklin Press & Highlands Maconian*, February 10, 1949, for an attempt to extend the 1889 corporate limits, which failed in the General Assembly.
[30]Interview with Bill Holt, October 14, 1993. Bill Holt's father, A. C. Holt, as noted earlier, married Gertrude Cobb.
[31]Interview with Joe Reese, December 1, 1993.

Albertina Staub
Left: Miss Staub. *Right:* unidentified. Biological Station directors.
Taken in the 1930s. Courtesy of Hudson Library.

J. Jay and Mary Chapin Smith
Portraits made ca. 1890. Courtesy of Earl Young.

Incorporation: 1895–99

Tis day in the mountain country,
For the sky is touched with light,
Like the tint of the coming color,
Or a rosebud folded tight.

The first fair gleam of morning,
So slight it never mars,
But only seems to heighten,
The beauty of the stars.

The songs of the birds are hushed,
The singers have gone to rest,
But still in the cozy room,
Are the sounds that we love the best.[1]

By 1895 the Hudson Free Library Association had enough books in its cozy room to consider owning real estate, so it incorporated.[2] It appointed Miss Albertina Staub, age twenty-nine, who looked like her name, short, prim, and precise, as its sixth librarian at "the munificent salary of $10.00 a year."[3]

Projected into the future of H. G. Wells' *Time Machine*, which was published in this year, ten dollars might seem

---

[1]Laura Hawkins, in T. W. Reynolds, *High Lands* (Highlands, 1964), p. 52. Laura Hawkins, known as the mountain poetess, wrote this poem in the 1880s. See also Frances Baumgarner Lombard, *From the Hills of Home in Western North Carolina* (Whiteside Cove, N.C., 1972, repr. 1993), pp. 20–24.
[2]Notice of the petition for an act of incorporation by the legislature was given in the *Blue Ridge Enterprise* as a "Notice" as early as January 22, 1885. For the actual year of incorporation, see the minutes of the annual trustees meeting, August 1, 1946.
[3]Mary Chapin Smith, *History of the Hudson Library Association* (Highlands, 1931), p. 3.

entirely inadequate for a librarian's annual pay. Mary Chapin Smith's ironic use of the word "munificent" in her history implies that even in 1931 ten dollars was regarded in retrospect as small pittance. Indeed, it would appear today as unthinkable!

On the other hand, in the 1890s expenses were considerably less than they are today. Overnight lodging at the Central House cost one dollar,[4] a dollar and a half at Highlands House.[5] Good wood, advertised as "sawed true to measure,—no swearing in the kitchen," went for eighty-five cents a cord.[6] A construction worker could expect to earn a dollar thirty a day.[7] Groceries sold in Highlands at ten cents a pound for fresh pork, twelve cents for a dozen eggs, and from twenty-six to thirty-five cents for a pound of Java Coffee.[8]

One further consideration when compared with the schedule of a full-time year-round librarian a century later, Miss Staub's work load was a light one: two hours once a week. All sides considered then, ten dollars was no small reward for a librarian's part-time dedication in 1895. It was far more than volunteer librarians earned, and at least one of those librarians who worked free of charge for the sake of the town's readers and the literary arts felt that those who accepted pay in all conscience should have declined it.[9]

---

[4]"Hotel Directory," *Asheville Carolina Mountains,* June, 1893.
[5]Advertisement for Highlands House, *Mountain Eagle,* March 31, 1892.
[6]Ibid.
[7]Betty Holt, *History of the First Presbyterian Church: Highlands, North Carolina, 1885–1985* (Highlands, 1985), p. 6.
[8]"Highlands Current Prices," *Blue Ridge Enterprise,* January 22, 1885.
[9]When Gertrude and Dolly Harbison were paid salaries of twenty-five dollars in 1928, the objection of their predecessor Miss Lucy Elliott was that she and her sister, Charlotte, had donated their services free of charge. Interview with Dolly Harbison, September 22, 1993.

In any event, regardless of whether Miss Staub deserved more or less pay, the library's cash reserves in 1895 were $21.88,[10] barely twice her annual salary, and the trustees' need for money was very great.

With Miss Staub at the helm of a newly incorporated association and book donations on the increase, an additional job was now in the offing. Someone needed to identify valuable editions and to cull out the "cheap trash" that people wanted to discard by "dumping" it on the library. The job was given to a book committee headed by Mary Chapin Smith. A "high mark" was now set as the aim of the library. This meant that the book committee became heavily engaged in literary censorship, "sifting the books, rejecting the absolutely harmful and vulgar, and also freeing the shelves from much that was not only antiquated but valueless."[11]

In a free society there are legitimate objections to such an aim, especially where it relates to the printed word. If, as the proverb says, books are the children of the brain, then to discard or destroy a book is to discard or destroy the brain that produced it. "As good almost kill a man as kill a good book," said a great English opponent of censorship. "Who kills a man kills a reasonable creature, God's image; but he who destroys a good book kills reason itself, kills the image of God, as it were, in the eye."[12]

Mrs. Smith, librarian Staub, and Mrs. H. P. Selleck (the third member of the committee) were undeniably highly educated and of fine ability and culture. Nonetheless, how does one decide in a free society who is adequately qualified to dictate the tastes of a complex reading public? The committee was charged with de-

---

[10]Smith, *History of the Hudson Library Association,* p. 3.
[11]Ibid.
[12]John Milton, *Areopagitica* (1644).

termining which books were good and which were "harmful trash."

Their stated goal, which was admirable, was that the library should offer "the best in science, nature study, literature, history, travel and general subjects as well as in fiction, just as far as possible."[13] The three committee members obviously accepted the notion that if books never corrupted anyone, then they never improved anyone either. If good books educated, then so did bad books, meaning that bad books miseducated, misinformed, and misguided. So censorship became a moral imperative.

Rather than debate the faults and virtues of censoring books, it might serve a more practical purpose to agree at this point that governing a library differs from governing a country in one essential respect. The government of the United States is restrained ideally and legally by its constitution's first amendment from any encroachment on free expression. On the other hand, a library enclosed in a six-shelf bookcase (or whichever four walls may contain it) is restrained primarily by physical space. Libraries throughout the world are physically unable to include all that is written among their holdings.

In the case of the Hudson Library, space being its limiting factor, books that were wearing out had to be discarded, and room made for new books on arrival. So for the next thirty years until she retired from the board at age eighty—according to a later librarian who served near the end of her long reign—Mary Chapin Smith "had the run of what books were bought for the library, which meant they weren't bought for the library but for *her*. She *ran* the library with Albertina Staub."[14] Fortunately for

---

[13]Smith, *History of the Hudson Library Association*, p. 3.
[14]Interview with Dolly Harbison, September 22, 1993.

the library, she was a well-educated graduate of Wheaton College, "precise, very particular." Furthermore, the intended results, more often than not, approximated her noble aim.

Beginning in 1898, the year of the Spanish-American war over Cuba when Spain ceded Cuba, Puerto Rico, Guam, and the Philippines to the United States, the little library in Highlands opened twice a week; and in subsequent years, three times a week during the summer.[15] The summer visitors were now charged fees to keep the library free for the year-round residents, as originally intended by Ella Hudson and Louise Wells. No one considered this change in policy unfair. On the contrary, the summer visitors had been requesting such a change, and they readily contributed a grand total of six dollars, twelve dollars, and eighteen dollars, respectively, during the next three summers to cover increased summer costs.

Donations of books also increased. Mary Chapin Smith remarked that "it seemed to be understood that only books worth while were desired."[16] Apparently word had gotten out that the book committee saw a difference between good books and cheap trash, preferring donations of the former to dumping of the latter. A donor's reputation was now at stake! So the library received a number of valuable editions. Most valued among them were a full set of Dickens, several quality magazines, and a subscription to *St. Nicholas Magazine.*

The arrival of each new issue of *St. Nicholas*, as though it were the old gentleman himself, was eagerly awaited by every child.[17] *St. Nicholas* contained the latest literary in-

---

[15]Smith, *History of the Hudson Library Association*, p. 4.
[16]Ibid.
[17]Interview with Dolly Harbison, September 22, 1993. *St. Nicholas: An Illustrated Magazine for Young Folks* (New York) was published monthly from 1873 to 1940. Joel Chandler Harris, whose fame rests on his creation

stallments by popular and subsequently famous American authors. Ongoing works appeared by Louisa May Alcott, Mark Twain, Rudyard Kipling, Palmer Cox, Howard Pyle, Andrew Lang, and Joel Chandler Harris. Mary Chapin Smith marveled that "nothing was ever so much appreciated by the children and young folks, both resident and visiting,—and their elders were not far behind. Even when read to pieces the fragments were treasured and read again."[18]

In the final months, as the nineteenth century drew to a close and the Hudson Library struggled on a small scale to survive, a sad but touching bit of news reached the little town of Highlands from the Shortoff home of Louise Emmons Wells. Her parents—the parents also of Ella Hudson—had lived with her now for seven years. Highlanders knew them quite well and held them in high esteem for their kindness and courtesy. In 1899 they quietly passed away.

Reverend Emmons, a once-popular Unitarian minister of the Dr. Channing type[19] in Boston, at age ninety-one had possessed the stately bearing of a gentleman of the old school and was extraordinarily compassionate and mindful of the needs of others. His wife, age seventy-nine at her death, had always had a solicitous interest in the

---

of Uncle Remus, contributed his *Daddy Jake, the Runaway* (1889) and *Chronicles of Aunt Minervy* (1899) as installments to *St. Nicholas* before they were published in book form, so the *St. Nicholas* versions of these works, rather than the books themselves, are valued as authentic first editions.

[18]Smith, *History of the Hudson Library Association*, p. 4.

[19]Dr. William Ellery Channing, a Congregational minister in Boston, in his conviction that Calvinism was not for him, preached a sermon in 1819 entitled "My Sympathy" that resulted in the establishment of Unitarianism. As the intellectual "Apostle of Unitarianism," he exercised wide influence through his sermons and writings on social and philanthropic issues of his time. A Unitarian camp and conference center, known as The Mountain, currently exists on the Dillard Road near Highlands.

welfare of her neighbors and friends and a noticeable affection for children. Had it been just one or the other of this pair—the Reverend Henry Emmons or Elizabeth—who had died on this overcast day in late November, the news would have been sad certainly, but not as singular as it turned out. As it was, Mrs. Emmons died at seven in the morning, her husband at four in the afternoon of the same day.

T. Baxter White, who was the Highlands correspondent for the area newspaper,[20] remarked that "their departure within such a few hours of each other, was a singular coincidence. Beautiful in their lives, in death they were not divided."[21] Bess Hines Harkins, also known as the earth child of Highlands, once depicted how much the complete life of such a mutually devoted and well-loved couple meant in a spiritual sense to those who remained behind:

Call Him God, or call Him what you will:
I only know there is a Power to fill
the receptive soul with all that's Great and Good:
That the Life Abundant is Truth understood.[22]

Ella Hudson's parents were buried in the family plot at the entrance to the Highlands Cemetery.

---

[20]T. Baxter White was the Highlands correspondent to the *Franklin Press & Highlands Maconian* from 1889 to 1911, signing his column "Bx." His son Elias D. White corresponded with the paper after their move to Lordsburg (now La Verne), California.
[21]"Obituary [Rev. & Mrs. Henry Emmons]," *Franklin Press*, November 29, 1899.
[22]Bess Hines Harkins, "Definition," *Earth Songs* (San Benito, Texas, 1975), p. 14.

The Smiths on the Bridge
J. Jay and Mary Chapin Smith on the path to Smith Cottage (now Hildegard's) and Smith House (now Highlands Inn), ca. 1910. Courtesy of the Bascom–Barratt estate.

H. M. Bascom and Daughter Louise
Taken ca. 1900. Courtesy of the Bascom-Barratt estate.

Trials and Tribulations: 1900–1914

My hill land is so cold and lean
It is the last to put on green
In winter first to put on snow
In spring the last to let it go
Here I labored, here I delved
Swung the ax-blade, hickory helved
Here I drove the walking plow
Sweated here and wiped my brow
Where my father earned his bread
Planted, sowed and harvested.[1]

With the close of the nineteenth century, the century of steam, and the death of Queen Victoria, whose influence had dominated the Western world for six imperialistic decades, the new century of electricity and discovery of the atom was born. Max Planck in the first year of the twentieth century had just formulated his quantum theory, leading Albert Einstein, five years later, to develop his now-famous Special Theory of Relativity, and the atomic age began. A fundamental idea to emerge from the new and revolutionary focus on quanta was the uncertainty principle, a notion not unfamiliar to those associated at this juncture with the Hudson Library.

The big world will no doubt view the Ladies' Floral and Industrial Society of Highlands with scant regard, but with Albertina Staub's ten-dollar annual salary in arrears, a thirty-dollar donation by these sacred ladies of the flowers was salvation on a universal scale. The

---

[1] Will Christman, in T. W. Reynolds, *Born of the Mountains* (Highlands, 1964), p. 35. Will Christman was known as the farmer poet.

trustees paid Miss Staub her due, and the library began the new century with a clear conscience debt free.

In 1903, the year of the first flight by the Wright Brothers and S. P. Ravenel, Sr.'s completion of his turnpike toll road from Cashiers to Highlands, the blessed Floral Society went the way of all flesh (the title of the new book just published posthumously by Samuel Butler). It willed its membership to the new Horticultural Society, its assets to the library, and answered the call of the wild (the new book by Jack London). Its legacy of $135 bought many books in those early years for a grateful library, whose holdings, however, like a well-fed hermit crab, were beginning to test the limits of its borrowed chamber.[2]

By 1904 the town's population of 450 had increased by only fifty percent, but the number of volumes in the library had increased more than eightfold. Miss Staub decided to list the holdings and published in 1906 a catalogue of the Hudson Library, containing eight hundred titles arranged in sixteen categories. It included several very recent publications that today stand as classics: Arthur Conan Doyle's *Adventures of Sherlock Holmes*, Rudyard Kipling's *The Light That Failed*, Henry James's *Awkward Age*, and Jack London's *Call of the Wild*. Several classics that were also recent publications but had somehow escaped the library's shelves were Joseph Conrad's *Lord Jim*, Doyle's *Hound of the Baskervilles*, Kipling's *Just So Stories*, London's *Sea-Wolf*, and James M. Barrie's *Peter Pan*.

As a matter of course, the library bought a number of its books, but the majority of its holdings were donated. When the Library Association was first incorporated in

---

[2]In 1903 the library had 567 volumes. "Educational Records Date from 1885," *Franklin Press*, Teacher Training ed., April 10, 1930.

1895, it held a sale of incidental articles and flowers that netted twenty-two dollars for the purchase of books.[3] The Highlands amateur string quintet gave a fund-raising concert, and in 1904 an impersonation of David Garrick and a tenor concert by several Floridians combined to net twenty-two dollars, again for the purchase of books. Except for these three fund raisers, however, the library didn't initiate benefits for itself until the mid-twenties.

So the association relied almost entirely on membership fees, fines, seasonal and monthly subscriptions, and small contributions for income, including the rent shelf. Consequently, if ten to twenty books were added by purchase in a year, as contrasted with eighty to two hundred by gift, the library quickly depleted its cash on hand.

Something so simple and basic as the gift of a glass door, which made the library room accessible from the street rather than through the schoolroom, a great inconvenience to many, the trustees welcomed especially in 1906. "This was as good as an extra window for light," exclaimed Mary Chapin Smith, "and gave us great comfort."[4] The library's needs were quite modest; its attitude, refreshingly appreciative.

In 1906 death took Ella Hudson's sister, Louise Emmons Wells.[5] At sixty she had lived twice as long as her younger sister, whom she had nursed through her last days. Having also cared for her parents during their final years with her in Shortoff, she was dearly loved by family, neighbors, and friends. It was she who had requested that the library bear the name *Hudson* and had

---

[3]Mary Chapin Smith, *History of the Hudson Library Association* (Highlands, 1931), p. 3.
[4]Ibid., p. 4.
[5]Louise Emmons Wells is buried near her sister and parents at the entrance to the Highlands Cemetery. The grave of her daughter, Mary Elizabeth Wells (1882–1965), is now next to her own.

seen to it that the boxes of books were properly preserved by the town.

In the year of Mrs. Wells' passing, one book, which Dr. Mary Lapham of the Sanatorium gave to the Hudson Library, began a long and treasured career as the single volume that for the next half century would rank with *St. Nicholas* as the most sought-after item on the library's shelves. Jan Chambers Chmar remembers the tattered copy of this little book, so old that it had practically disintegrated in its journey from hand to little hand. It was Margaret Sidney's *The Five Little Peppers and How They Grew*. "I remember books in that library that were years old, but that one," Jan Chmar asserts, "was the oldest of them all. That one, and Mary Poppins' sequel."[6]

Every child in Highlands from age three and up who had read any book at all or been read to knew about the incident in *The Five Little Peppers* where Phronsie gave a gingerbread boy to the rich old man summering at the village hotel. How much that spontaneous little act would change the lives forever of nearly every character in the book! Indeed, how that turning point changed so many of the lives of its little readers, who came away with a sudden and strong sympathy for, if not empathy with, the agony of poverty!

While the children in the library were facing issues of material deprivation and spiritual strength, the adults on the library board were facing the agony of apathy. One of the reasons that there are no extant records of the Library Association's meetings during this formative time

---

[6]Interview with Jan Chambers Chmar, September 24, 1993. Mary Chapin Smith, in her *History*, calls this book *The Ten Little Peppers* and says it was bought for $10.80. Smith, *History of the Hudson Library Association,* p. 4. Under the pseudonym "Margaret Sidney," Harriet Lothrop published her story first in 1880 in *Wide Awake* magazine, not in book form until 1881. The book was so popular that it sold two million copies in fifty years.

in its early life may be, as Mary Chapin Smith reports in her history, that the board couldn't muster a quorum. A meeting required no more than five people, but interest in the library had apparently declined.

On one occasion Mrs. Smith literally had to drag individuals off the street to convene the board, because all but three members had come up with some reason not to attend. "You know how it is," she waxed biblical, "some have bought five yoke of oxen and another has married a wife, 'I pray thee have me excused.'"[7] It was during this period, in 1908, that the board amended its constitution to read, "The number present shall constitute a quorum."[8] The library barely survived.

In 1910 T. Baxter White decided to retire from twenty-one years as second president of the library's trustees and was making preparations to leave Highlands. With old age setting in and his children grown up, he sold his house of thirty-five years and his business to join his son-in-law and daughter, Mr. and Mrs. Frank Sheldon, in La Verne, California. Then in a sudden change of heart, inspired by his love of Highlands and its grand old mountains, he tried to buy back his house and business and persisted for several weeks before being persuaded at last to part. For the people of Highlands his had been a long-time familiar figure: an elderly gentleman with mustache and beard, mounted with saddlebags upon his horse, selling fire insurance along the Macon County roads.[9] They would miss him even as he would obviously and painfully miss them.

---

[7]Smith, *History of the Hudson Library Association,* p. 5. The allusion is to the parable of the great supper in Luke 14:16–24, especially 18–20.
[8]Ibid.
[9]"Macon Pioneer Passes Away: T. Baxter White, for Many Years a Resident of Highlands, Died on July 14, at La Verne, California," *Franklin Press,* August 4, 1922.

In the year that a nine-year-old golfer named Bobby Jones won his first title, the Junior Championship of Atlanta, and Charles Kettering produced the first electric self-starter for automobiles, the Hudson Library bought the James Rideout lot next to the Episcopal Church on East Main Street for sixty dollars.[10] That same year in Highlands, 1911, thirty-eight-year-old Charlie Wright received the sixteenth gold medal awarded by the Carnegie Foundation, valued at $2,000, and an additional $2,000 honorarium for rescuing Gus Baty from a fall off Fool's Rock on Whiteside Mountain.[11] The town was still agog over the details of his two-hour ordeal on the great vertical granite slope, when Charlie and his wife, Helen, with the proceeds from the Carnegie award bought from Sumner Clark, Sr., the four acres of land where Helen's Barn now stands.

The lot that the library bought was much smaller than the Wright acreage, where for half a century the town would revel in the foot-stomping music of such musicians as Bill Wilson, Bobby Talley, Floyd Lamb, David Potts, and Willard Crisp.

He could fiddle all the bugs off a sweet-potato-vine.[12]

---

[10]Lieutenant James Rideout managed a boarding house, Satula House, near the present Catholic Church, which he had built originally as his residence. He also managed one of four general merchandise stores in the town, located on the southeast corner of Fourth and Main (currently the location of Old Edwards Inn). He came to Highlands in 1882 as a baker from Maine by way of Florida.

[11]See accounts of the rescue in Reynolds, *Born of the Mountains*, p. 7, and Gert McIntosh, *Highlands, North Carolina . . . a walk into the past*, rev. ed. (Birmingham, Ala., 1990), p. 63. For the most comprehensive and graphically described account, see Bill Marett, *Courage at Fool's Rock* (Highlands, 1975). The Carnegie Foundation did not bestow gold medals lightly. By the time Charlie Wright received his medallion, the foundation's 840th award, it was only the 16th gold medal awarded since the foundation's establishment in 1904. See *Carnegie Hero Fund Commission* (Pittsburgh, Pa., 1914).

[12]Stephen Vincent Benét, "The Mountain Whippoorwill" (1923), stanza 22.

Callie Beale bucked and winged till her wig turned sideways. Callie Beale could really buck dance! Wallace Henry would ask all the girls to square dance.[13] There would soon come a time when buck dancing, square dancing, and mountain clogging would be a popular pastime during the Highlands summers.[14] The great rhythm of feet, like jungle drums, shaking the ground blocks away would be heard as far away as the new library, on its lot at the other end of town.

The year after Mary Chapin Smith succeeded T. Baxter White as trustee president, Albertina Staub closed the book on sixteen years as librarian. That is not to say that Miss Staub would not be around for the next thirty years, for even today people still remember Albertina Staub's association with the library. "Everything was in such order when Miss Staub was around," according to Louise Edwards Meisel, whom Miss Staub taught the library's system of filing cards in metal boxes twenty years after her own retirement.[15]

Unfailingly, Miss Staub's controlling influence extended beyond the library, even in the late 1920s, for Louise also remembers the time when she wanted very much to sit next to Gene Murphy on a return motorcar trip from a party. She remembers Miss Staub's being there along with Mrs. John Durgin and a number of other older people. Miss Staub had never learned how to drive a motorcar and usually sat in the front with the chauffeur

---

[13]Interview with Harriet Zahner van Houten, September 30, 1993.
[14]The first dance in Helen's Barn was held on May 14, 1932. It was free and a huge success: "the talk of the town for days afterward." The girls wore summer dresses and heels, according to Mrs. G. Maxwell (Annie Linn) Armor. But within short time dancing at Helen's Barn became the target of pulpit-pounding local preachers. See A. J. Baty, "Helen's Gamble," *North Carolina State* (September, 1982), pp. 12–14.
[15]Interview with Louise Edwards Meisel, September 29, 1993.

because, as Joe Reese recalls, she said it "showed ownership."[16] She generally wore a white skirt and spread a white napkin on the seat. Everyone else sat in the back. However, on this occasion when the party was over, Miss Staub deliberately stepped into the back and sat between Louise and her date. Her date, Louise admits, "had TB," but "a healthy TB."[17] Still, there was no countering Miss Staub.

Probably after Miss Staub's resignation as librarian in 1911, until 1915, Mary Chapin Smith served concurrently as trustee president and acting librarian. As noted earlier, there are no extant records for the period, neither trustee minutes nor newspaper reports.[18] Nevertheless, in her *History* Mrs. Smith indicated that during this time she was in the reading room "every library day" and that at the end of each day it was her task "to close up."[19]

So one may safely assume that she managed the library at the time when Woodrow Wilson, who had once summered in nearby Horse Cove,[20] was rising to power and there was hope that intellect would thrive in realms of authority in the United States. With the United States Forest Service beginning to buy large parcels of land surrounding Highlands for watershed protection, the town was feeling increasingly secure.

---

[16]Interview with Joe Reese, December 1, 1993.
[17]Interview with Louise Edwards Meisel, September 29, 1993.
[18]Trustee minutes for the years before 1926 have disappeared, and the fire that swept the Franklin Press on December 20, 1922, destroyed all issues between 1903 and 1919.
[19]Smith, *History of the Hudson Library Association*, p. 8.
[20]See "28th U.S. President Once Visited Here," *Franklin Press & Highlands Maconian*, September 6, 1956. See also T. W. Reynolds, *High Lands* (Highlands, 1964), p. 41, and Thomas B. Crumpler, "History of Highlands" (an unpublished manuscript), p. 31. Woodrow Wilson, age twenty-two, having just graduated from Princeton University, was one of Mr. John R. Thompson's summer boarders for his vacation in 1879 in Horse Cove, before he entered law school at the University of Virginia in the fall.

World politics were a person's last concern during the advent of the first Charlie Chaplin movies, which appeared on the silent screen in the Masonic Hall in Highlands as they spread across the nation. *Making a Living* was making the rounds, and Charlie's antics with Marie Dressler in *Tillie's Punctured Romance* convulsed crowds across America. Such amusements were ironic backdrops for that fateful day in June—the twenty-eighth—in 1914 when a Serbian nationalist assassinated the heir to the Austrian throne. For the next three years everybody declared war on everybody, and world politics became a household concern.

If in the early days of the war America, or Highlands in particular, was not directly involved in this overseas cataclysm, it wasn't that people were callous and didn't care. It was that the peace-loving Woodrow Wilson, seeking to preserve American neutrality, survived reelection in 1916. Nevertheless, the tragic loss in the previous year of 168 American lives with the German sinking of the *Lusitania* had already set the stage for America's determined plunge in 1917 into the conflict.

During the three years, then, before the immersion of the United States into the horrors and heartbreak of tank warfare, the town of Highlands found itself involved with matters so mundane as the wettest year in its recorded history[21] and the appearance of the first motor car in town.[22] The little library existed in a euphoric state of transition, thrilled about a momentous change just over its immediate horizon.

---

[21]"Miss Harbison Recognized," *Highlander*, September 27, 1973. Professor Harbison recorded 120 inches of rain in 1916, a record for Highlands until 1979. In 1916 the Toxaway Dam broke and Asheville experienced its great flood.
[22]Interview with Bill Holt, October 14, 1993, and Dolly Harbison, September 30, 1993.

The Hudson Library
Built in 1915. Courtesy of Miss Dolly Harbison.

The Town-Clock School
Built 1915–18. Courtesy of the Bascom–Barratt estate.

Lucy P. Elliott
Taken ca. 1914. Courtesy of her daughter, Esther C. Shay.

Christina A. Rice
Taken in December, 1921. Courtesy of her son, W. Herbert Rice.

A Home of Its Own: 1915–25

And when in country dwellings,
The shaded lamps burn bright,
While wondrous works of science,
Make our great cities light.

The mountain children gathered,
Around the warm hearthstone,
Dream not of other households,
More brilliant than their own.[1]

By 1915 the town had turned its full attention to the pressing needs of the Hudson Library. With current holdings of fifteen hundred volumes, the association was in desperate need of its own home. Mary Chapin Smith observed that "the shelves of the little room became full to overflowing, there was not space for a wren's nest, and we must have more room."[2] Although only a sixth of an acre, the Rideout lot represented an exciting opportunity for the butterfly to escape the confining walls of its chrysalis. Libraries have an inherent tendency to outgrow their protective cocoons even before the adults form and metamorphosis gives them occasion to spread their golden wings.

The Hudson Library was no exception, for where does one store so many books in a cute little many-windowed room already filled to capacity by the overflow from an overcrowded school? The creature's swelling was cracking the shell. Indeed, in this year construction was also under

---

[1] Laura Hawkins, "Let There Be Light" (c. 1883), in T. W. Reynolds, *Southern Appalachian Region* (Highlands, 1966), vol. 1, p. 33.
[2] Mary Chapin Smith, "Library Active at Highlands," *Franklin Press*, July 5, 1928.

way of a new two-story school building to the rear of the Academy. "Now it was serious," exclaimed Mary Chapin Smith. "We were like the old woman who lived in a shoe, only we had so many books we didn't know what to do. We must build."[3]

Huger (pronounced "U-gee") Elliott, whose family had a summer home on Satulah, designed the new building. Mr. Elliott was a director of the Museum of Fine Arts in. Boston. A graduate of the Columbia University School of Architecture and with two years of study at the École des Beaux Arts in Paris, he had taught architectural design at the University of Pennsylvania and at Harvard before becoming a director, initially of the Rhode Island School of Design and then of the Boston Museum. He would later hold directorial and teaching positions at the Philadelphia and New York Metropolitan Museums of Art.

The difficult and time-consuming task of raising the $553 needed by J. Walter Reese[4] to construct the 1,300-square-foot building had taken almost two years. Beginning with an unsolicited gift of $100 from Mrs. S. P. (Margaretta) Ravenel, Sr., and including a benefit sponsored by Bug Hill (Dr. Mary Lapham's tuberculosis sanatorium on the hill, where the current Civic Center stands),[5] creative minds had met to stage every

---

[3]Mary Chapin Smith, *History of the Hudson Library Association* (Highlands, 1931), p. 5.

[4]J. Walter Reese was the son of Robert W. Reese, who moved from Franklin to Highlands when he painted the Presbyterian Church. See Betty Holt, *History of the First Presbyterian Church: Highlands, North Carolina, 1885–1985* (Highlands, 1985), p. 6.

[5]Dr. Mary Lapham, according to Thomas B. Crumpler in his unpublished manuscript, "History of Highlands," was "a much-loved family doctor for the people of Highlands and of the vicinity. House calls made in the middle of the night involving a 10 mile horseback ride were commonplace for her. In addition she became internationally famous for her innovative methods of treating tuberculosis. She is cited in the medical literature as being one of the group of 5 doctors in this country who introduced and popularized

conceivable means of raising the cash. There were a loan exhibit, card and lawn parties, a concert, flower show, and travel lecture. There were cash donations, one of which was $50 from Miss Minnie Warren, who every Christmas remembered the librarian, whomever she might be at the time, with a check for $100.[6]

Moreover, the giving didn't stop when the building began. The townspeople merely turned from contributing cash to donating valuable material goods: windows, doors, fixtures, an angle lamp and rugs, a large reading table, cement for the chimney (which Walter Reese volunteered to build without charge), rock for the foundation, mill work, and the loan of a machine for making cement bricks.[7]

The whole town helped carry the fifteen hundred volumes from the little wing of the schoolhouse to the fine new building on Main Street. To celebrate the cooperative effort, the Hudson Free Library Association was dedicated on Independence Day, July 4, 1915, thirty-five years after its inception in a few boxes of books, thirty-one years after its formal birth in a borrowed room.

If a room without books is like a body without a soul, as Cicero once exclaimed, then this one-room structure certainly sheltered a free soul. In one sense it was the smallest building around, but in another very important sense it was the tallest. It had more stories than any other in town. That's why the children loved it so.

For the new building's dedication Mary Chapin Smith had originally prepared a six-page library history.

---

therapeutic pneumothorax or artificial collapse of one lung. She also became the first woman ever to be president of the American Thoracic Society, a national medical group specializing in respiratory diseases" (p. 22). Bug Hill was built in 1908.

[6]Interview with Dolly Harbison, September 22, 1993.
[7]Smith, *History of Hudson Library Association,* pp. 6–7.

However, by popular request, in the interest of brevity on that auspicious day, she reluctantly agreed to delete from her oral remarks the countless names of people who had labored indefatigably in the library's behalf. However, in her written *History of the Hudson Library Association* published in 1931, she claimed to have restored the "many names that were like a constellation" in the formative years of the library's youth and adolescence.[8]

The library's new home was small, larger than formerly, but nonetheless small. It was quite simply a one-story gray frame building with a low hip roof. The appearance of the new building, although attractively designed by an accomplished artist, really wasn't important. For some thirty years the library had functioned without a building of its own solely as a service organization, ensconced in a cute little chestnut-paneled many-windowed room, lined where possible with shelves.[9] It had opened to the public only on Fridays (much later, on Fridays and Saturdays) with the ringing of a 360-pound school bell, heard under favorable conditions for a distance of three miles, as far north as Shortoff and east into Horse Cove.

Now settled in its new but still small quarters—its first real home—the Hudson Library would serve as a monument to the Highlanders' desire to learn, but it would never look monumental. Joe Reese, the builder's son, recalls that "you could carry all the books that there were in a pickup and not have a good load."[10] In truth, whether a library, as a service organization, is housed in a classic-pillared marble temple, a downtown store front, or just a

---

[8]Ibid., *History of the Hudson Library Association*, p. 7.
[9]Helen Hill Norris, "Looking Backward [The Hudson Library]," *Highlander*, July 13, 1962.
[10]Interview with Joe Reese, December 1, 1993.

bookmobile is not nearly so important as what it contains and how it's used. Indeed, this is how the people in Highlands valued their small library.

Two now-famous books published in the same year that the Hudson Library occupied its modest home—one by W. Somerset Maugham, the other by Joseph Conrad—epitomize by their titles alone the classic conflict that the little library in Highlands had just resolved (and was always resolving) between the boundless striving of the soul and the restrictive confines of space: *Of Human Bondage* and *Victory*. It may be no mere coincidence (to take the analogy a step further) that the world's first talking film made its première in the year that the Hudson Library was reborn. In 1915 D. W. Griffith produced his *Birth of a Nation*.

Incidentally, to cement conclusively the relative importance of the big world mirrored in the small, this was the year that Albert Einstein postulated his general theory of relativity. That was something to ponder while sitting upon Sunset Rock[11] on the roof of the world, gazing at a little village floating on a plateau in an ocean of mountain peaks extending to the horizon beyond. For in this year Captain S. Prioleau Ravenel's children had donated the Rock to the town in memory of their parents and for the restoration of soul that it would afford to countless residents and visitors who might luxuriate in its profoundly peaceful, panoramic view.[12]

---

[11]The view is known alternately as Sunset Rock or Sunset Rocks.
[12]"Highlands' Fitting Tribute to Samuel Prioleau Ravenel," *Franklin Press & Highlands Maconian,* August 29, 1940. Captain Ravenel, who had died in 1902, was a man of "strong personal and independent spirit, cultured and affable, and as true as steel to friends." See his obituary in "Highlands," *Franklin Press,* May 28, 1902. He built the first summer home, called Wantoot, the showplace of Highlands, on the north ridge of Sunset Rock overlooking the deep valley of Horse Cove. It is now known as Playmore, or the J. Blanc Monroe House.

One of the first patrons of the Hudson Library in its spacious new home, a young author of his first book of poems published in 1915,[13] was the now-famous Stephen Vincent Benét. Pulitzer Prize author of the Civil War poem *John Brown's Body* and author of the delightful book read by nearly every student today as a relatively painless assignment in school, *The Devil and Daniel Webster*, Stephen spent the summers of his teens, before beginning his studies at Yale, in Highlands.

He was shy, chubby, wore thick-lensed spectacles, and read Latin poetry for entertainment.[14] He frequented the library when it was still in the wing of the schoolhouse, and when it moved, he moved with it. Like young Jesus in the temple, he could be found lost in a corner of the room, slumped over a shabby copy of *St. Nicholas*. Initially he was Mowgli, reliving the atavistic urge to understand the lore of the jungle while stalked by the green-eyed Shere Khan. Then he was Little John, thrusting the merry Robin Hood into the raging current with a single well-aimed parry; or he was Merlin, peering into the shimmering mists of the future or resurrecting an ancient magic from the past. He loved the thrill of rafting with Huck Finn and the chill of witnessing a dastardly murder in a moonlit graveyard. Through it all, young Stephen was never aware of the time, up to the very moment that Mary Chapin Smith, acting as interim librarian and "loth to interrupt such joys," pried him loose and drove him out at closing time.[15]

Since the great war was raging during Stephen's vacations in Highlands, he kept a map of Europe on the wall

---

[13]*Five Men and Pompey*, a collection of verse.
[14]Thomas B. Crumpler, "History of Highlands" (an unpublished manuscript), p. 31.
[15]Smith, *History of the Hudson Library Association*, p. 8.

in the post office. Relying on what he had gleaned from the newspaper before Mrs. Smith drove him out of the library, he would designate with colored pins on the map the current locations of the armies of the Central Powers and the Allies and would gladly update interested residents who gathered to hear details of the latest news.[16]

Not long after the library's move into its new building, Miss Lucy Elliott took over as librarian. She had chaired the building committee that supervised implementing her brother Huger's design for the new library. Her sister Charlotte would follow her a year later.[17]

She and Charlotte had been reared by a strong, Savannah-bred mother, Lucy Huger, married to a former Confederate army surgeon and Tulane University professor of philosophy and medicine, Dr. J. B. Elliott.[18] Culture and intellect were undeniably strong forces in their home.

Lucy herself was extraordinarily well read. Her daughter, Esther Shay, describes her as familiar with all the classics before 1900.[19] A graduate of Sophie Newcomb

---

[16]Crumpler, "History of Highlands," p. 31.

[17]Mary Chapin Smith in her 1928 history in the *Franklin Press* (see "Library Active at Highlands," July 5) lists Lucy and her sister Charlotte Elliott—in that order—as having followed Miss Staub as librarians. In her 1931 *History of the Hudson Library Association,* she reverses the order: first Charlotte, then Lucy. The 1928 chronology is more likely the correct one, since in the 1931 *History* Mrs. Smith feels the need to introduce building committee chairman Lucy Elliott, an unknown, as Huger Elliott's sister (p. 7), meaning she wasn't librarian as of that time in 1915; and we know that Lucy married Warren Cunningham and moved to New York in 1917 (telephone conversation with her daughter, Esther Cunningham Shay of Scarsdale, N.Y., December 6, 1993). Simple logic dictates therefore that Lucy Elliott was most likely librarian beginning after 1915 and ending in 1917, when her sister Charlotte filled the gap left by her departure. There are no library or newspaper records during this period to support a definitive statement.

[18]"Mrs. Elliott Dies Thursday," *Highlands Maconian,* October 7, 1931.

[19]Telephone conversation with Esther Huger Elliott Cunningham Shay of Scarsdale, N.Y., December 7, 1993.

College at Tulane University, she used to remark that she was educated by decayed gentlewomen who taught her French and German. She read novels in both these languages, lamenting that she had not learned German better when she embarked on Thomas Mann. Gibbon's *Decline and Fall of the Roman Empire* was a favorite with her.[20]

Miss Lucy introduced into the library the best translations of ancient Greek literature and the finest classics in English fiction.[21] In particular, she focused on the novels of George Meredith: *The Ordeal of Richard Feverel*, *Evan Harrington*, and *The Egoist*, as well as collections of his poetry. There was something inspiring about Meredith's ready acceptance of life as a process of becoming. He saw life as an intellectual evolution devoid of excessive sentimentality, selfishness, and vanity, and she passionately shared his view of intellectual growth as an essential part of life.

"She was the best-read woman I've ever known, without being a professor," says Mrs. Shay, "and a very fine pianist, who practiced six hours a day until she had a family and had to give it up."[22]

Upon Miss Lucy's marriage to Warren Cunningham and departure for New York in 1917, her sister replaced her as librarian. Miss Charlie (pronounced "Shar-lee," but also called Darchie) was poured from a different side of the same family mold. She was a lady about town whom everyone knew as quite civic minded, and she took her job at the library quite seriously. During one bitterly cold winter she considered opening the library so important that she would trudge down from her home on Satulah

---

[20]Telephone conversation with Esther Shay, December 7, 1993.
[21]Smith, *History of the Hudson Library Association*, p. 9.
[22]Telephone conversation with Esther Shay, December 7, 1993.

Mountain despite subzero gusts of wind.[23] She had a beautiful fur coat but never wore it and, when asked why, remarked that she considered it "too ostentatious."[24] This was when American men were fighting a grueling war!

Adults liked Miss Charlie. Children in the library, such as Dolly Harbison in her teens, remember her as rather stiff—not that they feared her; they respected her.[25] She was a tall, stunningly handsome woman who had a sense of who she was. She never married, more out of obedience to her father than out of choice, for she had two heavy interests—one a first cousin, the other a Catholic—both of whom her father rejected, and in keeping with the customs of her time she complied with his will.[26]

Nevertheless, she retained her independence through a single-mindedness about her beliefs. In the 1930s the sign she would attach to the hood of her beat-up Chevrolet would read, "Up car has right of way," and she fully expected down cars to pull over on her way up Satulah to her home. Indeed, on her way back down, she would reverse the sign, which read on the other side, "Down car has right of way."[27]

Miss Charlie had a singular personality. During her tenure as librarian, she didn't trust her new Model T[28] alone with a mechanic. If it didn't run properly and she had to take it to Hines' & Zoellner's Garage (currently the Condiment Shop on Church Street), she would put on a duster and crawl under the car with the mechanic to check out his work.[29] Never mind that she lacked

---

[23]Smith, *History of Hudson Library Association*, p. 10.
[24]Interview with Louise Edwards Meisel, September 29, 1993.
[25]Interview with Dolly Harbison, September 30, 1993.
[26]Telephone conversation with Esther Shay, December 7, 1993
[27]Ibid., and interview with Jan Chambers Chmar, February 23, 1994.
[28]Joe Reese had taught her how to drive it. Interview, December 1, 1993.
[29]Interview with Louise Edwards Meisel, September 29, 1993.

mechanical ability! Her being there would assure that he did the job right.

Even more unforgettable than Miss Charlie's delightful eccentricities, which were legendary, was the striking image she presented in 1923, after her tenure as librarian and after the Nineteenth Amendment had given women the vote—indeed even as advocates were proposing the Equal Rights Amendment for the first time. Expressing her opposition to the town's proposal to run water lines up Satulah, which threatened to destroy the beautiful hemlock-lined roads, she donned bloomers and middies and challenged H. M. Bascom for the mayorship of Highlands.[30] With arms akimbo and those gorgeous Huger-blue eyes, she lost the race for mayor, but her self-assurance won the respect of all who witnessed her brash chutzpah.

The irony of the affair, as it turned out, was that in 1925 when the springs on Satulah dried up and property owners had to beg the town to put in water lines, homeowners on the mountain had to pay for them themselves. The town had done all it was going to do.

Miss Charlie frequently entertained family and old friends at her home. When hard times set in during the early 1930s, she had to let Zella Wilson go, who kept house and cooked and was as much loved as any member of the family. Miss Charlie then learned to cook. She learned from a recently published copy of the *Joy of Cooking*. She hated cooking, becoming, nonetheless, quite an accomplished chef.[31]

Much of what Miss Charlie gave the library, to which she felt quite dedicated, involved public relations. More-

---

[30]Interview with Mrs. Rudolph (Winnie) Hertzberg, September 30, 1993.
[31]Telephone conversation with Esther Shay, December 7, 1993. Rombauer's now-classic *Joy of Cooking* was published in 1931.

over, she, like her sister before her, served as librarian without charge.

It was during Miss Charlie's tenure as librarian that Highlanders tuned their radios every Saturday morning to hear her brother Huger, who was now a director of the Metropolitan Museum of Art in New York City, talk about art.[32] It was also at this time that the first real movies offered an alternative to reading in Highlands. Before 1920 occasional movies provided by the county had been shown in the Masonic Hall. However, when Mr. Henry Worrell Sloan arranged to have movies shown in the school auditorium, "some of the young people in Highlands were so anxious for the moving picture show to come that they met it at Scaly."[33]

The most popular movies were Westerns, especially *The Virginian*, which some of the teenagers had read in the library. They cavorted about the streets of Highlands, impugning one another with insults meant to invoke the classic retort of the day: "When you call me that, smile!"

Henry Sloan is remembered not only for the movies that he introduced to the town but also for the vast number of books and magazines that he contributed to the library.[34] A retired cotton broker and landscape architect from New Orleans, he offered thirty-five-cent tours through the paths and terraces of his Cheeononda Garden[35] on the western slope of Satulah, replete with purple rhododendron and flame azalea, fragrant roses,

---

[32] "Mrs. Elliott Dies Thursday," *Highlands Maconian*, October 7, 1931.
[33] "Highlands Locals," *Franklin Press*, July 2, 1920.
[34] Interview with Louise Edwards Meisel (who worked for the library from 1928 to 1932 and is mentioned in Mrs. Smith's history).
[35] "Cheeononda" in the Indian language means "little hills upon little hills," like the series of terraces that climbed the slope of Mr. Sloan's natural garden. See Sarah Hicks Hines, "Mountain Paradise Found in Garden of Cheeononda," *Franklin Press & Highlands Maconian*, June 30, 1932.

iridescent irises, and copious grapevines. He invariably gave the proceeds to the library and the school. A voracious reader, he bought new works of fiction and donated them to the library, along with high-class magazines, like *Studio* and *Arts Illustrated*.

In 1922 word was received from California that the library's longest-serving trustee president had died at the age of eighty-seven and "like a shock of ripened wheat garnered in the harvest, passed to his eternal reward."[36] This was a year after S. T. Kelsey had passed away in Massachusetts at eighty-nine. Thomas Baxter White had provided the first stock of goods for Highlands. His opening a post office had saved Highlanders a four-mile walk or ride by horseback down the steep mountain trail to Horse Cove to retrieve the mail. For several years he served as justice of the peace, while contributing his time to promoting education, temperance, and religion. For twenty-one years he was the only correspondent from Highlands to the newspaper in Franklin. After his move to California, he became as much respected as he was in Highlands for his integrity and kindliness and appropriately enough was buried in Evergreen Cemetery there in La Verne.[37]

When Christina Anderson Rice succeeded Charlotte Elliott as librarian in 1921, Warren G. Harding had just replaced Woodrow Wilson as president. The literary world was thriving on masterworks that would endure. Edith Wharton received the Pulitzer Prize for her *Age of Innocence*. Works were appearing by John Dos Passos, Sherwood Anderson, F. Scott Fitzgerald, Willa Cather,

---

[36]"Macon Pioneer Passes Away: T. Baxter White, for Many Years a Resident of Highlands, Died on July 14, at La Verne, California," *Franklin Press*, August 4, 1922.
[37]Ibid. This burial ground, containing the White family plot, is now known as the La Verne Cemetery.

Katherine Mansfield, and Eugene O'Neill in America and Ezra Pound, Virginia Woolf, James Joyce, and T. S. Eliot in England. Mrs. Rice had considerable literary talent of her own. Her poems (in Mary Chapin Smith's estimation) celebrated "her beloved mountains with beauty, deep insight and feeling."[38]

There is a crag on Blue Ridge Crest,
I dearly love to climb.
There on the soft green moss I rest
In solitude sublime.

I look across to Highlands Falls
And hear the water roar,
It seems to me a voice that calls
From all time gone before.

And just beyond there rises high
Old Whiteside's hoary head,
It reaches almost to the sky
Above the laurel bed.

And all around there seems to be
No living thing at all,
Just mountains, clouds, and me,
And God, up over all.[39]

---

[38]Smith, *History of Hudson Library Association*, p. 9.
[39]Christina Rice, "Clouds," an unpublished poem, written ca. 1923. In the possession of her son, W. Herbert Rice. Another poem, "Love," written about the same time and also unpublished, reveals a delightful side of Mrs. Rice:

Once, I judged love from the books that I read.
I thought Cupid the spirit of song.
Then, I judged life from what people said,
I now know my judgment was wrong.

For I've had some experience with love myself,
And I've passed thru great struggle and strife,

She had a thorough knowledge both of the library and of the people who frequented it. She steered children and adults alike not only to the best books on the shelves but also to the books best suited for them. She introduced Margaret Gilbert (now Hall), the ten-year-old friend of her daughters Elizabeth and Eloise, to that marvelous story by Dinah Maria Mulock Craik about the lonely little boy confined high up in a tower who found happiness and became a king. This book, *The Little Lame Prince*, Margaret read during the summer of 1922, sitting on the second-story porch of the Central House.

During that summer she also loved reading Annie Fellows Johnston's Little Colonel stories. How much better they were than those saccharine Elsie Dinsmore tales,[40] which Martha Finley had written as Sunday-school stories for girls but which Margaret Gilbert hated, bound in their blue and red covers with a pansy imprinted on each. Elsie was such a goodie-goodie! How many Little Colonel tales would it take to clear her memory of that cloyingly sweet little girl who refused to play the piano for her parents and their company because it was Sunday and at last fainted away like a little martyr to her faith? Margaret wanted to give her a swift kick![41]

Christina was married to Luther Rice, who ran a thriving butcher shop and grocery store (next to where Wit's End is now), so she didn't require compensation. She was just looking for something to do apart from, or perhaps because of, rearing five children and writing a

---

I now know that Cupid is a mean, sneaking elf,
   And the way to judge love is from life.
[40]Several popular titles in this series by Martha Farquharson Finley were *Elsie at Home, Elsie in the South, Elsie's Young Folks, Elsie and Her Loved Ones,* and *Elsie on the Hudson.*
[41]Interview with Margaret Gilbert Hall, November 11, 1993.

few poems that were never published.[42] At one point when her husband suffered a long illness, she had to rely on Miss Charlie's taking over her duties. At another time Miss Rebecca Nall stepped in as acting librarian.[43] Miss Nall had been a teacher and principal of Highlands School[44] and years later would serve as eighth and eleventh president of the library's trustees.

On the whole Mrs. Rice ran the library precisely, authoritatively, like the executive of a corporation. Although not yet forty, she began to experience a serious decline in health. She loved her work at the library, and her organizational abilities were indispensable to its efficient operation. It was with considerable reluctance, therefore, that in 1923, two years before her death, she submitted her resignation to the board.

It was with the same measure of reluctance that Leila Lewis Marett took over the librarianship. Her husband, S. T. Marett,[45] directed Highlands' first bank (currently the Highlands Gem Shop), which had just opened that year, and she felt no pressing need for employment. Nor had she the inclination to work at the time.[46] On the other hand, she didn't have much to do at home, and the library desperately needed her, so she accepted the job—conditionally, of course: without pay.

---

[42]Interview with Dolly Harbison, September 22, 1993.
[43]Smith, *History of the Hudson Library Association,* p. 10.
[44]"News of Week of Highlands," *Franklin Press,* September 3, 1920.
[45]Pronounced "Már-ett." S. T. accented the first syllable. His brother, George, who ran the general store, accented the second syllable: "Ma-rétt." According to George's wife, this was how it was spelled [Interview with Dr. William C. Marett, January 28, 1994]. S. T. was more reserved, more businesslike than George, according to Bill Holt, who says that when as a young man he would bring a dollar or two to deposit in his savings account, Mr. S. T. Marett would always say, "It isn't what you make that counts, Richard, it's what you save." Interview October 14, 1993.
[46]Interview with Dolly Harbison, September 22, 1993. The Highlands Bank closed during the crash of 1929.

Mrs. Marett's background was not strictly literary, but she had stamina and considerable executive ability. Replacing the old method of checking out and receiving books with a far more organized and efficient system, she impressed the State Library Commission with professional reports of the library's circulation, its holdings, and the sources of its book additions during each year. She began to enforce more rigidly the regulations regarding the borrowing of books and the timely collection of fines on overdue returns. Upon her retirement in 1926 the library's holdings had attained roughly four thousand volumes, almost tripling during the decade after the library's occupancy of its new home what had taken three decades of purchases and donations to accumulate before the move.

During Mrs. Marett's tenure as librarian, the son of Highlands' co-founder Samuel T. Kelsey, Dr. Harry Kelsey of Baltimore, donated to the library in 1925 the pocket compass that fifty years earlier his father and Clinton H. Hutchinson had employed on top of Satulah to lay out the town of Highlands. It had served to designate an east-west line through the dense primeval forest that was cut to form Main Street and then to sight Hutchinson's house, Connemara (later Patrick T. Farnsworth's house), to the north and Kelsey's house, Kanonah Lodge (later Professor Harbison's house), to the south. Preliminary to Charles Slagle's professional survey three years later, this was the first survey of Highlands. Now the little compass, secured in an attractive case, became a valuable part of Highlands' early memorabilia treasured by the library.

At this time young Margaret Gilbert, still frequenting the library for new books to read, had moved permanently to Highlands, her father having set up his dental practice in the Masonic Lodge. It was now that Mrs. Marett introduced her to the magic of *The Secret Garden*, the warmth and humor of *Little Women* and Lucy Montgomery's *Anne of Green Gables*. She shivered under the curse of Hawthorne's *House of Seven Gables* and Poe's *Murders in the Rue Morgue*, both of which primed her to read Bram Stoker's *Dracula* from her library at home. That scared her to death! Not the blood, but the notion that he had hair in the middle of his hands![47]

One of her favorites from the Hudson Library was Alexandre Dumas' *Count of Monte Cristo*. For weeks she suffered through Edmond Dantès' unjust imprisonment and thrilled to the drama of his escape and rise to a powerful and darkly mysterious avenger of all who had wronged him. For Margaret Gilbert the library was the fountainhead of her glowing imagination.

Primary among Leila Marett's contributions to the library, apart from organization and efficiency, was the training in library work that she gave her successors, two refined and accomplished daughters of Professor Harbison, whose names for the next half-century would be synonymous with that of the Hudson Library.

---

[47] Interview with Margaret Gilbert Hall, November 11, 1993.

Miss Gertrude Harbison
Librarian, 1926–1974. Taken in 1974. Courtesy of Hudson Library.

Miss Dolly Harbison
Assistant, 1926–75. Taken in 1975. Courtesy of the Hudson Library.

Gertrude Harbison: 1926–30

Spring came over the mountain
Tardy and flustered;
She rushed through the valley
Apologetic as she left
A thrush in perfect pitch
With humming lilac buds.
Sidestepping spots of snow
High on the ridge, she came
Bouncing through the woods
Tossing sundrops into the warming air,
Raising violets from their winter bed
And kissing all the buds awake.
Tossing back her laughing head she spilled
An apronful of daffodils.[1]

"Take courage, brother. The Devil's dead." These were Mary Chapin Smith's words of advice to Gertrude and Dolly Harbison, who "never had it in our minds to take over the library. We were just there to help. So when Mrs. Marett announced that she was resigning and recommended that we take over, we were chagrined," says Dolly Harbison. "I remember Mary Chapin Smith telling us at the trustees' meeting: 'Take courage, brother! The Devil's dead.'"[2]

This year, 1926, was a year of many consequential beginnings. It was the year that Britain, under George the Fifth, welcomed the birth of Elizabeth the Second. It

---

[1] Dee McCollum, "Spring 1981," *The Summer Mountain: Poems of the Hills* (n.p., 1986), p. 13.
[2] Interview with Dolly Harbison, September 22, 1993. The quote comes from Charles Reade's *The Cloister and the Hearth*, chapter 24: "Courage, mon ami, le diable est mort!"

was the year that Hirohito became Emperor of Japan. It was the year that Hemingway published *The Sun Also Rises*; T. E. Lawrence, *The Seven Pillars of Wisdom*; and Duke Ellington's first records appeared. Two of the most popular songs this year were "Bye, Bye, Blackbird" and "I Found a Million-Dollar Baby in the Five-and-Ten-Cent Store." Jack Dempsey lost the heavyweight boxing championship of the world, and the American escapist Harry Houdini died, as did the greatest influence on twentieth-century world poetry, the German poet Rainer Maria Rilke.

In this year the population of the United States topped 115 million; North Carolina, 3 million; and the circulation in the Hudson Library approached four thousand, its membership four hundred. In this year Gertrude Harbison became Highlands' longest-serving librarian, and Dolly, her able assistant.

It was the year before when construction had begun under Mayor Henry M. Bascom on Highlands' water supply, electric, and sewer systems. It was the year after when a twenty-five-foot dam and 300-horse-power hydroelectric plant were built on the Cullasaja River,[3] forming Lake Sequoyah,[4] replacing kerosene lamps with electric light bulbs on the walls of almost every business

---

[3] Cullasaja is Cherokee for "sugar water" or "sweet water." The Cullasaja is also called Sugar Fork.
[4] The lake was named Sequoyah, in the words of Sarah Hicks Hines, "because nothing but an Indian name, expressive more than anything else, of the towering mountains, tumbling torrents, and lonely crags, would be fitting; and because Sequoyah, the Indian, was as outstanding among his tribe as our beautiful lake is outstanding among other lakes." Sarah Hicks Hines, "Sequoyah Name Given to New Highland Lake," *Franklin Press*, June 26, 1930. There were four other artificial lakes in Highlands in 1927: Mirror, Lindenwood (built for Captain S. P. Ravenel, Sr., and renamed in 1931 Ravenel Lake), Harbison (now Harris Lake, named for Rebecca Harris, who bought it from Professor Harbison), and Ravenel (actually Osserogo but owned by the Ravenels). Lindenwood was used for boating and bathing.

and home, the Hudson Library included, and offering water from a faucet instead of a pail.⁵

The year 1926 in Highlands rode the crest of a wave, built up by the swiftly vanishing past and just now breaking on the threshold of the modern age. The reins of a library still very much in its teens were being handed to a young woman just out of her teens but of the old school of good breeding and a classical education.

Miss Gertrude Harbison was the daughter of the Hudson Library's fourth librarian, Professor Harbison, who at this stage in his illustrious career had completed a period of collecting plants for the Biltmore Herbarium on the estate of George W. Vanderbilt and was the southern collector for Dr. Charles Sprague Sargent and the Arnold Arboretum. Miss Gertrude possessed a razor-sharp mind, and word had it that she could remember things from the time she was three years old. Lucile Pierson Reese recalls how she never forgot anyone's birthday. Miss Gertrude kept to herself more than her sister, Dolly. Miss Dolly's personality was more demonstrative. However, both sisters, when they weren't recommending a book to read or enticing a child with a summary of its plot, left library patrons, more often than not, on their own.

Jan Chambers Chmar saw Miss Gertrude as rather stern, a librarian first, and Miss Dolly as more affable, a person first.⁶ Everette Wilson felt that both sisters were rather reserved. "You found out about the outer rim of them, but the second and third layer, you didn't get to know."⁷ Bill Holt recalls, however, that both ladies had a

---

[5]"Highlands is Enjoying New Power Supply," *Asheville Times*, April 17, 1927, and interview with Dolly Harbison, September 22, 1993. See also minutes of trustees meeting, September 12, 1927: motion passed that "electric lights be installed in the Hudson Library."
[6]Interview with Jan Chambers Chmar, September 24, 1993.
[7]Interview with Everette Wilson, September 28, 1993.

habit of speaking quite fast, which in his view reflected the speed of their thought.[8] There was no doubt that they were highly educated, yet at the same time, in the assessment of Sarah Thompson McNamee, "so precious, sweet, and kind."[9] Jeremy Wilcox felt that no two librarians could have been better cast.[10]

The first year after Miss Gertrude assumed the reins, the library spent $120 on "72 fine books," in the proud opinion of the book committee.[11] Among fictional works they bought P. C. Wren's best seller *Beau Geste*, George Moore's historical romance *Héloise and Abélard*, John Erskine's idol-breaking *Galahad*, and Dorothy Canfield's American study, *Her Son's Wife*—all published within the previous five years. For nonfiction they bought Henry Drummond's *Ascent of Man*, William H. Hudson's tropical romance *Green Mansions*, and his autobiographical *Far Away and Long Ago*, Baird Spalding's *Life and Teachings of the Masters of the Far East*, *Revolt in the Desert* by T. E. Lawrence, and Robert L. Mason's *Lure of the Great Smokies*.

For the children they acquired a number of books that became highly popular over the years: a new book by A. A. Milne, called *Winnie the Pooh*, Frances Hodgson Burnett's *Cozy Lion*, two of Lucy Fitch Perkins' twins series: the *Filipino Twins* and the *Colonial Twins*, and three of Laura Lee Hope's Bobbsey twins books.

Gertrude and Dolly knew, as the book committee knew but never told the children, that Laura Lee Hope was a man who wrote under so many pen names that every

---

[8] Interview with Bill Holt, October 14, 1993.
[9] Interview with Sarah Thompson McNamee, October 27, 1993.
[10] Interview with Jeremy Wilcox, December 4, 1993.
[11] "Report of the Book Committee on Books Purchased from August, 1926, to November 1927," in Secretary's Book, Hudson Library Association, 1926-54.

child today has read one or more of his books in series. His most popular series, of course, was the Rover boys by Arthur Winfield, which Bill Holt and Herbert Rice read as children in Highlands.[12] However, when he wrote the Tom Swift series—Harry Wright's favorite as a young boy[13]—he was Victor Appleton. He was Carolyn Keene when he wrote the Nancy Drew mysteries before turning them over to his daughter, Harriet Stratemeyer Adams. Then she became Franklin W. Dixon, and wrote the Hardy boys stories.[14]

These are things a wise librarian doesn't volunteer to tell a child, for what child reading *Snow Lodge* or *Blueberry Island* by Laura Lee Hope could remember or even pronounce the name of their real author, "Edward Stratemeyer," much less understand a "pseudonym"? For Anne Altstaetter (now Rhodes) it was enough that the library carried the Bobbsey twins, the Rover boys, and Tom Swift, whoever wrote them. She could check them out and read them all summer long perched way up high in the cleft trunk of the huge old pine tree in her yard, as though leaning against the cross-limbed back of a natural chair, stopping only occasionally to gaze at her home far below.[15]

Anne Altstaetter was a summer visitor, like many others who swelled the ranks of the summer population. These summer children counted their lives as mostly lived

---

[12]Interview with Bill Holt, October 14, 1993, and Herbert Rice, January 10, 1994.
[13]Interview with Harry Wright, October 29, 1993.
[14]See "Stratemeyer, Edward," in George Perkins et al., eds., *Benét's Reader's Encyclopedia of American Literature* (New York, 1991), pp. 1024–25.
[15]Interview with Anne Altstaetter Rhodes, October 31, 1993. Anne's parents, Colonel Frederick William and Rebecca Raoul Altstaetter, owned Rosemary, their home, and Laurel Lodge, which they let to renters, on the southwest corner of Main Street at First (location of the furniture store today).

in Highlands, the rest of the year spent in hibernation in their winter homes, impatiently anticipating their return to the wonderful views and cool mountain air of their summer homes.

Nancy Jussely (now Lyle) was the daughter of a sea captain, who was often away on long voyages from his home in the low country of Georgia and South Carolina. Her mother would pack a couple of large trunks and whisk her three young daughters away to spend the summer with their cousins Sarah and Bess Hines in Highlands. It was a long trip in the 1920s: first by train with an overnight stop, then by the mail touring motor car up the long, narrow dirt road. However, at the top was a whole summer of hiking, swimming, boating, teas at the lovely Sloan's estate, silent movies at the old schoolhouse on the hill, with Aunt Bessie Hines accompanying the action on the screen with appropriate piano music, church activities and bazaars, favorite books to read at the library, and dance classes a short way up Satulah. Quite a few girls in or approaching their teens regularly attended Elizabeth Lyon's Modern Dance Class. Miss Lyon had taken lessons while in Europe from Isadora Duncan and had brought back perfectly gorgeous silk pieces, which she draped over the body suits made by the mothers of her students out of sleeveless undershirts, dyed in bowls of hot strong tea.[16]

The year after Miss Gertrude took over as Hudson librarian, 1927, which was that awful year that the blight killed the great chestnut trees and left their dominance of the forest to the oak and the hickory,[17] the newly created

---

[16]Letter to the author from Mrs. David (Nancy Jussely) Lyle of Rock Hill, S. C., November 4, 1993.
[17]Before the blight, chestnuts were gathered by the bushel and sold, but the gatherer had to get out early before the wild hogs got them all, running from tree to tree. Interview with Louis Edwards, September 30, 1993.

Highlands Museum, of which Professor Harbison was a trustee, requested permission of the library board to construct an annex onto their building. Mr. William M. Cleaveland had just donated to the museum his father's collection of Indian relics, which needed proper housing. Additionally, the museum needed a room for their offices and meetings.

The new room, added to the east side of the building, would revert to the library when the museum moved out (as it turned out, in twenty years), so the library had a great deal to gain in allowing for future expansion by granting the museum permission to build on. When construction began the next year, the noise was no more distracting than the thrilling news that Charles Lindbergh had successfully landed his *Spirit of St. Louis* in Paris and the Babe had scored his sixtieth home run. Indeed, the slow, whimsical strains heard from construction workers in 1928 came from the latest hit that lamented toting bars and lifting chains with a body soaked and racked in pain.

"Blue Skies" and "My Blue Heaven" remained popular in Highlands throughout the summer of 1928 until one day in mid-August when eight inches of rain deluged the town, the most ever in a twenty-four-hour period of its recorded history.[18] It was Heaven's way of confirming Highlands—nestled among the whispering pines and hemlocks on a shoulder of the mountain called Satulah—as the wettest spot east of the Rockies, albeit with fewer rainy days than Asheville, the driest spot in the state.[19] These facts were carefully recorded by Gertrude Harbi-

---

[18]Gertrude Harbison, as reported by John Parris, "Roaming the Mountains [Gertrude Harbison]," *Asheville Citizen*, September 20, 1973. Reprint in "Miss Harbison Recognized," *Highlander*, September 27, 1973.
[19]Ibid.

son, who took her job of daily observer for the National Weather Service as seriously as her role of librarian. She had inherited the official designation from her father in March, just five months before this year's record rain.

While the library was expanding, construction began simultaneously on the Franklin Road to Highlands. Workers, indeed stouthearted daredevils, carved a ledge halfway up a 500-foot precipice just wide enough to thread a passage through the cleavage of Cullasaja Gorge. The whole town celebrated, for after years of petitioning the state and federal governments and years of official postponements, the project was at last under way.

There was really no comparison between what the state spent on the Herculean task of traversing the gorge and what the Hudson Library collected in two-cent overdue fines. However, relatively speaking, the system worked out by Gertrude Harbison to allow new books to pay for themselves was every bit as clever as the methods employed by the state road department to move solid granite. Beginning with the 1928 publication of Stephen Vincent Benét's Pulitzer-Prize-winning *John Brown's Body*,[20] the library put new books on a table and checked them out at ten cents a day. When a new book had paid for itself, it was shelved with the older ones.[21]

In the case of *John Brown's Body*, portrayed as one of America's classic epic poems—a stroke of genius in its realistic and profoundly sympathetic depiction of the Civil War by an acknowledged master of lyrical beauty and deep-rooted patriotism—the waiting list was so long that the book never reached the shelf. The library and its literate patrons considered Stephen Vincent Benét a

---

[20]This novel-in-verse was completed on a Guggenheim fellowship and won the Pulitzer Prize in 1929.
[21]Interview with Louise Edwards Meisel, September 29, 1993.

native son, or at the least a part of the furniture from its early days.[22]

The excitement over *John Brown's Body* escaped the children of the library, for the thrills of the very young centered on the new English translation of Felix Salten's *Bambi*,[23] published in 1928, and on *John Martin's Book* with its puzzles, rhymes, and oatmeal-paper pictures to color. The early grammar school children, like Marion Day (now Arnold),[24] read *John Martin*, because they could check it out for a week, while the older grammar school students fought for *Child Life*, which had a more advanced selection of poems, stories, and puzzles.

The *Book of Knowledge* attracted children of all ages, for each volume contained stories and poems, to be sure, but also instructions on how to make things. A child could make a kite right there at the table and take it home.

A favorite book of Virginia Edwards (now Fleming) by Ernest Seton Thompson, which accomplished the same purpose as the *Book of Knowledge*, was the foxed and

---

[22]*John Brown's Body* (New York, 1928) is no longer available at the Hudson Library, although a copy can be obtained from the Macon County Library in Franklin or the Western Carolina University Library in Cullowhee. Incidentally, an excellent book for young beginning writers, who might aspire to follow in Benét's footsteps, is *Stephen Vincent Benét on Writing* (Brattleboro, Vt., 1964), which is a collection of a great writer's essays and letters of advice to a young beginner on how to write and how to get published. A good sampling of Benét's poetry and prose can be found in the two volumes of his *Selected Works* (New York, 1942), *Volume I: Poetry* and *Volume 2: Prose*. These volumes are available in Franklin and Cullowhee. The one book by Benét held by the Hudson Library is *James Shore's Daughter* (1934). Other works held in Cullowhee are *Heavens and Earth*, *They Burned the Books*, *Western Star*, *Zero Hour: A Summons To Be Free*, *Last Circle: Stories and Poems*, and *Thirteen O'Clock: Stories of Several Worlds*.

[23]*Bambi* was originally published in 1923 in German. Felix Salten was a pseudonym of Siegmund Salzmann, a Hungarian critic and writer of adult novels and plays besides animal stories for children.

[24]Interview with Marion Day Arnold of Macon, Georgia, October 29, 1993.

buckled copy of *The Two Little Savages*. This story of two boys who had decided to live like Indians told how to make a fire or a bow and arrow. Virginia remembers that when she and several young friends in the woods near her home made a teepee out of feed sacks, modeled on the one constructed by the little savages, one little savage lit a match inside and set it on fire. They had to dump it in the creek.[25]

Anne Altstaetter chose an entirely different set of books to read. She lived vicariously the life of an English child in Frances Hodgson Burnett's *Sara Crewe* and the enormously popular *Little Lord Fauntleroy*, *The Little Princess*, and *The Secret Garden*. Then she followed the life of a Swiss mountain child in Johanna Spyri's *Heidi*, *Mazli*, and *Children of the Alps*. She recalls a truly exciting story in which a hole was bored all the way through the world.[26]

The older children, in their early teens, checked out Louisa May Alcott's *Little Women*, *Little Men*, *Eight Cousins*, and *Rose in Bloom* and steeped their minds in the Limberlost country of Gene Stratton Porter's *Freckles*, *Laddie*, and *Girl of the Limberlost*. In 1927 the first Jalna novel appeared by Mazo de la Roche, and each new sequel carried the Whiteoak family a generation further in its highly readable and instantaneously popular account of very different individuals growing up within the same family in Canada. In the end the library carried all twelve of the series, for the children loved them.

---

[25]Interview with Virginia Edwards Fleming, September 29, 1993. Louise and Virginia Edwards and Marion Day were all three descendants of Jonathan Heacock, one of the original settlers of Highlands, arriving from Minnesota in 1880. Louise and Virginia were his grandchildren through his daughter Helen, who married G. D. Edwards, and Marion was his grandchild through his daughter Martha, who married Emory Day.
[26]Interview with Anne Altstaetter Rhodes, October 31, 1993.

Some seventy-five percent of those who frequented the library on Saturday, apart from the dozen or so adults who came regularly, were children.[27] Louise and Ralph Sargent donated generous quantities of the books they had bought for their own children. The Sloans, Ravenels, Foremans, Crosbys, and Bascoms also gave books. The Durgins contributed a number of Westerns. Indeed, J. H. "Papa" Durgin, one of Highlands' pioneer settlers who came from Massachusetts in 1883, was a proper subject for a Western himself, having served as a scout and Indian fighter in his younger days and for five years in the late 1860s with General Custer. He took part in some of the hardest-fought campaigns directed by that daring and headstrong leader.[28]

John Durgin could ride a horse at a mad gait one day and be champing at the bit for a repeat performance the next, which had earned him the post of personal courier for Custer. That he miraculously survived so many dispatches without a scratch, though plenty of nearlys, won him the nickname "Reckless Jack." One wonders if Custer might have survived the infamous battle at Little Big Horn that wiped out his command in 1876 if Reckless Jack had not received his discharge from the army five years earlier, this man who could slip through the skirmish line as though it were the rear guard and, digging spurs into his mount, fly over the country like no other messenger to gather reinforcements. John Durgin passed on to the Hudson Library many books from his personal collection pertaining to the West for those who might wish to live vicariously the life that he had lived in actuality.

---

[27]Minutes of the trustees meeting, August 31, 1931: "75% of the readers are children."
[28]See "Highlands Man, 95, Has Had Dangerous, Colorful Career," *Franklin Press & Highlands Maconian*, September 22, 1938.

Young Bill Holt read every Western he could find by Zane Grey—especially *Riders of the Purple Sage* and *The Last of the Plainsmen*. He devoured each new wilderness adventure that the library acquired by James Oliver Curwood—another favorite of Harry Wright[29]—especially *The Grizzly King* and *The Valley of Silent Men*.[30]

If Virginia Edwards wasn't reading a donated *Yearling*, or Harry Wright, a copy of *Tom Sawyer* or *Huckleberry Finn*, then four or five children would gather around the latest issue of *St. Nicholas* to read the answers to the puzzles and the riddles in the previous issue or to read a poem or short story by Highlands' own Bess or Sarah Hines. *St. Nicholas* was as much an outlet for creative local talent as it was a popularizer of established authors. Louise Edwards saw her pen-and-ink drawings published in several issues.[31] Louise Bascom Barratt published children's dialogues;[32] and Dorothy Farnsworth, poetry and songs.

Dorothy Farnsworth rarely, if ever, published under her own name. Her writing career began with a poem that she had published when she was thirteen. Over the years she used twenty-one pen names, with a different reason for each one. The name she used for her verses was Robert Emmet Ward, and for her songs, Ann F. Barr, both in the United States and in England. In the May, 1930, issue of *St. Nicholas* she would one day publish her poem "Consider the Llama" under the name Robert E. Ward. Reginald Birch, the artist for *Little Lord Fauntleroy* and other works by Frances Hodgson Burnett, would illustrate the poem. Mrs. Farnsworth claimed a preference for

---

[29] Interview with Harry Wright, October 29, 1993.
[30] Interview with Bill Holt, October 14, 1993.
[31] Interview with Louise Edwards Meisel, September 29, 1993.
[32] For a list of Louise Bascom Barratt's children's stories, see Appendix VI.

writing humorous verse, as she would rather see laughter than tears.[33]

Children all over the United States and England wrote St. Nicholas to tell him how much their whole family loved his magazine and couldn't get along without him. They told him stories about themselves and found their letters printed in "The Letter-Box" each month. Eleven- and twelve-year-old girls wrote about how anxious they were to read the lovely *Lady Jane* each month and how the story would be spoiled if Lady Jane didn't get back to her relatives.[34] Eleven- and twelve-year-old boys wrote about how fascinated they were with *The Boy Settlers*, especially the part where the Howells and Bryants crossed the Mississippi.[35] If children found any fault at all with the many serialized stories in *St. Nicholas*, it was that they were all too short, for reading this magazine every month became in truth an addiction.

For the library to be crowded required only four or five children at a time, except during the rainy season when the number increased dramatically. Still, it was never noisy. Talking was not allowed. Some children, like Robb White and his little sister Becky, came almost every library day. Invariably each would perch quietly over a book on the floor, chin in hand, feet in the air, having discovered one of the least frequented cubicles, like the botany or birds section or the chemistry shelf where the books were dated, so as not to be disturbed or get trampled underfoot.

---

[33] See Sarah Hicks Hines, "Farnsworths Study Science and Arts at Highlands Home," *Franklin Press*, May 15, 1930. Mrs. Patrick T. (Dorothy McPherson) Farnsworth was also a sculptor, her most admired bronze being a girl's head, entitled "Melisande."

[34] *Lady Jane*, a novel set in New Orleans, by Mrs. C. V. Jamison.

[35] *The Boy Settlers*, the third book in the series *The Boy Emigrants* and *The Fairport Nine*, by Noah Brooks, a personal friend of Abraham Lincoln.

Years later Robb would repay the library of his childhood by writing books himself for children to read in their own libraries.[36] He would fill his own books with adventures of which most people only dreamed. In Highlands he and Becky found adventures enough, for besides reading, he loved swimming and was an extraordinary diver, while she rode horseback, her long curls flying, along the scenic trails and woodland paths around the town.[37]

Outside Highlands, Robb would one day do all those things he had read about. He would attend the U.S. Naval Academy at Annapolis. He would pilot a plane high above the clouds, serve in a submarine deep beneath the waves, and on a carrier and a battleship on the calm and stormy surface of the sea. He would learn how to sail with and against the wind. On resigning his commission in the Navy, he would become a wanderer, like Ulysses or Sinbad or Richard Halliburton. He would travel to the caves of Kurdistan, have his own private island in the Caribbean, and build a beach house in Malibu.

He would one day fulfill the goal he had set for himself when he was thirteen, living his future vicariously in the aisles of the Hudson Library. He would become a writer and write short stories and adventure books for young people, like *The Survivor, Silent Ship, Silent Sea,* and *No Man's Land.* He would write screenplays and TV scripts and thrilling books for movies, like *House on Haunted Hill, Up Periscope,* and *Thirteen Ghosts.*

Indeed his life itself, so filled with adventure, would be filmed at his home in the Caribbean and be called *Our Virgin Island.* If his friends in Highlands knew none of his many novels, they would at least know *Our Virgin*

---

[36]Interview with Louise Edwards Meisel, September 29, 1993.
[37]Interview with Anne Altstaetter Rhodes, October 31, 1993.

Island for the part of his life that he had passed summering in this small town. In the end he and his wife would settle down with their basset hound in Arizona. He would grow orchids but never stop writing, for since thirteen that would have been his dream.[38]

The reality at the base of this dream was that he and his little sister Becky came almost every library day in their youth and read everything that Miss Gertrude or Miss Dolly would suggest, and more.

Unlike Robb and Becky White, Allen Ordway was never at the library itself, except to check out a whole stack of books once a week and bring them back from home, already read, right away. His father worked in 1928 and 1929 on the Franklin Road. However, his mother, when she wasn't educating the prisoners in Franklin, was educating Allen. What he got from the Hudson Library and his mother was his entire schooling. Ordinarily, Miss Gertrude or Miss Dolly held the line, allowing patrons to check out no more than three or four books on any one day, but for Allen they stretched the rules just a bit, allowing him to take out whole armfuls every week.[39] From their erudite education inspired by their professor father, the Misses Harbison knew instinctively the truth of Rabelais' maxim, that a child is not a vase to be filled but a fire to be lit.[40]

---

[38] Robb White was born in the Philippine Islands, the son of a missionary who moved eventually to Thomasville, Georgia, which now claims Robb as its native son. Other adventure books for young people by Robb White are *Candy, Surrender, The Survivor, The Haunted Hound, The Lion's Paw, Midshipman Lee of the Naval Academy, Sailor in the Sun, Three Against the Sea, Torpedo Run, No Man's Land,* and his works include one adult book of fiction, *Run Masked. Deathwatch* and *Fire Storm* appeared during the 1970s.

[39] Interview with Virginia Edwards Fleming, September 29, 1993.

[40] The sixteenth-century French literary giant and physician Rabelais displayed in his own life the never-ending quest for knowledge, so char-

Allen would return his books—all of them—on time. This was not always the case with others. Periodically Gertrude Harbison would declare a day of amnesty, when people could bring back books that were overdue without fear of penalty. On one occasion a patron returned an entire armload of books. However, some would haphazardly leave them on the porch in the rain, and many in this way were lost.[41]

Then there was the time in 1930 that the library lost (and never found) Edna St. Vincent Millay's *Buck in the Snow*.[42] Louise Edwards searched high and low for this title. "Someone just snitched it," she concluded. "It was brand new."[43] Books by Millay and Edith Wharton were in high demand, that is, at high risk. "So we created an oddity in office," explained Mary Chapin Smith. The trustees appointed Mrs. J. A. (Bessie) Hines official book chaser. The job was not at all pleasant. People took offense. Mrs. Smith observed: "the greater the sinner the more was the sinner offended!"[44] When Mrs. Hines tired of the task, she turned the chore over to Mrs. A. J. Salinas, a highly trained and most successful retriever.

On the whole, people returned their books, even the folks who trudged up the steep Passmore Trail[45] once a week from Horse Cove or the long trek from Shortoff, tot-

---

acteristic of the Renaissance thirst for erudition and of his own satiric masterpiece, *Gargantua and Pantagruel*.

[41] Interview with Louise Edwards Meisel, September 29, 1993.

[42] Mary Chapin Smith, *History of the Hudson Library Association* (Highlands, 1931), p. 10.

[43] Interview with Louise Edwards Meisel, September 29, 1993.

[44] Smith, *History of the Hudson Library Association,* p. 10.

[45] The footpath made by John Passmore to deliver the mail between Highlands and Horse Cove. It went straight up the Highlands mountain and, as Frances Lombard observes, "was steep as a horse's face." See Frances Baumgarner Lombard, *From the Hills of Home* (Whiteside Cove, N.C., 1972, repr. 1993), p. 76.

ing flower sacks to haul back the scores of books their friends had requested that they check out.[46]

When the state completed the grading of the Franklin Road in 1929, the year that Raoul Altstaetter and Margaretta Duane (now Wood) galloped their horses through Highlands and were arrested for speeding,[47] two momentous events occurred that hurled the library initially—and subsequently the town, the country, and the world—into a new view of prosperity. On August 10 Bobby Jones, double champion of both the United States Amateur and the United States Open Golf tournaments and touted as "the most famous golf player in the world,"[48] played an exhibition match to christen the new Highlands nine-hole golf course.

Important for the little institution on East Main Street, this event laid the groundwork for a benefit played two years later for the library. Gertrude and Dolly Harbison joined the more than fifteen hundred golf enthusiasts at the reception to honor Jones, who had scored a sixty-six on nine holes played twice, since that's all the Highlands course had.[49] Little did anyone suspect that Jones' next game on this course would effectually lift the library from the nadir of its fiscal existence to such heights that the staid and sober Mary Chapin Smith would "faint away with joy and gratitude."[50]

---

[46]Interview with Louise Edwards Meisel, September 29, 1993.
[47]Interview with Anne Altstaetter Rhodes, October 31, 1993.
[48]"Highlands to Unveil Monument to Founder: Three Events Will Be Celebrated There on August 10," *Asheville Citizen*, August 1, 1929.
[49]Jones paired up with Mary Rogers, winner of the Biltmore Forest Invitational Tournament, against Scott Hudson, Jr., president of the Atlanta Athletic Club, and Crawford Rainwater. See Evangeline McLennan Davis, *The Lure of Highlands* (Highlands, 1981), p. 23. Admission to the exhibition was a dollar.
[50]Smith, *History of the Hudson Library Association*, p. 12.

However, that event is for a later accounting in this history. The other event of the year, which not only affected the library, the town, and the country but threw the whole world into a state of crisis, occurred on October 28—Black Friday—the day the U.S. stock market crashed with a value loss of $26 billion. Ironically, the two tunes most popular just before the market's collapse were "Stardust" and "Singing in the Rain."

But there would be no singing in the Highlands rain, for the bubble had burst. The road to salvation that the sacred ladies of the flowers had funded at the turn of the century with a splendid donation of thirty dollars abruptly disintegrated in a dead end. In 1928, before the crash, Mrs. Harvey L. Parry's Camp Parry-dise Players staged Browning's *Pied Piper of Hamelin* as a benefit on the grounds of Smith Cottage. It had netted sixty dollars, above the fifty dollars in the library treasury.[51] The board had felt prosperous. It had voted to give the librarian and her assistant an annual salary of twenty-five dollars each.

A second performance by the Parry-dise Players in 1929 had netted almost as much again. However, in 1930, after the crash, the library's bank balance dropped to four dollars, with an eighty-eight-dollar insurance premium due in two months' time. This was the year that Millay's brand-new *Buck in the Snow* mysteriously disappeared. Funds were too scarce to buy recently published copies of Hemingway's *Farewell to Arms*, Thomas Wolfe's *Look Homeward, Angel*, Faulkner's *The Sound and the Fury*, and Erich Remarque's best seller *All Quiet on the Western*

---

[51]Camp Parry-dise for girls was established on Little Scaly Mountain in 1924 by Judge Harvey L. Parry of Atlanta. Judge Parry died August 5, 1931. The site is currently occupied by The Mountain, the Highlands Unitarian camp and conference center.

Front. A third Parry-dise performance in 1931 netted eighty dollars to pay off the insurance premium but left a very small amount in the librarian's hands for running expenses, a mere thirty-three cents in the bank[52] and, with Judge Parry's death, no prospects for the coming year.

---

[52]Smith, *History of the Hudson Library Association,* p. 11.

Satulah Road
View north from Sloan's Gap toward town. Taken in the late 1920s.
Courtesy of the Bascom–Barratt estate.

Highlands Inn and the Water Fountain
Fourth and Main. Altitude oak on the right. Taken summer, 1930.
Courtesy of Hudson Library.

Summer Guests: 1931–39

Ever the cool, sweet rain
   falls on the green, green mountains;
Ever it overflows
   from the misty skyland fountains;
Ever the deep woods drink it—
   gratefully receives:
Pine and oak and hemlock
   fern and galax leaves
Drink of it and glisten,
   glisten and drink again,
For the beauty of the Blue Ridge
   is the bride of the mountain rain.[1]

Henry van Dyke, American clergyman, educator, and author of the now famous *Story of the Other Wise Man*, observed at the turn of the century, "The first day of spring is one thing, and the first spring day is another. The difference between them is sometimes as great as a month."[2] At an emergency meeting of the Hudson Library board, called in July of 1931 because the treasury had been "greatly depleted," the trustees considered two items of business: first, a preliminary report on a matter of immediate concern and, then, a plea for solutions to the long-term dilemma.

The preliminary report, given by Mrs. Marett, was that "a cow had been engaged to eat the grass in front of the library, but had done a very poor job."[3] Headaches come in

---

[1] Bess Hines Harkins, "Rainy Summer," *Unknown Seas* (Los Angeles, 1958), p. 16.
[2] Henry van Dyke, *Fisherman's Luck* (1899), chapter 5.
[3] Minutes of the called meeting, July 21, 1931.

pairs. The solution to the preliminary problem was to entrust Rebecca Nall's nephew, Thomas Greville, with the completion of the cow's work.

The solution to the long-term dilemma of how to replenish the treasury, however, came less easily. It was not until the next meeting that Mrs. S. T. Marett proposed a solution inspired by Scott Hudson, a principal founder of the Highlands Estates: a benefit golf game. Just like the one that had featured Bobby Jones two years earlier! Only one year earlier Jones had made the lowest score ever registered on the local links when he played a public exhibition game, featuring the king of golfers with the diamond king, Ty Cobb.[4] That event, in which Jones scored a record sixty-four, had attracted more than three hundred spectators. If anyone could save the library, it would have to be Bobby Jones!

The outcome of the highly publicized affair that took place on August 15, 1931, was that the Hudson Library netted nearly six hundred dollars, the most it had ever received from a library benefit.[5] At a subsequent called meeting, the trustees renewed the $25 annual salary for both Harbisons, invested $300 in Realty Trust & Saving Co. of Augusta at five percent interest, and as Mary Chapin Smith euphorically exclaimed: "there was near being the spectacle of a whole society fainting away with joy and gratitude. Only being very modern women we thought we wouldn't faint. We went instead to spend the money."[6]

---

[4]"Ty Cobb and Jones Golf Together: Bobby meets Diamond King," *Highlands Maconian*, September 10, 1930.
[5]A net balance of $580.75 was reported in the minutes of the Annual Meeting, August 31, 1931. See also "Library Fund Increased $500," *Highlands Maconian*, August 19, 1931.
[6]Mary Chapin Smith, *History of the Hudson Library Association* (Highlands, 1931), p. 12.

At the annual meeting the celebration continued. The trustees decided to publish Mary Chapin Smith's *History of the Hudson Library Association* at a cost of forty dollars. They paid her fifty dollars and set the price of the pamphlet at twenty-five cents a copy.

The board now planned extensive book purchases, beginning with the acquisition of Pearl S. Buck's best seller, *The Good Earth*. Physical improvements to the library building were in the offing, as well as benefits, which the library would sponsor itself.

During the next three decades library-sponsored fund raisers would include card parties, food sales, a movie benefit (which netted "very little," meaning five dollars), a children's party (a "marked success"!), and the first Silver Tea at Wolf Ridge, the lovely home of Miss Marguerite Ravenel. The event doubled the number of new members of the Library Association and led to annual Silver Teas years thereafter. Another golf exhibition with Bobby Jones netted $275 in 1940.[7] Garden tours, rummage sales, author readings, art exhibits, and plant sales added to the coffers right until 1961: the year of the first book sale, and the year following: the third-best fund raiser ever, the first Art Show, which netted $240.

So for the ensuing years beginning with 1931, the library's treasury increased dramatically: $100 in 1933, $200 in 1935 (from a third benefit featuring Bobby Jones), $300 in 1938, $500 in 1940, and so on. The librarians' individual salaries increased proportionately: $25 in 1931, $50 in 1936, $220 in 1942, $480 in 1946, and $1,200 in 1956. However, so did the summer hours of operation: from three days a week, totaling twelve hours, in

---

[7]"Highlands Highlights," *Franklin Press & Highlands Maconian,* August 15, 1940.

1936 to every working weekday, totaling thirty hours, in 1956.

Beginning in 1931, therefore, with membership approaching five hundred and circulation five thousand, the library experienced a significant growth that directly paralleled the growth of the town and the nation. The permanent population of Highlands at the time stood at 447 with a summer count of approximately three thousand.[8] The Chamber of Commerce was founded in this year, the biggest tourist season ever.[9]

Before 1931 Highlands—and the Hudson Library—had grown by impulses, rather like a tree than a mushroom. The latest impulse had begun just before the Depression; the previous impulse, just before the war. Both had been arrested by catastrophe on an international scale. However, the town and the library now found themselves on the threshold of a new start that would eclipse all other impulses in the history of both. New blood was arriving every day. The town (with its electric, water, and sewer systems installed) and the library (with its expanded inventory, physical improvements, and financial house in order) stood strong on a broader and firmer foundation. The U.S. population, at this juncture in history, having grown by 50 million in five years, peaked in 1931 at 170 million.

However, as every teenager knows, intuitively if not directly, from aching experience, great bursts of growth entail considerable pain. The library's circulation was on the increase to the same extent that its books were wearing out. The trustees gave about thirty Sunday

---

[8]"Social and Personal News from Highlands," *Highlands Maconian*, July 29, 1931.
[9]"1931 Proves Biggest Tourist Year: Most Visitors Ever to Come," *Highlands Maconian*, September 30, 1931. The first chamber had twenty-two members.

school books that no longer appealed to the reading public a more appropriate home. Most of the readers being children, many library volumes that had suffered damage had to be retired. So for the next decade mending books ate up a librarian's hours to the point that the board chose to supplement annual pay. In 1936 the trustees paid Dolly Harbison twenty-nine cents an hour for fifty recorded hours of mending and making heavy paper covers for 111 volumes![10]

By 1931 pavement of all roads leading out of Highlands toward Franklin, Dillard, Walhalla, and Cashiers was completed with crushed rock from the town quarry mixed with asphalt oil as binder.[11] The water fountain that had graced the intersection of Main and Fourth streets was dismantled and taken away. Bordered by large granite slab stones and chain-linked hitching posts and stocked with trout and goldfish, this fountain had always been the center of Highlands. Horses brought into town had watered here. Kids had balanced themselves along the top of the wall. "Adults warned, 'You'll fall in!'" recalls Marion Day Arnold, "but we never did."[12]

The road toward Horse Cove, as the only exception, was still a secondary dirt road and would remain so until 1942. This was the road at the end of which the library stood, as though on a country road, like the last bastion of rural charm frequented only by those who preferred the less traveled path. In the words of Mary Chapin Smith, the library—like Highlands—was not intended for those who traveled the hard-surfaced motor highways and raced through the center of town and on, "at 40 miles an

---

[10]Minutes of Annual Meeting, August 6, 1936.
[11]See "Highlands and Vicinity," map of September 13, 1931, showing main and secondary motor roads, roads passable by auto, poor roads or unopened streets, and trails. Copyrighted 1932 by Thomas N. E. Greville.
[12]Telephone conversation with Marion Day Arnold, October 29, 1993.

hour." It was meant instead for those who went about a little more slowly, to see the flowers and count the chipmunks that scampered across the dusty road. It was meant for those who wished for "a book and a shady nook" in Highlands' pride and joy.[13]

The library and the town were meant for the many visitors who kept coming back, season after season, to rejoice in the social as much as the rural charm there along the by-road and the high road, isolated but protected by Satulah's arms. In their own unique ways the library and the town prospered, not in the conventional sense of vigorous good fortune or financial success. Rather they thrived, as a golden butterfly thrives that measures its daily existence in the sun's warmth by the nectar of individual encounters, each holding no more universal significance than that of a single forget-me-not.

Despite a resolution passed by the library's board that residents of Franklin not be allowed to use the library,[14] more and more nonresidents in Highlands borrowed books. Furthermore, they sought to borrow more than two books at a time. By 1935, the year that the town installed a stop light at Fourth and Main streets and the number of summer homes in Highlands had increased to two hundred,[15] book space was scarce. The shelves were

---

[13] Mary Chapin Smith, "Center of Beauty's Realm Lies In Highlands' Country: Wonderland Is Described," *Highlands Maconian*, November 5, 1930.
[14] Minutes of trustees meeting, August 21, 1931. The Franklin Library had only recently reopened, having ceased to function several years prior to April, 1933. In this year Mrs. Margaret Ordway, wanting the Franklin library to serve the public again, re-established it in the Franklin Masonic Hall. She was the mother of Allen Ordway, as described above. See "Reopening of Library Urged: Mrs. Margaret Ordway Asks for Volunteers to Aid in Task," *Franklin Press & Highlands Maconian*, January 19, 1933.
[15] Mrs. T. C. Harbison, "Many New Homes Built at Highlands: Town Enjoys Building Boom, Business Section as Well as Residential Areas Improved," *Franklin Press & Highlands Maconian*, August 29, 1935.

overflowing. In 1937—while one of the most popular shows in the history of radio, "The Shadow," was teaching wrongdoers that "the weed of crime bears bitter fruit" and the Franklin Library was becoming the Macon County Library—new books, like Margaret Mitchell's *Gone With the Wind,* James Hilton's *We Are Not Alone,* and Lloyd C. Douglas' *White Banners,*[16] were replacing worn-out books in the Hudson Library, but space was available for only one hundred new volumes each year.

So in 1941, when the Highlands Museum moved out of its borrowed space in the library to occupy new quarters of its own and celebrated in the same way that the library had rejoiced when it outgrew its wing of the school, the library too rejoiced. Overnight the vacated room became the children's room.[17] Space was then made to transfer the original bookcase, the cradle that had contained the library as a babe, from the school lunch room into the main room of the library itself.[18]

Dolly Harbison recalls, however, that the plan never materialized. "The bookcase was as tall as a door and about as wide. It had two sections, a top and a bottom, and the doors opened out from the center, like a wardrobe, but it had been painted some awful thick gray, and we decided we didn't want it," she says.[19] Five years later, as will be seen, the library would receive from Dr. Alexander P. Anderson's estate two very attractive

---

[16]"New Books in Hudson Library," *Highlander*, August 17, 1937. This was the year that the Dillard Road to Highlands was being reduced from eighteen to fifteen miles and surfaced with crushed stone. See "New Highway Being Built," *Franklin Press & Highlands Maconian*, March 18, 1937.
[17]Minutes of Annual Meeting, August 7, 1941.
[18]Mrs. H. G. Story, "Children's Room Planned at Library," *Franklin Press & Highlands Maconian*, July 24, 1941. "The closed bookcase, used by the school lunch room for several years, is the original library and the trustees hope to get this bookcase for the children's room."
[19]Interview with Dolly Harbison, December 6, 1993.

enclosed bookcases, which would serve as a more appropriate home for the volumes that started the Hudson Library.

These bookcases would hold half a century of sentimental value, regardless of monetary worth, as is evidenced by one of the seventy titles that remain today: Mrs. Adeline Dutton Train Whitney's *Patience Strong's Outings*, a book bound upside down and indisputably from Worcester, but who has heard of it? Yet what woman wouldn't have her interest piqued on reading this one intriguingly contemporary paragraph from the 1869 outings of Patience Strong:

"I wonder if women ever will be finished. They've been added on to and taken off from, and lengthened out and cut short, and humped up and flattened down, and I don't know how many different things, since I can remember. I wonder if they'll ever find out what is just right and prettiest, and stop there and be comfortable."[20]

Instead of the enclosed bookcase, the trustees added a stove to the children's room, and Virginia Edwards Fleming remembers how the Harbisons would come early on cold days to build a wood fire.[21] Every working day, even the coldest, when winter chilled the mountain under gentian-blue skies, Gertrude (or as often Dolly) would leave her home beneath the frown of Satulah's cliffs,[22] where sister Margaret tended the fire, trudge the two-and-a-half-mile, deeply rutted course past Satulah Falls on the old Walhalla Road, climb to Sloan's Gap (also known as Buck Horn Gap), checking the little weather station along the way, and descend into town.

---

[20]Mrs. A. D. T. Whitney, *Patience Strong's Outings* (Boston, 1869), p. 185. For a list of all seventy titles, see Appendix V.
[21]Interview with Virginia Edwards Fleming, September 29, 1993.
[22]This two-story wood-shingled frame house with a barn was built on the east side of Walhalla Road at Old Orchard Road. All four of the Harbison

On occasion some kind soul—like Harry Wright, Judge Leo Burke, or Bill Holt—would give her a ride into town. However, even on days when storms or fog settled on Satulah's bluffs and vision reached no more than ten feet in front of her nose, she would descend into town. Opening the library, she would gather wood from behind the green curtain and stoke the stove.

> *Winter on the warpath,*
> *Icicles fo' swords.*
> *Cabin walls a-creakin'*
> *As the heat warps the boards.*
> *Wind in the chimbley*
> *Cryin', "Oo-oo-oo!"*
> *Mighty glad of supper,*
> *And a good fire, too!*[23]

Mary Pugh Matthews recalls how her mother would drop her off at the library, and Miss Gertrude would have her read to her. When Mary missed a word, she had to reread the sentence for each missed word, again and again and again until she got it right. When she finally returned to sit on the porch of Chestnut Lodge in the late afternoon, here would come Miss Gertrude, treading up the chestnut-shaded Satulah Road toward Sloan's Gap, past Mary Pugh, and call out, "Hello, Mary, have you done your reading?"[24]

---

children—Margaret, Gertrude, Dolly, and Tom—had been born in the Kelsey house after S. T. Kelsey left for Linville, N.C., in 1893. The family moved to the M. I. Skinner house (called Glencroft, renamed Trillium Lodge) in 1909. Then in 1920 Professor Harbison contracted with W. M. Cleaveland to build just south of Satulah, and the family moved in 1921.

[23]A verse from a poem by Robert Emmet Ward, the pseudonym used by Highlands' Dorothy Farnsworth when she had it published in the January, 1930, issue of *St. Nicholas Magazine*. See "Highlands Writer's Poem To Be Reproduced For Blind Children," *Highlands Maconian*, December 3, 1930.

[24]Interview with Mary Pugh Matthews, September 28, 1993.

The lasting effect that the library had on Mary would be seen when in 1984 she established a memorial fund of $5,000 in honor of her parents, Franklin and Lea Pugh, to provide income for the purchase of children's books for the library.[25]

For many of the children of Highlands, Miss Gertrude and Miss Dolly were their guiding lights, and the library meant everything to them. During the week they had school and Christian Endeavor on Sunday evenings to occupy their time, but the most exciting event, apart from an occasional hayride, was the library on Saturdays. "Our lives would have been very bleak without the library," says Sarah Thompson McNamee.[26]

Her mother, Helen McKinney Thompson, believed that there was no better friend than a good book: "a friend that does not intrude but, when approached, yields the best thought and wisdom of the age."[27] She would let her eldest daughters Peggy and Sarah walk to the library from their house where the funeral home now exists, barefoot along the dusty road. They would stay the whole day on the one day, Saturday, that they didn't have their younger sister, June, and six little brothers in their hair.

They read Gene Stratton Porter's *Freckles* or *Girl of the Limberlost* or Jean Webster's popular book about *Daddy-*

---

[25] Minutes of trustees meeting, October 17, 1984. The Lea and Franklin Pugh Memorial Fund has grown until today, ten years after its establishment in 1984, over $6,000 earns interest that is used to buy children's books.

[26] Sarah was the daughter of Dr. Percy Thompson and Helen McKinney Thompson, who was previously married to Jamie Cleaveland. Her brothers by Jamie Cleaveland were George, Henry, and Wendell. Her sisters and brothers by Percy Thompson were Peggy, June, Buddy, and Richard. This made a total brood of eight. Dr. Thompson served Highlands from his arrival in 1917 until his early death at age thirty-five in 1931. It left the family destitute at the height of the Great Depression.

[27] Interview with Sarah Thompson McNamee, now living near Lake Junaluska, N.C., November 15, 1993.

Long-Legs, the anonymous benefactor of a little orphan girl. They read Alice Rice's *Mrs. Wiggs of the Cabbage Patch*, so that thereafter whenever a hardship arose in their lives—and hardships did come, to be sure—they would say with renewed patience, "every thing in the world comes right, if we jes' wait long enough."

It was Miss Gertrude who would say as they entered the door, "Sarah, you'd like this book," and hand her one of the Bobbsey twins, if Marion Day wasn't reading it, and give Peggy a copy of *Uncle Remus*. At day's end they'd take home some light novels for Mama: romances by Faith Baldwin, novels by Willa Cather, like *O Pioneers!* and *My Antonia*. For their brothers they brought copies of *John Martin* to work the puzzles, fill in the dot-to-dot pictures, read the short stories, and generally shred to pieces. Sarah has always wondered "why Miss Gertrude didn't get upset when we brought back those ragged *John Martins*."[28] Nor did Miss Gertrude seem to mind that every Saturday Sarah and Peggy left dusty bare footprints on the maroon runner that stretched from the door to the middle of the library floor.

On one Saturday Sarah found a spot way back at the end of the stacks near a window where she could sit cross-legged and read undisturbed all day long. "Miss Gertrude forgot I was there," she remembers. "Around six o'clock every Saturday night my mama served baked beans and brown bread, and I suddenly realized I was hungry, but that library door was locked good and fast. I screamed and screamed for twenty minutes before Mr. Fred Edwards heard me and hollered, 'Sarah, be calm! Help is on the way!'" Mr. Edwards sent Roliver Baty[29] in his

---

[28]Interview with Sarah Thompson McNamee, October 27, 1993.
[29]Roliver Baty was the son of Gus Baty, whom Charlie Wright rescued from Whiteside cliff.

truck to fetch Miss Gertrude and the key. After Miss Gertrude had let Sarah out, she told her that from now on, she was to let her know if she was going to be back there. Miss Gertrude was certainly sorry to have locked her in, but Sarah was not to let it happen again!

By 1935 or 1936, when Sarah was in her teens, Miss Gertrude introduced her to the beautifully fashioned romances of Grace Livingston Hill. She would hand Sarah the latest arrival, *Rainbow Cottage*, and watch her light up with unbridled joy. However, before she let Sarah take it home, knowing how her brothers chewed up the *John Martin*s, she'd admonish, "Now, the children must not tear the leaves out of this book."

Miss Gertrude always advised the Thompson sisters what to read, perhaps believing like the English novelist Graham Greene that it is only in childhood that books have any deep influence on our lives. She also taught them what she knew about plant life, which was extensive, and about the stars. The girls learned to love good reading material.

Of course, there was the one time that Sarah got caught reading one of those true confession books that was circulating in the school. "My mother beat me with the book," she recalls, "and said to me, 'Don't tell me this came from the library.'" The next time her mother saw Miss Gertrude, who had heard of the incident, Miss Gertrude was quick to assure her that the library did not carry that kind of narrative and never would![30]

Sarah's sister, June, had a similar run-in with her mother over a questionable magazine, but the younger sister's favorite books were the resolutely cheerful *Pollyanna* novels by Eleanor Porter, the saucy *Anne of Green Gables* series, *The Secret Garden*, and *The Book of*

---

[30]Interview with Sarah Thompson McNamee, October 27, 1993.

Knowledge, where she got the idea to sell the *Grit* newspaper for ten cents. She got some little bit of each dime that she earned and has been a saleswoman ever since.[31]

Victor Smith recalls that the Harbisons went through all the magazines in the library and tore out the naughty bits. *Life* magazine, especially, fell victim to their censorship, even the pages that showed African natives. Ethel Calloway remembers their hiding new books behind the green curtain if they felt them to be improper. "Gertrude was a moralist. She didn't want to contaminate the community," Ethel remarks with a twinkle in her eye. "I used to ask Miss Gertrude if she would like to go get her mail while I kept the library for her. Then I'd grab a book from behind the curtain to take it home, read it, and bring it back. Gore Vidal was one of those who landed behind the curtain."[32]

What attracted Victor Smith to the library in particular was *Tom Sawyer* and *Huckleberry Finn* and books he had to read for school reports, like the interminably long but popular romance of the Napoleonic era, Hervey Allen's *Anthony Adverse*, which had just come out in 1933. Victor regarded Miss Gertrude as somewhat stern and aloof, while Miss Dolly was a bit warmer, friendlier, and smaller. Her being smaller made her more "one of us," he recalls.[33] June Thompson found herself a bit afraid of Miss Gertrude. She was stoic and refined, rather reserved, and "formidable," as compared with Miss Dolly, whom June felt was more "folksy and everyday."[34]

Sarah Thompson McNamee, apart from what she learned from Otto Summer's math classes in the High-

---

[31] Interview with June Thompson Medlin, wife of the Reverend Dr. W. T. Medlin of Black Mountain, N.C., November 9, 1993.
[32] Interview with Ethel Calloway, November 8, 1993.
[33] Interview with Victor Smith, November 1, 1993.
[34] Interview with June Thompson Medlin, November 9, 1993.

lands School, credits the library, and in particular Miss Gertrude and Miss Dolly, with the balance of her education before she left in 1939 for college.[35] Marion Day Arnold remembers that the library was all the young people had, especially in the winters, which were terrible, just "snow and ice, snow and ice."[36] Many of the youth in Highlands, who didn't frequent the Dugout[37] and even those who did, found considerable excitement, ensconced in a captivating book in a cozy nook in the library and lost to the outside world.

Ethel Calloway read Zane Grey, but she loved the English romances of Georgette Heyer and Victoria Holt.[38] Anne Altstaetter's world was that of the romantic young librarian in Margaret Widdemer's *Rose-Garden Husband* or the charming adventuress who loved a young doctor in *Wishing Ring Man*. Then she found the *Graustark* novels[39] and for most of one summer thrilled to stories of love behind the throne that thrived in the romantic kingdom of George Barr McCutcheon.[40] She would check out these novels from the library but read them perched in her pine throne in her yard.

June Thompson preferred historical novels, books by Bess Aldrich, whom her mother also enjoyed—novels

---

[35]Sarah Thompson, valedictorian of her class at Highlands School, would graduate from Queens-Chicora College in Charlotte in 1941 and return to teach fourth grade at Highlands School before leaving again to serve as a stewardess for Delta Air Lines in 1942. Her sister June would attend Western Carolina Teacher's College, graduate from Queens, and work as Secretary of Children's Work in the Women's Society of Christian Service.
[36]Telephone conversation with Marion Day Arnold, October 29, 1993.
[37]Children weren't allowed to attend Monday, Wednesday, and Saturday dances at the Dugout, a roadside tavern built in 1937 on the Highlands-Franklin federal highway on the shore of Lake Sequoyah. It was sold in 1961. The restaurant . . . On the Verandah exists there today.
[38]Interview with Ethel Calloway, November 8, 1993.
[39]*Graustark, Beverly of Graustark*, and *The Prince of Graustark*.
[40]Interview with Anne Altstaetter Rhodes, October 31, 1993.

about pioneer mothers in Nebraska and Iowa, such as *A Lantern in Her Hand, A White Bird Flying,* and *Miss Bishop.* The library had just acquired in 1939 the *Song of Years.*[41] Ten years later June would return to discover on the shelves "the sweetest little book," Bess Aldrich's latest, *Journey Into Christmas.*

In the meantime, she and her mother thrived on the family stories of a new author, Alice Sligh Turnbull. Miss Dolly recommended *Rolling Years* and *Remember the End.* In 1947, after June and her sisters had finished Queens College and were able to handle a liberal Presbyterian clergyman, she checked out the highly popular *Bishop's Mantle.* Five more years would pass before *The Gown of Glory* would appear, but already she was an avid Turnbull fan. One of her sister Sarah's favorite authors was Grace Livingston Hill, whose novels the younger sister regarded as "trash, because they didn't have any history to them."[42]

In 1939 the library enjoyed a nostalgic visit from Mr. and Mrs. A. W. Hudson of White Plains, N.Y. Mr. Hudson was Ella Hudson's son; the library was his mother's namesake. He told Miss Dolly how pleased he was with what the present library had become from its humble origin in the "old cupboard," as he called it, with its six shelves. He left a very generous gift for Miss Dolly "to buy something for the library that it would not otherwise have."[43] The amount of the gift was twenty dollars, and with it the library bought a new table, which was badly

---

[41]Gertrude Harbison, "Hudson Library Notes," *Franklin Press & Highlands Maconian,* July 13, 1939. See also the reprint of her article in "The Hudson Library," *Mountain Trail,* July 14, 1939.
[42]Interview with June Thompson Medlin, November 9, 1993.
[43]"Mr. and Mrs. A. W. Hudson Visit Highlands," *Franklin Press & Highlands Maconian,* April 20, 1939.

needed.[44] It was this table that thirty-four years later would astound a number of trustees and volunteers, but that story will follow in its proper place.

The library in this year, the year that it bought the *Wizard of Oz*, was not ready for modernization. Marion Day Arnold recalls that when she was nineteen and volunteering to work in the library, she had just learned the Dewey Decimal System[45] but found that none of these white-haired people were keen on the idea. Apparently Albertina Staub had tried to introduce it in the early thirties, but nobody understood it, so they gave it up.[46] Indeed, why go to the trouble of classifying all these books with numbers and letters when one card for each borrower was enough? When someone wanted a book, Miss Gertrude or Miss Dolly checked it out on his card. When he brought it back, she checked it in on the card.

Anyway, Miss Gertrude and Miss Dolly already knew where all the books were, every one of them. For anyone who didn't, the arrangement was alphabetical by author. Not by author within a section, mind you, like fiction or science or regional books! No need for that. The whole library, except for children's books, was arranged by author alphabetically from the A's on the first shelf to the Z's on the last. A patron just had to know who wrote the book he wanted. If he didn't know, he could ask Miss Gertrude or Miss Dolly. As often as not, he got the book without even having to use his card. They knew him, and knew he'd bring it back.

Two years before the library's occupation of the children's room, the Satulah Club came to the trustees with a

---

[44]Minutes of trustees meeting, July 1, 1939.
[45]The decimal system of classifying books originated in 1876 with Melvil Dewey, director of the New York State Library and founder of the N.Y. State Library School and the American Library Association.
[46]Telephone conversation with Marion Day Arnold, October 29, 1993.

special request. The Satulah Club was an outgrowth of the old Highlands Improvement Society, which thirty years earlier had paid five hundred dollars to preserve the summit of Satulah Mountain for public use.[47] Now, in 1939, the club sought the library's permission to build a Satulah Room at the rear of the building with $825 and a bond that it had recently received as a gift. The additional room, according to a resolution that the library passed, would serve as a meeting place for Satulah Club members as long as they needed it, but would be called the Hudson Library Annex and, in the event the club no longer needed it, would belong exclusively to the library.[48]

The wording of this resolution would prove vital forty-one years later when the two organizations clashed briefly over ownership and control of the room. At the time of the Satulah Club's proposal, however, with safeguards appended, both parties readily accepted it. The upshot of the offer was that the library in essence was expanding by accretion, like a coral reef choosing which ornaments to adopt.

Despite the library's expansion, perennial problems, like regressions in the teenager that it still was, kept cropping up. A potential defect in the architect's original plan for the library's construction on the Rideout lot kept raising its surly head in the minutes of the trustees. The

---

[47]Professor T. G. Harbison wrote about this gift of the summit of Satulah Mountain by the Highlands Improvement Society in terms of genuine pride. The top of Satulah, he exclaimed, "is OURS, ours to keep forever. No money grubbing skinflint without any soul can ever acquire this top and then put up a toll gate to charge admission to what he the same as stole from God. I mean just what I say. No man has a right or can acquire a right to charge his fellow man toll to visit the tops of God's mountains." T. G. Harbison, "Highlands Site of Beautiful Estates," *Franklin Press*, Teacher Training ed., April 10, 1930.

[48]See Resolution of September 29, 1939, in Secretary's Book, Hudson Library Association.

problem was library drainage! Back in 1927 the matter had been simple: the gutter pipe at the corner of the building nearest the porch terminated at precisely the height to splash the porch and everybody on it, and in a heavy rain it did so very thoroughly.[49] The pipe was therefore extended to the ground.

In 1929, however, the drains had choked up and were in dire need of reopening.[50] So Mr. Sloan had been called in. In 1931 the board, at a specially called meeting, had considered filling the yard to the level of the street, making a lawn, and planting a hedge in front of the lot. However, when Tom Harbison's work estimate figured at seventy-five dollars plus ten dollars for fertilizer and seed, the board had ditched the plan.[51] In 1932 Gertrude Harbison reported that at last "the drainage problem had been solved." The culvert was rerouted under the sidewalk, diverting the water from a neighboring spring to the east side of the building instead of through the yard.[52]

Like original sin, however, the difficulty wouldn't leave. In 1939 the problem was still surfacing. The library wore a damp, musty odor that it could not eradicate. In addition, the small bridge in front needed repair. So when the Satulah Club sought permission to build on, the library ingeniously decided to split the cost of draining the whole lot, work that included a special "guarantee for twenty-five years."[53] Twenty-five years! Headache free until 1964!

Then came 1945, six years into the guarantee. The board felt that the inferior condition of the bridge and the

---

[49]Minutes of trustees meeting, August 8, 1927.
[50]Ibid., August 8, 1929.
[51]Ibid., September 18, 1931. This estimate was prepared by Tom C. Harbison, Professor Harbison's son, who died in a tragic accident in 1959.
[52]Ibid., July, 1932.
[53]Ibid., October 19, 1939.

ditch warranted bringing the problem to the attention of the mayor. In 1947, eight years into the guarantee, the board referred the matter to the town council.[54] In 1975, after the guarantee had expired, the drainage situation was so severe that the vents in the foundation were left open throughout the winter to prevent moisture from accumulating underneath the building. As a result, cold gusts of wind cooled the ducts and put the furnace under substantial strain. In addition, the front door stoop began to sag because the porch floor had settled up against the building.[55] So the board paid $200, without quibble, to end the problem conclusively.

By 1976 bad drainage had brought all beautification projects to their knees.[56] Miss Dolly recalls that the yard was a "swamp."[57] It's little wonder, therefore, that in sheer desperation the trustees cried out in 1978: Let the drainage problem be fixed! "With whatever methods necessary!" Polyethylene was laid under the building, the brush was cut away, and the town board agreed to excavate a drainage ditch.[58]

Three years passed without incident. Then came the winter of 1981. Ronald Reagan became the fortieth president of the United States. His budget proposed the greatest-ever tax and spending cuts. Iran had just released all fifty-two U.S. hostages. The Hudson Library was beginning to consider whether to construct a new building to replace the one it had outgrown or to add a two-story structure to the rear on the same lot. One sentence looms large in the minutes of that January meeting of the

---

[54]Ibid., June 25, 1947.
[55]Minutes of trustees meeting, September 29, 1975.
[56]Ibid., July 27, 1976.
[57]Interview with Dolly Harbison, September 22, 1993.
[58]Minutes of trustees meetings, July 19, October 18, and November 15, 1978.

trustees: "A brief discussion was held concerning the need for more adequate drainage of surface water in front of the library building."[59]

---

[59]Executive board minutes, January 21, 1981.

Fourth Street on the "Hill"
Looking toward Main Street. Taken in 1950. Courtesy of *Highlander*.

The Alexander P. Anderson House
Front, east face. Windmill of the water tower shows over the top.
Taken January 31, 1920. Courtesy of Lucile Reese.

Honored Losses: 1940–53

Late summer—
and the Joe Pye weed grows tall.
The blackberry vine hangs heavy
along the old stone wall.
The sun's a lazy riser
as it tops the mountain peak.
The purple phlox are flourishing
beside the meadow creek.

The produce trucks are rolling
down the winding country road,
bedded high with cabbages,
hampered by their load.
Red Service leaves are signaling
their signs of coming fall—
late summer in the highlands,
and the Joe Pye weed grows tall.[1]

As may be seen much later when the library has moved into its new building after 1985, some problems never cease, regardless of where or how far one flees. The library's drainage problem persisted for the seventy years that it occupied Huger Elliott's masterwork of architectural design. On the other hand, never did the matter dampen the enthusiasm shown for the library by its patrons or its librarians. Admittedly, the building smelled musty, damp, and mildewy. The rooms were rather dark on overcast days, particularly before the kerosene lamps on the walls gave way to electricity in

---

[1] Virginia Edwards Fleming, "Late Summer," *So Tender the Spirit* (Highlands, 1985), p. 11.

1927, but afterward the library still existed in a perpetual twilight.

It was also cold, especially during that winter in early 1942 that brought the second-deepest snow ever recorded in Highlands.[2] From one-and-a-half to two-feet deep between drifts! It piled up for three days at the beginning of March in a blizzard that left the town totally isolated for a week. In previous winters, after snows of a foot or so, the children and many adults would don their ice skates and sail out over Lake Sequoyah and Mirror Lake, sometimes frozen to a depth of fifteen inches. However, this winter the townspeople were snowbound for the whole week. It was perhaps the only extended period that the Misses Gertrude and Dolly failed to open the library, notwithstanding that Miss Gertrude braved the bitter cold and waist-high drifts to document the record snow at her weather station, hung with yard-long icicles, on Satulah.[3]

With the thaw and the arrival of spring, the last of the main roads in Highlands had been paved with asphalt surfacing, signaling a new era in the town's and library's growing involvement with the outside world. On the international front the United States was at war, having responded decisively to the Japanese bombing of Pearl Harbor, the same year that Upton Sinclair published *Between Two Worlds* and *Dragon's Teeth* to update his *World's End* series to include the onset of actual hostilities. The world was in an existential crisis that uprooted some forty-seven Highlanders from their homes and

---

[2]"Deepest Snow: In Highlands History Last Week; 18 to 20 Inches," *Franklin Press & Highlands Maconian*, March 12, 1942. This account ignores the "deep snow" of 1886.

[3]See Gertrude Harbison, in "Miss Harbison Recognized," *Highlander*, September 27, 1973.

planted them on totally alien soil.[4] Many would return, like Val Pierson—his was a miraculous escape[5]—after four years of helping to win a grueling and destructive war. However, some few, like James Baty and Albert Rogers and Henry Zoellner,[6] who used to call the square dances, would never see again the green unspoiled hills of home. For a community the size of Highlands, the loss of one life diminished the town as crucially as if the altitude oak were uprooted from its honored spot where it always stood between the Central House and the Highlands Inn.[7]

Indeed, the natural loss of some of its time-honored citizens was already diminishing Highlands. With Professor Harbison's passing in 1936,[8] the few remaining stalwarts of the old guard—the library's and town's early founders—were Mary Chapin Smith; her husband, J. Jay Smith; H. M. Bascom; and Albertina Staub, all of whom death took between 1940 and 1942.

---

[4]See list of forty-seven Highlanders in service in "Highlands Highlights," *Franklin Press & Highlands Maconian*, December 17, 1942.
[5]Lieutenant Val Pierson, a paratrooper from Highlands, was captured by the Germans on September 15, 1943, but escaped by jumping from a moving train. He hiked the mountains and returned to duty on October 18. See "Val Pierson Dies Here," *Highlander*, January 6, 1972. His wife, Norma "Boots" Pierson, would serve as president of the library's trustees on four separate occasions from 1965 to 1987.
[6]William Henry Zoellner was an artist as much as he was a musician. His grave is in Margraten Cemetery. His family struggled for three years before deciding to leave him where he "rests in peace with his comrades in Holland" and erect a memorial in the Highlands Cemetery. See "Highlands Highlights," *Franklin Press & Highlands Maconian*, April 8, 1948.
[7]The "altitude oak"—or "charter oak," as it was sometimes called—stood encircled by a rock wall. It was called the "altitude oak" owing to the plaque affixed to its base designating Highlands' average altitude of 4,118 feet. Lucile Pierson Reese knew it simply as "the big old oak tree in the middle of the street." Interview with Lucile Pierson Reese, November 27, 1993.
[8]Professor Harbison, at age seventy-two, had been appointed curator of the University of North Carolina Ashe Herbarium, the position he held until his death in Chapel Hill, N.C., on January 12, 1936. He was seventy-four when he died and is buried in the Highlands Cemetery

> *Death paused awhile without my door;*
> *I did not bid him enter in,*
> *For joys of Paradise can nevermore*
> *Seem sweeter than they seem, in spite of sin*
> *And wo, the joys of this dear earth.*[9]

Mary Chapin Smith died at the age of eighty-five in 1940. A descendent of old New England families, she had grown up in Massachusetts and graduated from Wheaton Seminary (now Wheaton College), founded by her Aunt Eliza Wheaton. In the earliest days of Highlands' founding she and her husband, J. Jay, lived in Smith Cottage (now Hildegard's Restaurant), built in the early 1880s by her widowed mother, Cynthia Loomis Chapin.[10] From the late 1880s until 1925 she and J. Jay ran the Smith House (formerly Highlands House), which had been a wedding present to her and her husband from her aunt Eliza.[11]

As president of the library's trustees and chairman of its book committee for the fifteen years that embraced the turn of the century, she was instrumental in the library's selection of books of high quality because of her own broad familiarity with the best in literature. In addition to her history of the library's first fifty years, she also composed poetry for newspapers and magazines.

Her interests, however, extended beyond literature. Since childhood, she had loved music and art and had been a devoted student of botany. Flowers, trees, shrubs, and birds were a great joy to her in the woodland setting of Smith Cottage, where her personal garden emulated

---

[9] Mary Chapin Smith, "Sweet Mother Earth," *Earth Songs* (Boston, 1910), p. 7.
[10] "The Gray Cottage Has Interesting History," *Highlander*, May 26, 1966.
[11] "J. J. Smith's Life Sketched," *Franklin Press & Highlands Maconian*, September 11, 1941. Mary Chapin and J. Jay Smith were married on July 20, 1886. "Mrs. J. J. Smith Dies Tuesday," *Franklin Press & Highlands Maconian*, April 4, 1940.

the Anne Hathaway Garden in Stratford, England, in its exceptional beauty.[12] She reflected her love of nature in her art and poetry, having painted before her arrival in Highlands for Asa Gray, the botanist, and published in 1910 a book of her own verses, entitled *Earth Songs*, which Marion Day Arnold remembers as one of her favorite books of poetry.[13]

Mrs. Smith was one of the organizers of the Highlands Improvement Society in 1905, for which she wrote a brief history[14] and which later merged with the Highlands Community Club to form the present-day Satulah Club. She had been an active member of both the Floral and Horticultural Societies, as well as the Highlands Museum and Biological Laboratory.

At the time of her death, her civic contributions to Highlands were regarded as indispensable. Friends portrayed her as "keenly interested in the civic welfare and beauty of the town," and in her passing depicted Highlands as having "suffered a distinct loss."[15]

The very next year, 1941, death took her husband, John Jay Smith, who at the time was Highlands' oldest citizen and co-developer.[16] He had arrived from Penn-

---

[12] See the illustration "The Smiths on the Bridge" on page 37 above.

[13] Telephone conversation with Marion Day Arnold, October 29, 1993. Many of the poems in Mary Chapin Smith's *Earth Songs* were published originally in *Watson's Jeffersonian Magazine, Journal of Outdoor Life, Taylor-Trotwood Magazine,* and *Book News.*

[14] For Mrs. Smith's history of the HIS, see "Women Do Much for Highlands: The Highlands Improvement Society Sponsors Many Things Benefiting the Town and Vicinity," *Franklin Press*, July 5, 1928. The Highlands Community Club, with which it merged in 1934 to form the Satulah Club, was founded in 1925.

[15] "Mrs. J. J. Smith Dies Tuesday: Highlands Pioneer Was Poet, Artist and Botanist," *Franklin Press & Highlands Maconian*, April 4, 1940.

[16] "J. J. Smith's Life Sketched: Served Town as Mayor; Road Builder; Artist and Craftsman," *Franklin Press & Highlands Maconian*, September 11, 1941.

sylvania in 1878 and set up the first saw and planing mill in the region. His mill furnished the material used in constructing all the houses built during the thirty years after his arrival. Joe Reese remembers buying shingles and corn meal at his mill.[17] For a number of years, while Miller Henry and his brother Joe ran the mill for him, Mr. Smith served as postmaster and as mayor, having achieved on one occasion the unusual distinction of receiving every vote cast. His work as road surveyor led to his laying out the Dillard Road, which for many years Highlands residents knew as Smith's Road.

A large stout gentleman who wore brown leather leggings over his pants' legs and shoes,[18] Mr. Smith had a hobby of wood carving. At first he made vases, bowls, trays, lampshades, and furniture from native woods, but later he constructed pictures depicting the scenery of the Highlands mountains. He created landscapes from mosses, ferns, and bark with delicately tinted bits of cotton that gave one the impression of viewing an actual scene through an open window.

One of these scenes, a beautifully crafted forest tableau, still hangs in Hildegard's Restaurant, his former home. A larger scene depicting Dry Falls (then known as Cullasaja Falls) with the macerated wood pulp of a hornet's nest was lost in a fire that consumed Kenyon B. Zahner's house on Billy Cabin Ridge, where it hung until the early 1970s.[19] Another picture of a waterfall—possibly Bridal Veil, also made from hornet's nest, bark, and moss —belonged to Charlie McDowell, who says he burned it before he knew who had made it. "Twenty-twenty hindsight. I should have kept it!" he admits with a

---

[17]Interview with Joe Reese, December 1, 1993.
[18]Ibid.
[19]Interview with Harriet Zahner van Houten, September 30, 1993.

chuckle.[20] In actuality, J. Jay Smith's many contributions to the welfare of Highlands consisted more in memories of the man than in what physical handiwork he bequeathed to the ravages of time.

In 1941 the Hudson Library received a unique gift from a former resident of Highlands, a new book that fulfilled its famous author's lifelong dream. Dr. Alexander P. Anderson, its author, was the Clemson professor who discovered the method of exploding or puffing starch granules of wheat and rice that brought him world fame for the commercial production of the popular breakfast cereals, Quaker Puffed Wheat and Quaker Puffed Rice. As a child, he had grown up on the McGuffey *Readers*, which for thousands of young Americans during the last half of the nineteenth century were their first schoolbooks. These eclectic readers consisted of six books in a graded series.[21]

Born five years after publication of the *Sixth Reader*, Alexander Anderson, like the rest of the educated youth of America, had learned from them how to read. They had given him the basis for pursuing a specific career in science—indeed, had prepared him generally for a rich and full life—but had left him keenly disappointed as a child that there was no seventh reader to satisfy his insatiable curiosity. So for the next fifty years he wrote short sketches, stories, and poems about life in the frontier days of Minnesota where students had used the McGuffey *Readers* in lonely country schools. He gathered illustrations until he had accumulated 625 pages of a *Seventh*

---

[20]Interview with Charlie McDowell, October 30, 1993.
[21]In the century and a half since their publication between 1836 and 1857 more than 120 million copies of McGuffey's *Eclectic Readers* in original and revised editions have been sold. They combined moral lessons with selections from literature and helped shape the tastes of generations of Americans even into the twentieth century.

Reader, which he published in 1941 and dedicated to his wife Lydia, "The Sweetheart of the Valley: My Only One."

In 1907 Professor Anderson had moved to Highlands, nine years after his marriage there in the little town, and built a truly beautiful summer home bordered by Fourth, Fifth, and Pine streets (known after 1926 as the William W. Sullivan house, where Nations Bank and Carolina Square now exist).[22] With his book's publication in 1941, he gave a copy to Highlands and its library as a token of his appreciation of the community. The *Seventh Reader* waits today among the first books from the original boxes, preserved in the enclosed bookcases for some precocious child whose curiosity might enjoy a fascinating primer of life. Set in a wholesome environment, it portrays farm work as being hard but breeding courage and resourcefulness into the spirit. It may be coincidence, though entirely appropriate, that the enclosed bookcases containing Dr. Anderson's book originated from his own library, as a gift to the Hudson Library by his daughter Louise in 1946.[23]

The books that Professor Alexander had read and reread himself as a child, when he frequented the school library ten miles from Red Wing, Minnesota, were not the usual choice of the average American student. They were Alexander Pope's translations of Homer's *Iliad* and *Odyssey*, *Gulliver's Travels*, and especially Jane Porter's historical romance, *Scottish Chiefs*, about the life of

---

[22]For a description of Professor Anderson's uniquely innovative house and windmill, see Lee B. Copple, "Professor Anderson's Windmill," *One Man's Highlands* (Highlands, 1975), pp. 92–95. See also the illustration on page 108 above. It was known as the Whittle residence before William Woodward Sullivan bought it. In 1961 it was sold and later razed.

[23]"Museum Given Bookcases By Mrs. Sargent," *Franklin Press & Highlands Maconian*, January 24, 1946. Dolly Harbison has confirmed that the two bookcases containing the birth books are indeed the ones donated by Louise Anderson Sargent. Interview with Dolly Harbison, December 6, 1993.

William Wallace and the great battle of Bannockburn when Robert Bruce sent King Edward II with his tail between his legs scurrying out of Scotland.

Dr. Anderson's daughter, Louise Anderson, grew up in Highlands on the McGuffey *Readers*, married Dr. Ralph Sargent, and served on one occasion as president of the library's trustees. She still lives in Highlands, and has donated to the library many of the books that she and her husband bought for her children when they, too, were first learning to love to read.[24]

Dr. Anderson chose the stories for his *Seventh Reader*, intending to excite the imagination, in the same way that William Holmes McGuffey would excerpt only one chapter of Louisa May Alcott's extremely popular *Old-Fashioned Girl*, enticing the child who read it to find the novel itself for the rest of the story. He would print only one of Longfellow's poems, "The Village Blacksmith," while letting his reader know that there were many, many more favorite poems by this popular American poet. A teenager might settle down with the *Sixth Reader* and find fascinating poems and short works of no more than five pages by Sir Walter Scott, Washington Irving, Shakespeare, Edgar Allan Poe, and Elizabeth Barratt Browning and would invariably check the library for more works by these and other newly discovered authors. Indeed, by 1941 such a youngster now had what Dr. Anderson had never had but desperately craved as a child: a continuation of the series, a *Seventh Reader*.

In 1942, with both Mr. and Mrs. Smith deceased, Highlands again lost its oldest citizen, and the library, one of

---

[24]See "Dr. Anderson: Scientist, Compiles New Reader," *Franklin Press & Highlands Maconian*, August 21, 1941. See also the reprint of this article in "Alexander P. Anderson's 'Seventh Reader' Among New Library Books," *Mountain Trail*, August 22, 1941.

its most ardent supporters. Henry M. Bascom, always dressed as a gentleman in coat, vest, and tie, embodied all the qualities that a library might seek to instill in an ideal individual. To support his younger sisters and brother, Henry had apprenticed himself at age eleven to a tinsmith, so that his education derived almost entirely from omnivorous reading. Quite capable of quoting large sections of Shakespeare and the Bible by heart, he read throughout his life at least one—often two—books a day.

He came to Highlands shortly after Kelsey discovered it, in May of 1881, burdened with a single lung, which all insurance companies considered a bad risk. Yet before his death at age eighty-eight, he had served Highlands for a total of at least sixteen years as its mayor and as road commissioner, while engaged in establishing a drug and general merchandise store (especially with one-cent stick candy and five-cent big Baby Ruths for the kids), a hardware store, a sheet metal and plumbing shop, and a shoe shop, in addition to buying and selling real estate and insurance, constructing Davis House (later Tricemont Terrace, Lee's Inn), and generously supporting both the school and the library in Highlands.

A friend astutely characterized his romantic style of life, marveling that, "with his business acumen, charm of manner, and square dealing, had he lived in New York City instead of this remote village where he chose to make his home, he would have been a second J. Pierpont Morgan."[25] Yet he always took the time to read the comic strips with young Craig Cranston when the *New York Tribune* arrived.[26]

---

[25] "H. M. Bascom Final Rites: Prominent Highlands Resident Dies at Home of Daughter in N.Y.," *Franklin Press & Highlands Maconian*, March 5, 1942.
[26] Interview with Craig Cranston, October 18, 1993.

The Hudson Library owes its existence in its present quarters to this man's son-in-law, George Watson Barratt, who saw in H. M. Bascom's daughter Louise the incarnation of art and in the character of her father the product of earnest reading—two ideal qualities that in 1985 would fuse books and paintings under the same roof. Furthermore, just as Ella Hudson's tragic death had prompted the original library's birth, so also would the natural deaths of H. M. Bascom and, later, Watson Barratt give birth to a new home for a well-established library that had outgrown its aging quarters. The first inspiration for this fortunate chain of events was the unforgettable and respected character of H. M. Bascom.

The death of Miss Staub, at age seventy-six in 1942, four months after H. M. Bascom's demise, closed the book on fifty-five years of her association with Highlands. Besides her role as Hudson librarian, during the sixteen years that she had nursed it through the turn of the century, she had contributed her exacting talents to the Highlands Museum and Biological Laboratory as one of its founders. She had assisted Jim Hines as postmaster when the Edwards building at Main and Fourth housed the old post office. After leaving the library, she had eventually turned her business-like and commercially friendly manner to selling real estate and insurance for J. Quincy Pierson at one of Highlands' oldest insurance agencies, located in the Edwards building.

Her father, Professor Albert Staub, a Swiss immigrant, had taught with Professor Harbison in the Highlands Academy soon after the family's arrival from Atlanta in 1887. Living in Ohio, where Albertina attended Urbana College, and then Savannah before moving to Atlanta, the Staub family in all likelihood had instinctively gravitated toward the heights of Highlands as reminiscent of the mountainous terrain of their native land. Miss Staub had been born in northeast Switzerland in the little village of Netstal, nestled on the road between Lake Wallen and the 6,440-foot Alpine Klausen Pass. She spent the last years of her life very much like the first years, steeped in nature in the heart of towering mountains. She was laid to rest without survivors in the Highlands Cemetery by the minister of the Presbyterian Church, in whose church she had taught Sunday school during her younger days. Her students still remember her in this capacity today. The list of her active pallbearers reads like a roster of Who Was Who in Highlands for the year 1942.[27]

The Hudson Library had now lost one of its earliest librarians, but one of its most competent still guided its fate. Miss Gertrude's chief interest, apart from conservation, astronomy, world affairs, and American politics, remained focused on books, and always—though less overtly than was apparent in her affable sister Dolly—on young people!

A young person who regarded the library as one of her four best friends during the early forties was Marna Cobb (now Chalker). It was not infrequent to find her reading in the library alone, just her and Miss Gertrude and Miss Dolly. Her favorite book, as it was for many of the youth in Highlands, was the little collection *One Hundred and One Famous Poems*, in which she especially loved Longfellow's "Hiawatha's Childhood" and Joyce Kilmer's "Trees." She remembers the oval pictures of each author and even selections lovingly committed to memory from Sandburg's description of the fog "that comes on little cat feet" and Tennyson's marvelous description in the "Eagle":

---

[27]"Miss Staub Passes," *Franklin Press & Highlands Maconian*, July 2, 1942.

He clasps the crag with crooked hands;
Close to the sun in lonely lands,
Ring'd with the azure world he stands.
The wrinkled sea beneath him crawls;
He watches from his mountain walls,
And like a thunderbolt he falls.

However, the book that bothered her, indeed scared her the whole time she was reading it, was Dickens' *Great Expectations*, because she never could understand the eccentric Miss Havisham, moreover feared her intensely.

It was Miss Dolly who introduced her to the book that gave her a beautiful philosophy of life, Oscar Wilde's *Happy Prince*, where the little bird takes all the jewels and gives them to the poor without their ever knowing their benefactor. "Anonymous love," Marna calls it.[28] It was an accomplished fact that when Marna wasn't out with Sarah Hall, Mary Bascom Cook, or Anne Anderson, then she was with her fourth friend, the library.

Two sisters who served Miss Gertrude and Miss Dolly as library hounds during the early 1940s were Jessie and Nancy Potts (now Owens and Coward, respectively). Nancy remembers the Harbisons as being from unfamiliar backgrounds. "They were different from us, wore their hair in braids around their heads, walked five miles over the mountain and back, between their home and the library, but we had tremendous admiration and respect for them."[29] Miss Dolly was also Nancy's Sunday school teacher at the Presbyterian Church.

What Nancy remembered most about the library was the windows, which pushed out. They were anchored by

---

[28]Interview with Marna Cobb Chalker, November 17, 1993. Marna is the daughter of Wilton H. Cobb, a former mayor of Highlands.
[29]Telephone conversation with Nancy Potts Coward of Sylva, N.C., November 27, 1993.

metal rods on which screws were tightened to lock them open or closed. She felt as if she were in one of those old, old churches or cathedrals in England. Though there was a mustiness, "there was an aura to the place" that endeared her to it and that she never forgot. What she loved almost as much as the library were the Silver Teas given at Miss Marguerite Ravenel's beautiful home, Wolf Ridge, up on the mountain.[30]

In 1944, as the world watched the heavy air raids against London and Berlin and the United States secretly prepared D-day landings in Normandy, trustee president Rebecca Nall approached the town board for the first time for official support of the library.[31] The board responded by making its first appropriation of $100, the beginning of annual contributions that would continue until an increase to $250 in the mid-sixties, $500 in 1977, currently $750. Meanwhile, the library applied to the state for aid in library maintenance.

Then came 1945, the year of the atomic bomb and the end of World War II, the year that the library received an unsolicited gift of $200 from the erstwhile estranged Franklin Library! This offer came from the town whose residents the Highlands library had resolved fourteen years earlier not to allow use of its facilities. Responding in kind, however, the trustees of the Hudson Library invited the Franklin Library to tea.[32] The incident was not insignificant, for when the library adopted a new constitution in 1946, the document contained a clause expanding membership to include not just citizens of Highlands but visitors as well, thus dissolving the official ban against Franklin residents who had found the library

---

[30]Telephone conversation with Nancy Potts Coward, November 27, 1993.
[31]Town board minutes, April 3, 1944.
[32]Minutes of trustees meeting, August 28, 1945.

in Highlands worth the perilous trip up the gorge. Indeed, the ban must have applied in name only, for in reality Miss Gertrude had been serving Franklin residents as early as 1939. One Franklin citizen, who signed her name M. P. J. to the published poem "My Friends at Highlands," offered this appreciation in her town's newspaper:

A special place I hold in my heart
For the kind Librarian, who keeps a chart
Of special Mystery Stories for me.
Discriminating as she can be
She adds to my pleasure a part.[33]

One possible motive for the library's new open-door policy was the sudden reduced circulation among Highlands school children, as the school's PTA began channeling funds into buying books for its own library. Also, for the scientists in the region, the death of Dr. E. E. Reinke the year previous had led his family to donate his extensive personal book collection to the Highlands Museum and Biological Laboratory, which he had served as first director. His books formed the nucleus of a new scientific library, very much like the boxes of books that had established the Hudson Library, so that scientists in the Highlands region now had a drawing card in a library of their own.

Consequently, to preserve its membership, which had dropped from 451 a decade earlier to 50 in 1946,[34] the trustees of the Hudson Library joined the N.C. Library Association and sent Gertrude and Dolly Harbison to meetings in Asheville. This was the year of Churchill's Iron-Curtain speech in America, and the library, too, was

---

[33]M. P. J., "My Friends at Highlands: An Appreciation," *Franklin Press & Highlands Maconian*, July 20, 1939.
[34]The latter report of memberships was made at the trustees meeting of October 2, 1944, listing 50, before plans were discussed to enlist new members at the meeting of July 10, 1946.

having its share of new problems. On the positive side, it had sufficient funds for the first time in its history to announce a budget for the coming year,[35] but its patrons were rereading old books.

For a young boy, like Harold Reese, the books were all new, for he recalls checking out Defoe's *Robinson Crusoe* and Edgar Rice Burroughs' *Tarzan*.[36] However, one-half of the library's holdings were either outdated or worn out. Jan Chambers felt that there was not a new book on the shelf,[37] except for occasional recent acquisitions, like Betty Smith's *A Tree Grows in Brooklyn,* Somerset Maugham's *Razor's Edge,* and a new dictionary that replaced the "old one 45 years old."[38] Patrons were not returning overdue books, but this was a separate issue from the aging problem, easily resolved by preparing a slot in the library door to facilitate book returns when the library closed.[39]

No one could hold the librarians—Gertrude and Dolly—entirely responsible for the aging of the library's holdings. The reading material was still good, as originally advertised, but now mostly unbound and old! It was not until 1947, the year that future president Gerald R. Ford, Jr., attended the wedding of Sooky Terhune in Highlands,[40] that the trustees gave their librarian "permission to buy books at own discretion."[41] Before this, a trustee resolution was prerequisite to the librarian's purchase of

---

[35] See "133 Members Join Library in Campaign," *Franklin Press & Highlands Maconian,* September 19, 1946.
[36] Interview with Harold Reese, November 2, 1993.
[37] Interview with Jan Chambers Chmar, September 24, 1993.
[38] Minutes of Annual Meetings, August 3, 1945, and August 3, 1946.
[39] "Highlands Highlights," *Franklin Press & Highlands Maconian,* September 11, 1947.
[40] A. J. Baty, "Helen's Gamble," *North Carolina State* (September, 1982), p. 13.
[41] Minutes of trustees meeting, August 7, 1947.

"a bucket, a mop and a bottle of O. Cedar oil"[42] or an expense as meager as twenty-five dollars on new books.[43]

One of the volumes that the library acquired at this time was a book of rhymes just published by the building's own architect and his wife, Huger and Elizabeth Elliott. Huger had written *An Alliterative Alphabet Aimed at Adult Abecedarians*, and she—a student of Howard Pyle—had illustrated it, having previously illustrated a number of volumes, including Charles and Mary Lamb's *Tales of Shakespeare*.

In the same year that he published his book, Huger and his sister Charlotte passed away. The loss was a dual one for the library, their being the architect and an early librarian of its present quarters. The women of the Episcopal Church extolled their work as citizens of the Highlands community while expressing sincere grief over their departure. Not only had Huger designed the library; he had painted the four saints on canvass that once flanked the Episcopal Church altar and the elaborate grapevines in oil for the panels that graced the windows.[44]

As the decade of the forties came to a close, several more losses would deprive Highlands and its library of invaluable assets. In either 1936 or 1947 town officials cut down the revered altitude oak—along with two large red oaks—in Main Street. One of the unsolved mysteries of Highlands is when this well-loved tree was cut.

> *The trees in the streets are old trees*
> *used to living with people,*
> *Family-trees that remember*
> *your grandfather's name.*[45]

---

[42]Minutes of trustees meeting, July 29, 1930.
[43]Ibid., August 28, 1945.
[44]Interview with Margaret Gilbert Hall, November 11, 1993.
[45]Stephen Vincent Benét, *John Brown's Body* (New York, 1928), Book 4. From *The Selected Works of Stephen Vincent Benét*. Copyright 1927–28 by

There are those who remember that tree from when they were only old enough to do so in the forties, but others who were just as old yet don't remember it at all. Marion Day Arnold recalls writing a poem about the cutting of the tree in 1936.[46] The women in the old Satulah Club were upset and wanted someone to write something, which she did, imitating Longfellow's "Village Blacksmith," and the newspaper published it. Indeed, June Thompson Medlin wrote a poem about it also and was jealous that hers wasn't published.[47]

Nevertheless, Joe Reese claims he cut that tree down in 1947. "People wanted the street paved," he recalls, referring to the block between the Highlands Inn and the Episcopal Church. "The state said they'd pave it, but the trees had to be moved. I was on the street committee, and we had to take down all three."[48] People cried, he says, and his wife Lucile adds, "I've bawled him out a number of times. I haven't given him any rest since."[49] Whether the tree came down in 1936 or in 1947 remains, at the time of this history's publication, a curious puzzle.

In 1949, thirty-eight years after the Hudson Library's fifth librarian, Jessie White, had moved with T. Baxter White to California, a package arrived, addressed to Miss Dolly Harbison, showing that Highlands was still very much in the thoughts of its early pioneers. Miss White was sending what she claimed to be the original map of Highlands, made between 1881 and 1885 on durable pa-

---

Stephen Vincent Benét and renewed 1955–56 by Rosemary Carr Benét. Reprinted by permission of Brandt & Brandt Literary Agents, Inc.
[46]Telephone conversations with Marion Day Arnold, October 29, November 5, and December 9, 1993.
[47]Interview with June Thompson Medlin, November 9, 1993.
[48]Interview with Joe Reese, December 1, 1993. See also "Street Improvement Being Planned in Highlands," *Franklin Press & Highlands Maconian*, April 22, 1948, for the actual paving of the block the next year.
[49]Interview with Lucile Pierson Reese, November 27, 1993.

per with linen texture and was requesting that it be given to the Highlands Museum.[50]

The White family, though gone from Highlands after 1910 and remembered by few living here today, never forgot the town of their youth. As noted earlier, when T. Baxter White retired from his life as the first settler in Highlands, his departure was an emotional struggle in the midst of which he refused at one stage to leave, trying to buy back the property he had already sold. He had been the Highlands' correspondent to the newspaper in Franklin, and when the family moved, his son Elias kept Highlanders informed of their former citizens living in California as late as the forties, indeed until his sister Jessie's death in 1956.[51]

In the same year that Miss Jessie sent the map and while the new Highlands Community Hospital was under construction to facilitate the work of the town's sole resident physician, Dr. William A. Matthews,[52] a person very dear to the library, Louise Bascom Barratt, age sixty-four, passed away at her summer home, Chetolah, on Satulah mountain. She was the daughter of H. M. Bascom by his first wife, Ida Crockett, who had died soon after Louise's birth. Apart from her unstinting devotion to the library as patron and trustee, readers outside Highlands knew her as a writer. A dramatics major at Wellesley, she began her career as an author after college. She published popular articles, mostly romantic, in *Harper's Weekly, Good Housekeeping,* and *Ladies' Home Journal.*

---

[50]"Old Map of Highlands Presented Museum By Former Local Resident," *Franklin Press & Highlands Maconian,* January 27, 1949.
[51]See "Miss White, Daughter of Highlands Founder, Succumbs In California," *Franklin Press & Highlands Maconian,* April 12, 1956.
[52]The hospital opened its doors on January 25, 1951. It was renamed the Highlands-Cashiers Hospital in 1963 and moved to its present site between Highlands and Cashiers two days into the "storm of the century" in 1993.

Two stories, by their titles alone, reveal the characteristic thrust of her writings: "Aunt Sarah and the Policeman: How He Helped Her to Have Her Fling" and "Carrila's Corn: In which the Lady Makes Someone Eat 'Humble-pie and Grass and Weeds'—and How That Someone Was Not Always Her Father." Miss Bascom published a romantic "Story Time in Prose and Rhyme" series that ran for a year and a half in *Today's Housewife* and a second series, "Peacock Robe: A Story of Mystery and Love," which ran for five months and which her childhood friend and future husband Watson Barratt illustrated. She wrote for *Housewife*, *Youth's Companion*, and *Woman's Home Companion*.

Her writing embraced more than romantic or fictional topics. *Editor* magazine published over a dozen instructional articles on the craft of fine fiction, in which she taught how to write popular stories without sacrificing quality as well as how to get published. One of her best bits of advice she gave in "Three Secrets of Literary Success." Seeking to encourage the dream of aspiring young writers, however, she never lost sight of the absolute necessity for logical plot building and economy in writing. She even focused on mistakes to avoid in the creation of character and the use of language.

Besides articles, she published several plays and a biography of the American film comedienne Marie Dressler, whom she called *The Ugly Duckling*. Her monthly publications for the New York Central Railroad made her well known to every traveler by rail, who read her *New York Visitor* on trains, much like the in-flight magazines now placed on airlines. She also edited the *Sears Shopping Guide*.[53]

---

[53] For works published by Louise Bascom Barratt, see Appendix VI.

Her death deprived the magazine world of a highly accomplished writer, whose appeal to the mind and the heart reflected an all-too-rare combination of good sense and good taste. Perhaps these qualities were only extensions of her own beauty, which was regarded as classic.

Watson Barratt sustained a severe loss in the death of his wife. Their lives together had begun like a page from the famous courtship of the English poets Elizabeth Barratt and Robert Browning. Just as a poem by Elizabeth Barratt had attracted the attention and subsequent love of Robert Browning, so also had an article by Louise Bascom induced Watson Barratt to write congratulating her. They had known each other as neighbors while growing up in Salt Lake City but had taken separate paths when they departed for college, she to become an author, he an artist.

Yet even before his writing to commend her on her literary accomplishment, she herself, recuperating from an illness in the hospital, had picked up a copy of *Life* magazine, found in it one of his artistic accomplishments, and intended to write and express how proud she was of him. The impulse to write had been initially hers, but the first letter was his. They married in 1917.

After his wife's death, Watson Barratt retired from scenic design and theatrical production in New York. He returned to Highlands as manager of Tricemont Terrace, renaming it Bascom-Louise Hotel in 1951, as a tribute to his dear wife and H. M. Bascom, her esteemed father.[54] The gallery branch of the Hudson Library would bear the

---

[54] "Mrs. Barratt's Funeral Held in Highlands," *Franklin Press & Highlands Maconian*, September 8, 1949. See also "Highlands Highlights," *Franklin Press & Highlands Maconian*, December 7, 1950, about Watson Barratt's retirement and naming of the Tricemont Terrace the Bascom-Louise. In this same year, the Frank B. Cooks bought Highlands Inn from the J. Harvey Trices and became its sole owners.

same name at its festive christening thirty-four years later. In 1956, when Richard Lee bought the Bascom-Louise Hotel, it became Lee's Inn,[55] and Watson Barratt returned to the Broadway stage for the remainder of his life.

In the year that Communist China was born and the Library of Congress reported holdings of 8.6 million books as compared with the Hudson Library's five thousand, the library bought a new asbestolene roof, at a cost of eighty dollars and guaranteed to last for ten years.[56] Nineteen fifty was the year of modernization in Highlands. A new school building arose at the foot of Satulah Mountain, where it stands today. The new Galax Theater opened on Main Street, premièring the *Daughter of Rosie O'Grady* in Technicolor.[57] The new Catholic Church was erected on Fifth Street, where James Rideout's Satulah House (subsequently the Hall House, golf course, tennis court, lake, and dance pavilion) had existed. The new First Baptist Church had existed for only three years. A new toll road wound up Whiteside Mountain. Dolly Harbison had started a new Girl Scout troop in the children's room of the library.[58] New books began appearing on the shelves of the library—in particular, two of the most widely read works of their time, Gilbreth and Carey's *Cheaper by the Dozen* and Fulton Oursler's best-selling popularization of the Bible and Christianity, *The Greatest Story Ever Told*.

---

[55]See "Lee's Inn Celebrates 10th Anniversary," *Highlander*, May 5, 1966.
[56]In 1955, five years into the ten-year guarantee, the condition of the library roof had deteriorated so drastically that, in the advice of Dolly Harbison, "instead of patching up the present roof it would be better to put on a new one." Minutes of trustees meeting, April 16, 1955.
[57]"Highlands Highlights," *Franklin Press & Highlands Maconian*, May 25, 1950.
[58]Interview with Beverly Cook Quin, November 25, 1993.

G. Watson and Louise Bascom Barratt
Taken ca. 1925. Courtesy of the Bascom–Barratt estate.

The Bascom-Louise Hotel
Taken ca. 1953. Courtesy of the Bascom-Barratt estate.

A Free Spirit: 1954–72

I stretched my arms to the twilit skies
And set my spirit free—
It wandered o'er the miles of space
And then came back to me—

All washed clean from the golden light,
Radiant . . . and still . . . .[1]

In 1954, in a far-reaching historic decision under the Fourteenth Amendment, the U.S. Supreme Court outlawed segregation by color in the public schools. In the same year the Hudson Library, while celebrating its seventieth birthday, chose to delete the word *free* from its name, now amended to read the Hudson Library of Highlands, North Carolina, Inc.[2] Considering the one-dollar annual membership dues, perhaps the library sought to achieve total honesty in its title. The records give no reason for the change.

Ostensibly it was a sign of the times: the discarding of an outdated and arbitrary idea. In this year the notion that no one could run the mile in under four minutes fell by the wayside. Roger Bannister changed the world's view of what was impossible. It was not long after the library's name change that the trustees decided to keep the building open every day of the week, though not yet

---

[1] Bess Hines Harkins, "Remembered Spring," *Singing of the Heart* (Atlanta, 1943), p. 35.
[2] Minutes of annual meeting, August 5, 1954: Motion by Gertrude Harbison that "the name Hudson Free Library Association be changed to Hudson Library Association, dropping the word Free." The official certificate of incorporation was not amended, however, until December, 1956, to read "Hudson Library of Highlands, North Carolina, Incorporated."

every month of the year. They gave the librarian a forty-dollar raise, setting her salary at one hundred dollars a month.[3]

On the whole the 1950s and early 1960s brought to Highlands and to the library a growing focus on natural beauty. In 1953 the Highlands Garden Club adopted the library for projects that would improve and landscape the grounds, a tradition that has continued to this day, with other garden clubs joining in.[4] In 1957 the club considered restoring the trees that once grew in the center of Main Street, like the altitude oak, which until 1936 or 1947 had stood so tall and protective over the town. However, since the town council had begun to focus five years earlier on congestion in the center of Main Street[5] and now considered parking a problem, the club embraced the alternative of planting five dogwoods on each side of the street between Third and Fourth.[6]

By 1962 the Highlands Biological Station had established behind the museum, now known as the Nature Center, its Botanical Garden, which eventually would contain four hundred fifty labeled specimens of plants native to the southern Appalachians. The museum instituted classes and programs to teach natural history to adults as well as children in Highlands and to emphasize the special heritage that made Highlands unique in the biological, ecological, and geological world.

During this rebirth of enthusiasm over the Highlands environment, the library received and bought a large number of books on flora and fauna, beginning with the sale of Alice Lounsberry's *Southern Wild Flowers and Trees*, which Gertrude Harbison had obtained from a

---

[3]Minutes of trustees meeting, June 15, 1956.
[4]Ibid., November 25, 1953.
[5]Minutes of town council meeting, July 7, 1952.
[6]Ibid., April 1 and June 3, 1957.

dealer in out-of-print books and sold for fifty dollars. She used the proceeds to buy "much needed books on nature and books of local interest."[7]

In a community where natural beauty is not a cosmetic designed to adorn its form so much as its *raison d'être*, its primary justification for existence, it was no accident —though it was coincidence—that when the Hudson Library moved into its present quarters, a group of citizens from Highlands planted four large red maples in rock planters placed in the center of Main Street. The altitude oak, so painfully lamented in 1936 or 1947 when it fell, would be in 1985 severally restored. Ironically, it was the year previous, 1984—when the library had to clear-cut twenty-seven giant white pines for its new building—that the townsfolk would direct their despair, not at town officials this time, but at the library. More on this issue, however, when the time arrives.

With a town population of nearly six hundred[8] and library holdings of six thousand volumes, the town and library began the 1960s with essentially the same population and holdings that they would still control at the outset of the 1970s. Little changed in Highlands over this decade when the United States inaugurated its thirty-fifth and youngest president, saw him in short order assassinated, and then plunged into an agonizing and costly Vietnam War. Little changed in Highlands from the year that Robert Bolt premièred his *Man for All Seasons* and Peter, Paul, and Mary were crooning "Blowin' in the Wind" until the Broadway hits *Jesus Christ, Superstar* and *Grease* introduced the 1970s. The

---

[7]Minutes of trustees meeting, November 25, 1953.
[8]The population of the town in 1960 was 592. The township count was 1,418. In 1970 the town's population actually dropped to 583. See James A. Crutchfield, ed., *North Carolina Almanac and Book of Facts* (Nashville, 1988), p. 296.

town and the library coasted through the decade, like a youth growing in spurts, growing and ceasing growth to consolidate for another surge. That surge for both would occur in 1973.

Nevertheless, the town and the library did realize a few successes during the 1960s, though on a relatively small scale. Highlands celebrated in 1962 its first annual square dance. Concurrently the library was enjoying, as its central attraction for the children of the town, a Story Lady. Virginia "Ted" Wilcox, aided by her eager listeners, acted out *Winnie the Pooh,* Hans Christian Anderson's *Fairy Tales, Aesop's Fables,* Carl Sandburg's whimsical *Rootabaga Stories,* and many other children's stories.[9] By 1961 she had become the Pied Piper of Highlands, stealing the children from their homes every Saturday morning. Her story hour was so popular that it practically guaranteed a resurgence in the early seventies, when Mrs. John J. (Harriet) Brown and the Misses Harbison in 1972 brought in storytellers, puppeteers, and the Highlands Community Theatre group to stage a children's hour that initiated an annual affair.

In 1963 the library held its most successful fund raiser ever. A gem project made more money "than any two projects, taken together, in its history."[10] In a raffle of three cases of precious and semi-precious cut stones donated by friends of the library, the affair netted $1,220.[11] In the same year the library sponsored the movie *To Kill a Mockingbird,* featuring Highlands native actress Collin Wilcox, daughter of the Story Lady. In 1965 the Presbyterian Church honored Miss Dolly, a member

---

[9] See "Story Hour Big Success," *Highlander,* November 11, 1960.

[10] Helen Augur, letter to Miss Blanche Davenport, September 11, 1963. In Secretary's Book, Hudson Library Association.

[11] "Gem Benefit Big Success," *Highlander,* September 13, 1963.

of the Order of the Eastern Star,[12] as the first woman in Highlands to become Ruling Elder.[13]

During the rest of the decade, to pay for the purchase of current and popular books, like Victoria Holt's suspenseful, romantic *Mistress of Mellyn* and Helen MacInnes' thrilling *Decision at Delphi*, the library held Silver Teas, bake sales, and art exhibits, including a second gem stone raffle, all of which kept the association solvent: unchanged in essence but debt free.

All the while Miss Gertrude and Miss Dolly kept tucked away in their minds the reading preferences of scores of Highlands families. Their catalogued memories told them who had read what and who hadn't. So when Stevie Potts came in one day to say, "I've come for 'Teeve's book," Miss Dolly knew to choose another mystery that his father Steve would like. She also knew how much young Steve himself loved to read.

One sad note, however, marred the relatively static life of the sixties in Highlands. In 1962 Watson Barratt, age seventy-eight, the last of the Bascom-Barratt family, died in New York. His death was a significant loss not only to the town but more specifically to the library and the Highlands Community Theatre. Many of the theater's young actors and actresses owed their careers to Mr. Barratt's spirited support since its establishment in 1941.

A student of the American impressionist James Whistler and the children's illustrator Howard Pyle,[14] Mr.

---

[12]The Highlands chapter of the Order of the Eastern Star was founded in the Masonic Hall in 1949, with Miss Dolly's father, Professor Harbison, as worthy patron. See "OES Chapter Is Instituted in Highlands," *Franklin Press & Highlands Maconian*, May 5, 1949.

[13]See "Miss Harbison To Be Ordained as Presbyterian Ruling Elder," *Highlander*, February 12, 1965.

[14]"Library Benefits from Bascom-Barratt Bequest," *Highlander*, August 20, 1981.

Barratt had become a famous art director and scene designer. He spent almost fifty years of his life in New York, summering in Highlands. He designed a thousand plays on and off Broadway, beginning in 1918 with a commission for *Sinbad* and including stage sets for Melville Ellis and Elizabeth Marbury, which drew public acclaim as some of the most beautiful ever seen in New York. He was chief designer for the Ackerman studios, where he designed sets for the Winter Garden, Hippodrome, and high-class vaudeville. As art director of the Metro–Rolfe Moving Picture company, he created the surroundings for Ethel Barrymore. In 1924 he designed Sigmund Romberg's *Student Prince*. He also worked for many years with J. J. and Lee Schubert and served as art director for the St. Louis Municipal Opera. Staging productions in London, Paris, and at the World's Fair in Brussels, he brought the curtain down on his own long career with *Brigadoon* on his return to New York, where he passed away.[15]

Since his wife Louise Bascom had died thirteen years earlier, Mr. Barratt left no survivors other than the child of his own brain, the Bascom-Louise Gallery, which he created in his will and endowed as a branch of the Hudson Library.[16] He left Chetolah, the Bascom-Barratt house, which neighbored the Sloan property on Satulah and which he and Louise had inherited as a summer home from H. M. Bascom, to their closest friend Helen Augur until her death, which occurred in 1981. His own death in 1962, however, left no one in Highlands knowing his last wishes for the future library and gallery. His

---

[15]"Watson Barratt Dies in New York Hospital: Highlands Summer Resident Was Famous Theatrical Designer," *Highlander*, July 13, 1962. See also "Watson Barratt, Designer, 78, Dies," *New York Times*, July 8, 1962, for his full name at birth: "George Watson Barratt."

[16]See G. Watson Barratt, "Last Will and Testament," signed May 29, 1958.

attorney, who should have probated his will also in North Carolina, did so only in New York. Some twenty years would pass before Helen Augur's death would bring to light his life-long intent.

At the outset of the 1970s, on the threshold of a new era of the library, Mrs. William (Mary) Jewell of Atlanta donated six hundred used books and $1,500-worth of new books, a truly significant contribution in 1972 to a library already bulging at its seams yet desperately in need of new titles. An old order was about to pass.

The Hudson Library with Its 1927 and 1939 Additions
Taken in June, 1969. Courtesy of the Hudson Library.

The Hudson Library and Its Patrons
Taken in September, 1984. Courtesy of the *Highlander*.

The End of an Era: 1973–74

Gone the spiral stairway's trace
Where the white spiranthes climbed,
Gone the slender saffron's grace,
Following where the frost bells chimed.[1]

"The old order changeth, yielding place to new," cried Tennyson in his *Morte d'Arthur*.[2] The time was fast approaching when Miss Gertrude and Miss Dolly must leave their half-century's dominion over the library and give up the reins to unsure, untried hands. Small fears and particular concerns were already contributing to a growing tension as the trustees struggled to decide what to do with the incredible number of old books overflowing the shelves onto the floor and mounting in precariously balanced stacks like brittle stalagmites reaching for the ceilings of the children's and Satulah rooms. Old books were added daily like mineral-rich deposits to towers already poised—indeed destined in short time—to fall.

In 1973, while the nation focused on the Watergate break-in and cover-up, which would ultimately force an American president to resign, the Hudson Library quietly incorporated into the Fontana Regional Library system. Some benefits accrued, but many problems ensued. The library began to receive federal revenue-sharing funds through Macon County, and Fontana now and hereafter paid the librarian's salary.

The trustees would not know the amount of the revenue-sharing grant until the following year, when they

---

[1] Mary Chapin Smith, *Earth Songs* (Boston, 1910), p. 16.
[2] Alfred, Lord Tennyson, *Morte d'Arthur* (1842), line 408.

were astounded to learn that the Macon County Board of Commissioners had granted Gladys McDowell's request for $10,000. Earmarked for capital improvements over the next three years, it was sufficient for the trustee president Delores "Dee" Sherrill to take "a long, long time to calm down, I was so excited!"[3]

With the grant, however, came a new influence on the library. Marilyn "Lynn" de Ville chaired the committee whose job entailed the tremendous task of sorting and cataloguing the overwhelming number of books and magazines that had accumulated over the past many years on the shelves, the floor, behind curtains, and everywhere. Only by bringing in someone knowledgeable about the value of old books to decide what went and what stayed could the trustees accomplish such a complex job. Dee Sherrill recalls that board supports had been built in to keep the shelves from bowing beneath the weight of so many worn-out and outdated books that needed repair or rebinding or were simply inappropriate for a small public library. There was a big, big box of old, old newspapers. There were old maps and heaps of *National Geographic*.

Books were stacked so deep in the back of the children's room and in the Satulah Room that when the process of sorting them began, one volunteer found a table underneath that nobody knew was there, then a chair, and a wash basin. The table had been the gift of Mrs. Hudson's son back in 1939.[4] The stove in the Satulah Room had long been inaccessible so that the Harbisons had been using an electric heater near their

---

[3]Interview with Mrs. Worth (Delores) Sherrill, October 25, 1993. See also Helen Hopper, "Library Greatly Pleased with $10,000 Allocation," *Highlander*, February 7, 1974.
[4]Minutes of trustees meeting, July 1, 1939.

front desk. The toilet in the Satulah Room, which many patrons didn't even know was there, was still accessible but was broken, so that anyone in dire need went to Steve Potts's grocery store across the street.[5]

The Misses Harbison felt, according to Miss Dolly, that they "knew all the books in the library and didn't need to get it catalogued,"[6] which of course was true. However, Miss Gertrude and Miss Dolly would retire in 1974 and 1975, respectively, and who else knew all the books? So "the people from the Fontana Regional were quite helpful," admits Miss Dolly.[7] During the years 1973 to 1980, the library catalogued its books, beginning with fiction (F) and progressing through biography (B), mystery (M), children's books (J), and so forth. Twenty-six volunteers gave 1,138 hours to the task during the first year alone![8]

As the world's population peaked in 1974 at 3.8 billion, the library's holdings must have reached 13,500 because volunteers cleared out 3,000 books to sell at the Macon County Book Fair and another 2,000 for sale at the sidewalk tables during Highlands centennial week.[9] As reorganization got well under way, the library stayed open for the first time in its history throughout the winter of 1974–75. The old order was swiftly fading away.

The thoughts of those who knew this place of yore
Rush down the years and with mine own entwine,
The virgin forest towering on the hill
Has marked the hopes and fears of more than mine.[10]

---

[5]Interview with Mrs. Worth Sherrill, October 25, 1993.
[6]Interview with Dolly Harbison, September 22, 1993.
[7]Ibid.
[8]President's report to the trustees, August 27, 1973.
[9]Minutes of annual meeting, June 30, 1975.
[10]Mrs. A. R. (Lillian) Nall, "North Carolina Home," *Franklin Press & Highlands Maconian*, July 15, 1943. Lillian Nall was married to Miss Rebecca C. Nall's brother, Archibald Rockwell Nall. Interview with Emma Potts Pell, February 9, 1994.

These were hard times for Miss Gertrude and Miss Dolly. When an outside censor arrives to decide what book the Regional Library system considers worth keeping and which one has only extremely local interest at best, then many indigenous treasures that the Harbisons considered sacrosanct have suddenly become vulnerable. Whether by intent or accident, the books in the enclosed bookcases, the nucleus of the original library in 1880, were miraculously retained.

The records don't show what cherished gems went out with the chaff, and Miss Dolly won't specifically say, for indeed the Fontana Regional people—Mrs. Marita Quinnett[11] and Mr. John Woxny—were professionals. They helped choose and discard old, outdated textbooks and obsolete teaching-method books and even called in the archivist of the University of North Carolina to evaluate books, magazines, and newspapers that the library would certainly want to keep. The inevitable losses notwithstanding, Miss Dolly is quick to reiterate that "the people from the Fontana Regional were quite helpful."

Still, sometime between 1973 and the present, in the long process of discarding books regarded as dispensable, the book of poems by Stephen Vincent Benét's sister Laura as well as Mary Chapin Smith's poetic *Earth Songs* disappeared from the library's holdings, perhaps because someone deemed them too strictly local or did not recognize their local worth at all.[12]

---

[11]Mrs. Quinnett was later fired as director of the Fontana Regional Library System by its trustees, action taken on June 15, 1975, and replaced by Wayne Modlin of Richmond, Va., effective July 1.

[12]Mary Chapin Smith's *History of the Hudson Library Association* (Highlands, 1931), p. 6, refers to the gifted Benét family and especially Miss Laura Benét—the sister of William Rose and Stephen Benét—"whose poems we have in the library." Although her poems are no longer available in the Hudson Library, the Macon County Library in Franklin carries her novel *Enchanting Jenny Lind*. As for Mrs. Smith's own *Earth Songs*, a copy

Miss Gertrude didn't come in so often now, for her health was failing. Nevertheless, she kept the summer residents current through vital orders for Eugenia Price's *Beloved Invader*, Gore Vidal's *Burr*, and Morris West's *Salamander*. She acquired an up-to-date *World Book Encyclopedia* for the children. She welcomed books of local interest, like Elliot Wigginton's *Foxfire* series, Van Nopp's *Western North Carolina Since the Civil War*, and Highlands resident Hubert Shuptrine and James Dickey's *Jericho: The South Beheld*.[13]

Miss Dolly frequented the library regularly, sorting volumes along with Simone Kuehl (now Sorge), who volunteered to haul home a load of books every night in a straw bag to type cards for them, barring of course Tuesday nights when she kept the library open for the public. Estelle O'Brien sorted magazines: the *Saturday Evening Post, Collier's, Life, New Yorker*, and *National Geographic*. Harriet Brown arranged the *Highlanders* chronologically, Helen Chambers categorized and catalogued, inserting a pocket and card in each book.

As if there weren't already enough activity in the library with the creation of a new card file system, capital

---

donated by its author to the Cullowhee Normal and Industrial School in 1926 is held by the Western Carolina University Library. Richard Melvin of Highlands bought the Hudson Library's copy at a book fair in Franklin and returned it to Highlands, but apparently it, too, was discarded. On January 12, 1994, Miss Dolly Harbison donated one of her copies to the library, so Highlanders now have access to it in the bookcases housing the original volumes of the library.

[13] Artist-author Hubert Shuptrine, who lived in the Elliott house on Satulah, left Highlands in the mid-1970s but would return in 1987 to autograph his second book, *Home to Jericho*, an odyssey of his journey through fifteen states from Texas to Vermont, including North Carolina. See Sylvia Thomas, "Highlands Integral Part of Shuptrine's Art," *Highlander*, December 1, 1987. Both his books feature reproductions of his paintings of the people and places he encountered during his stay in Highlands and his subsequent travels.

improvements were now permitted by the revenue-sharing grant. Between 1973 and 1976 the library installed a new furnace to replace the unused wood stove, repaired the bathroom and connected to the town sewer system with modernized plumbing, mended the leaks in the Satulah Room, refurbished the children's room and decorated it with Priscilla Dunning's charming murals, and at long last insulated the building—walls, floor, and ceiling—to keep it warm year-round.

There's a sad, if not cruel, irony in the fact that even as the library was at last able to streamline its services and improve its facilities, the dedicated woman whom everyone had come to regard as inseparable from their library was about to retire. This librarian, who had weathered the two-and-a-half mile walk to and from her job every working day except during, but sometimes even during, winter's fury when she stoked the primitive stove with wood to keep warm, and who was always there to tell the children more about what they liked than they themselves knew so that many of the summer children wrote notes of thanks to their Highlands librarian when they returned to their winter homes far, far away[14]—this dedicated and seasoned librarian was after forty-eight years about to bring a quiet age to a peaceful end! Who still living today can remember entering this small-town library before 1974 when Miss Gertrude Harbison wasn't there?

On August 24, 1974—ninety years after its birth from a few boxes of books—the library honored Miss Gertrude and Miss Dolly for their fifty years[15] of service to the

---

[14]Interview with Dolly Harbison, September 22, 1993.
[15]If one adds the two years that the Harbisons trained under Mrs. S. T. Marett to the forty-eight years that they served as librarian and assistant, the fifty-year designation is correct for time served. Actual time in the capacity of librarians figures from 1926 to 1974.

community by holding a reception, attended by one hundred fifty appreciative admirers and nine past presidents of the trustees. The library building, we are told, "could never have looked lovelier than it did that afternoon,"[16] with a new coat of paint, graveled parkway and entrances, fresh curtains, polished windows, waxed floors, and sunshine. The encomium expressed by Bess Blair as mistress of ceremonies set the stage for an enormous overflow of praise and appreciation that climaxed in the presentation of a large scrapbook filled with notes and letters of love and thanks from the many people affected at one time or another through the years by these two lovely and loving women.

The trustees had commissioned an enlarged photograph of Miss Gertrude—and later of Miss Dolly—for the wall of the library. The two ladies were each given a handbag designed with exquisite needlepoint and containing a check to cover the cash contributions that were still coming in, and would continue until the end of the following week. It was a heartrending but heartwarming reception, acutely moving for all involved, but especially for the frail but resolute Miss Gertrude.

---

[16]See "Library Reception Is Well Attended," *Highlander,* August 29, 1974.

Gert McIntosh
Story hour with the children. Taken in April, 1981.
Courtesy of the *Highlander*.

Betty Service
Taken in June, 1979. Courtesy of the *Highlander*.

Transition: 1975–79

Please pull the cord
This is it. This is the age
Where I must get off
The moving sidewalk, let Time
Go on without me, remain
This age indefinitely . . . .[1]

Miss Dolly stayed on for another year as acting librarian until the trustees could find a replacement. With the library all cleaned up now, it opened its doors to public book reviews, children's films and story hours, and four years of Library Night.

Evening lectures in the Satulah Room focused on quilting, pottery, jewelry, silver hallmarks, Christmas in the mountains, the *Highlander* newspaper, crime control, and Albert Schweitzer. Large crowds came to hear Colonel Charles Ivins speak on Mao Tse-tung and the Republic of China, Ralph de Ville on "Shopping Round the World," and Jonathan Williams on "Aunt Mnemosyne's Punktatum Conserve, or How to Make Poems out of Macon County, N.C."

One of the poems that Mr. Williams read to his audience gave a crystal-clear definition of poetry:

whether it is a stone next to a stone
or a word next to a word,
*it is the **glory**—*
the simple craft of it.[2]

---

[1] Dee McCollum, "1982," *The Summer Mountain: Poems of the Hills* (n.p., 1986), p. 18.
[2] Jonathan Williams, "My Quaker-Atheist Friend . . .," *Get Hot or Get Out* (Metuchen, N.J., 1982), p. 126. Works by Jonathan Williams currently available in the Hudson Library are *An Ear in Bartram's Tree* (Chapel Hill,

The craft of poetry, for Jonathan Williams, is much like weaving or splitting shingles and not something made just to be sold. His books of poetry, with titles like *An Ear in Bartram's Tree*, *Blues & Roots/Rue & Bluets*, *The Loco Logodaedalist in Situ*, and *Mahler*, have had limited appeal. A poet has crafted them for poets, who are "an endangered species," Williams has astutely observed, "like the morel, the pileated woodpecker, and the rattlesnake."[3] That's why he founded in 1951 the Jargon Society to publish and support writers who lack the large public appeal needed to make the best-seller lists. These mavericks do not have wide appeal, Williams concludes, because of, or despite, their existence as poets who are "afflicted with both vision and craft."[4]

When Williams is not writing his own poetry or hiking in the woods—another of his favorite activities—then he is editing and publishing the books of other writers and poets at his mountain home near Highlands or in "19th century hiding," as he calls it, at a cottage in England. He still writes, walks, and publishes today.

Besides book reviews, story hours, and lectures, innovative changes characterized benefits for the library in the 1970s. Bake sales now gave way to art shows (the first one netting $770 in 1973),[5] home tours (the first one in 1978 clearing $450), and sidewalk sales of old books. A

N.C., 1969), *Elite/Elate Poems* (Highlands, N.C., 1979), *Magpie's Bagpipe: Selected Essays* (San Francisco, 1982), *In the Azure Over the Squalor: Ransackings and Shorings* (Frankfort, Ky., ca. 1985), and *Blues & Roots/Rue & Bluets* (Durham, N.C., 1985). See also the list in the Bibliography under "Poets of Highlands."

[3]"Poet, Publisher Jonathan Williams Unknown to Many Highlanders," *Highlander*, May 18. 1978.

[4]Ibid.

[5]The library's sponsorship of art shows, which began in 1973, appropriately foreshadowed the 1985 union of the library with the gallery, which would thereafter sponsor all art shows for the association.

children's summer reading program began in 1976, the same year that the column "Library Corner" began to appear in the *Highlander*. The newspaper now listed memorial fund donors, and the library resumed the first baroque chamber music series since the late 1880s, which would run for the next seven years.

In 1977 the town board increased its annual contribution to the library from $250 to $500. In the same year the county decreased its budget for the Highlands library from $4,500 to $3,000. Nothing had prepared County Manager Joel Mashburn for the hornet's nest he had stirred up when he accepted the invitation of the trustees to come and explain the $1,500 cut. An hour and a half and sixty questions later he departed fully aware of the Hudson Library board's dissatisfaction not just with the cut but with his rationalizations for it.[6]

By 1979 the library was applying for and receiving institutional grants and issuing a fund-drive letter. In 1980 Mountain Findings gave its first contribution of $2,000, which the next year amounted to $10,000, in 1982 $9,000, in 1983 $5,000. Beginning in 1981 the Woman's Club and Recreation Bridge group made contributions as well.

For the first time in 1974 the library ran a full schedule: Monday through Friday from eleven to five, open Wednesday evenings, and on Saturday from ten to two. Working five days a week, six hours a day, Miss Dolly was earning an annual salary in 1975 at her retirement of $3,360, an increase in forty-seven years of more than 13,400 percent.[7] In the same year the library turned to adding paperbacks to its holdings because it

---

[6]Minutes of trustees meeting, June 28, 1977.
[7]Dolly Harbison's starting salary in 1928 had been twenty-five dollars for the year.

could thus buy a larger number of currently popular books.[8]

Anne Ham now took over as librarian—a daunting experience considering the shoes she had to fill. It may be partly due to the library's successful transition from an outpost of the old to the vanguard of the new, but due also to Mrs. Ham's proficiency and effervescent personality, that by the following year circulation had increased fifty percent to level off at 9,000 in 1977, 9,800 in 1978.

That was the year that library patrons heard "spine tingling noises" periodically in the little foyer of the library, and the trustees had to decide "what to do about the resident rat."[9] The unanimous opinion of the board was to "call Terminix immediately." Six months later the board paid thirty-five dollars to "rid the library of a squirrel in the roof."[10] Miss Dolly, who still worked as a volunteer, claims that "they wanted to kill the squirrel, and I didn't want the squirrel bothered." Indeed, one summer when Miss Dolly was still assistant librarian, "there was a snake in the evergreens, and I would tell the children, 'Don't you bother my snake sunning on the evergreens!' It was just a garter snake." Miss Dolly loves all creatures of nature. Indeed, her aversion to the circus, which first came to Highlands in 1923, stems from her feeling that circuses mistreat animals.[11]

In 1978, as a final and fitting tribute to Miss Gertrude, who was by then well into retirement, the National Weather Board awarded her the highest honor that it could bestow on a volunteer observer: the Thomas Jefferson Award. John Parris praised her "rare and unselfish

---

[8]Minutes of trustees meeting, January 27, 1975.
[9]Ibid., March 22, 1978.
[10]Ibid., October 18, 1978.
[11]Interview with Dolly Harbison, September 22, 1993.

dedication to public service" in an article entitled, "She Watched the Skies for More Than 50 Years."[12]

Miss Gertrude would live a life of fading glory for two more years, long enough to hear talk of the need for a new and grander library than the one that she had shepherded so conscientiously through the wilderness. Like Moses on Mount Nebo, though, she would not enter the promised land. Gertrude McIntosh, an inexperienced but enthusiastic Joshua, in 1978 now took command. She was the one anointed to enter Canaan instead.

Oh, tell me what do the katydids sing
To the heart only half aware
A shrill staccato, quaint improvisings
A rustic harmonious aire . . . .[13]

Miss Gert, after a three-year interlude of Anne Ham, Melinda Russell, and Martha Keener, succeeded Miss Gertrude at a critical time when the library grew dramatically. Circulation in 1978, which figured at 9,800, increased fifty-six percent to 15,300 in 1979. It grew another thirty-two percent to 20,200 in 1980. Still another thirty percent to 26,200 in 1981. Then it leveled off at about 32,000 for the three subsequent years. The overall increase totaled 230 percent during the six years that Miss Gert reigned.

Miss Gert began her tenure by replacing Miss Gertrude's curtain over the closet with a folding door. That became her office. Cataloguing of the books was already well under way, but plenty of old books and old magazines remained. They filled four rows of shelves and one aisle, piled waist high: fifteen boxes jammed full. Three closets in the children's room held old copies of *Reader's*

---

[12]*Asheville Citizen*, September 3, 1978.
[13]Butler Sterling Harkins, "Elfin Strings," *Sequoia Bound* (n.p., 1978), p. 18.

Digest and stacks of the *Highlander* as well as ancient copies of the *Blue Ridge Enterprise*, the *Highlands Star*, the *Mountain Eagle*, and the *Highlands Maconian*. Miss Gert recalls that she had nightmares that the building would burn down, and the library would lose forever these old heirlooms, found nowhere else. She sent them to the North Carolina Archives for microfilming and didn't get them back for almost four years.

She found way back on a bottom shelf twelve pamphlets of Matthew Brady's photographic history of the Civil War, like veins of gold suddenly opened to the light. Nevertheless, such findings were rare. Many old books were just taking up valuable space. One book, she notes, "hadn't been checked out in seventy years."[14]

Other than having set up two church libraries, Miss Gert had no experience as a librarian. However, even as she was assuming her uncertain role, the fortuitous arrival of a first-class tutor practically guaranteed her success. Betty Service did for Miss Gert what Mrs. S. T. Marett had done for Miss Gertrude and Miss Dolly, albeit on a far more professional level. She drew from forty-eight years of experience as Sarasota's head librarian.

Having taken over Sarasota's library when she was only a high school senior in 1926—at a time when it was expedient to keep her impending marriage secret because the Women's Club, which ran the library, felt that the head librarian should be single—Betty Service directed the growth of that library's holdings from 2,000 volumes, crammed into wooden shelves bought from Sears, to two branch libraries of more than 220,000 books.[15]

---

[14]Interview with Mrs. Harold (Gertrude) McIntosh, November 2, 1993.
[15]Kathleen Flinn, "Librarian, Storyteller Betty Service Dies at 82," *Sarasota Times*, August 22, 1991. See also Lee Copple, "One Man's Highlands [Betty Service]," *Highlander*, June 28, 1979.

Her life paralleled the life of Miss Gertrude Harbison only in that they both began their careers in 1926 and retired in 1974. Both women loved books, indeed centered their lives on them. On the other hand, Mrs. Service's life in a town that swelled from no fewer than two thousand inhabitants to over 45,000 held more glitter and sparkle than Miss Gertrude's in a village that grew from 547 to 583 in the same period.[16] Miss Gertrude Harbison's collection of juvenile literature, when Miss Gert McIntosh inherited it, amounted to eighty or ninety books in the children's room. On a far different scale, Mrs. Service enlarged her children's section, which didn't even exist when she started, to 16,000 volumes in the children's library at Gulf Gate, now named in her honor.[17]

Comparisons of extremes serve little practical purpose other than to clarify rather than rank differences. In her own right, Mrs. Service was "a terrific, dynamic woman and a real inspiration," according to the head librarian who replaced her at the Gulf Gate branch in Sarasota. She had a special way of storytelling, according to another head librarian who replaced her at the Shelby branch. "She would run her hands through her reddish hair and gather her arms close to her chest, then lean forward to a crowd of hushed children at her feet."[18] These two qualities—her professional expertise and her flare for storytelling—made her the ideal mentor at the right time for Miss Gert, who faced the monumental tasks of discarding and ordering and cataloguing, which were

---

[16]For the census of 1947—population 547—see "A Brief History of Highlands, Highest Town East of Rockies," *Franklin Press*, July 5, 1928. For the 1970 census—population 583—see "'80 Census: Results Are In, County Population Up 25%," *Highlander*, July 24, 1980.
[17]Flinn, "Librarian, Storyteller Betty Service Dies at 82," *Sarasota Times*, August 22, 1991.
[18]Ibid.

already five years in the making upon her arrival untutored on the scene.

Betty introduced Miss Gert to the tools of the trade. At Miss Gert's request the trustees, who were meeting monthly now at the discretion of their president, Norma "Boots" Pierson, authorized buying the *Public Library Catalogue* both for fiction and nonfiction.[19] This professional reference replaced the skimpy but useful amateur volume, *Gold in Your Attic*.[20] Now anyone could determine, with less probability of regret, whether to keep or discard a book. The library bought the *Sears List of Subject Headings*—not the Roebuck version—and used it to categorize books of all kinds. The library subscribed to *Publisher's Weekly* and the *American Library Journal*, which helped considerably in the choice of children's books.

Beginning with five volunteers in 1978 and ending eight years later with twenty, the library always had several workers putting up books, shelf reading them by the Dewey Decimal System, covering frayed volumes and marking them on the spine, carding and filing them, answering reference questions, registering new members, and checking out, reserving, renewing, receiving, and reshelving books. In 1982 alone fifteen volunteers gave 250 hours to the library, many of them serving two or three times in a week.[21]

The number of magazines to which the library subscribed increased from two—*National Geographic* and *National Wildlife*—in 1978 to thirty-two eight years later. Besides the *Highlander* and the *Franklin Press*, the library subscribed to the *Asheville Citizen*, *Atlanta*

---

[19]Minutes of trustees meeting, November 15, 1978.
[20]Ibid., October 26, 1976.
[21]"Library Corner," *Highlander*, August 12, 1982.

Constitution, Christian Science Monitor, Wall Street Journal, and *New York Sunday Times.* It bought a new set of the *World Book Encyclopedia* for its young people and a six-year-old edition of the *Encyclopedia Britannica* for its adults. It added to its holdings large-type books and children's cassettes and eventually audio tapes. Soon after the move to new quarters, it stocked videos and received a collection of 750 classical records. It ordered and received regularly the *Reader's Guide to Periodical Literature* and the *Guide to National Geographic* for students doing research. It subscribed to *Value Line*—during six months to include the summer—for investors seeking reliable guidance.

Miss Gert loved encouraging children to read, and with Betty Service's prodding she introduced songs, finger plays, and puppets into the story hours to attract school children as well as kids from Highlands Head Start. When young Alex Sanchez cautioned a fellow student about tearing books in the library, he was imitating Dandelion, the puppet who blew a gasket about damaged books. Miss Gert ordered books by Eric Carle for children as young as three years of age, who would return to the library and ask, "May I have the book with the red car?"[22]

During the next eight years, from 1978—when the library bought *Georgia,* the first in a photographic essay series covering the southern states by local resident James Valentine[23]—until 1986, circulation of children's books and cassettes would increase from 1,500 to over

---

[22]Interview with Gert McIntosh, November 2, 1993.
[23]Minutes of trustees meeting, May 24, 1978. Nature photographer Jimmy Valentine's next book in the series, *North Carolina,* appeared in 1979. See "New Photo Book by Valentine Now on Sale," *Highlander,* November 15, 1979. He had published *Guale: The Golden Coast of Georgia* earlier and would publish *Florida* later.

11,500,[24] in part due to Miss Gert's "down-home friendliness," which made the library special to residents and visitors alike.[25] Wendy DeWolf and Betts Calloway told Miss Gert that the library was where they learned to love books because she herself loved them. Like an addiction, her enthusiasm was infectious.

One unique way in which Miss Gert stimulated circulation was by ordering several copies of the same book. She bought two copies of Helen Santmyer's *And Ladies of the Club,* and donors gave three more, yet all five copies were promptly checked out, and a waiting list applied to each one. In this way one book contributed through multiple copies to an increase in circulation.

By 1980, the year that Mount St. Helens erupted in Washington State, burst its seams, and spewed years of its pressurized contents into the sky, the library had attained the limit of 7,000 books on shelved volumes,[26] the maximum proposed back in 1915 when the architect designed the building. Circulation in this year was 20,200, thirty-one times greater than the population of Highlands.[27] Patrons had checked out 3,360 books in the month of July alone, the biggest count ever.[28] Twenty-five percent, or 840, of these represented juvenile circulation.

---

[24]See 1985–86 Annual Report to Hudson Library Association.
[25]"Commentary: Library Patrons Are Losing Special Friend," *Highlander,* February 3, 1987.
[26]Minutes of trustees meeting, June 18, 1980.
[27]Ibid., January 21, 1981. Town population in 1980 was 653, township 1,750. In "'80 Census: Results Are In, County Population Up 25%," *Highlander,* July 24, 1980, the town's population is listed as 637, but the James A. Crutchfield, ed., *North Carolina Almanac and Book of Facts* (Nashville, 1988) lists it as 653 (see p. 296), as does the U.S. Bureau of the Census in *1980 Census of Population* (Washington, D.C.). Interview with Elizabeth Bruce (December 14, 1993), who was sent from Cullowhee to Highlands for the recount.
[28]Hudson Library report for month of July, 1980.

Many students were now using reference books for reports and term papers, but the largest circulation was in easy-reader or preschool books. The library's programs for children were becoming the most popular in town. Twelve volunteers gave sixty hours a week to the children's summer reading program, during which time seventy children checked out 660 books in eight weeks. Total attendance at the Thursday movies and Saturday story hours stood at 250.[29] For the adults, volunteers fielded over twelve hundred reference and directional questions. Such a rapid increase in library use made necessary the purchase of a new charging machine to expedite the checkout process.

For the library to be crowded in the late 1920s, it required only four or five children at a time, although the rainy season brought in more. In the 1980s, however, it was not uncommon for twenty-five to thirty people to be using the reading areas of the library each day.[30] Gert recalls that she counted twenty-eight patrons on one occasion in that small library, many standing up to read the paper and magazines. She noticed that every seat in the main room, the children's room, and the Satulah Room was taken, and "that's when I knew we needed a new library!"[31]

No sooner did the thought of a new library enter Miss Gert's mind than thoughts of remaining in the old library expired with the death on April 17, 1980, of Miss Gertrude. Her passing did not make front-page news. The newspaper devoted no more than a single column to it on the obituary page. No editorial followed in any subsequent issue. As a life-long resident of Highlands, she

---

[29]Hudson Library report for September, 1980.
[30]Ibid.
[31]Interview with Gert McIntosh, November 2, 1993.

was credited with fifty of her seventy-six years as volunteer weather observer, librarian, and Biological Station trustee and treasurer. That in a thimble summarized a richly generous life.

Perhaps no article could adequately summarize such a life. Indeed, what more could this history add to what has already been said? Suffice it to say that death discovered a private treasure born to blush unseen when it took Miss Gertrude! It laid her to rest with her father, her mother, and her sister Margaret just beyond the crest of the hill at the right of the road in the Highlands Cemetery.

Growing Pains: 1980–84

*After the truck had roared
Down Main Street, and the
Children had filled the sidewalk
With long, shrill whistles;
After the skateboard and
Motor bike had noised beyond
Our ears, in the lull a song
From the throat of a grosbeak
Announced his return to Highlands.[1]*

So it was in June of 1980—while the literary world was raving over Forrest Carter's *Education of Little Tree*, the sensitive story of a Cherokee boy reared in the tradition of authentic values, and the social world writhed in the epidemic of Dallas fever, 89 million television viewers wildly impatient to know who shot J. R. —that John Reid, president of the board, apprised the trustees and membership of the possibility of having a new library building.[2]

The town of Highlands would apply for a matching-fund grant of $174,000 from the Appalachian Regional Council. If successful, the town would donate a site for the new library at the Recreation Park. Presumably, the town would acquire title and ownership of the facility but would relinquish control of the library proper to the Macon County Library System, into which the Hudson Library had just this year incorporated as a branch.[3]

---

[1] Dee McCollum, "Main Street: April," *The Summer Mountain: Poems of the Hills* (n.p., 1986), p. 13.
[2] Minutes of Annual Meeting, June 18, 1980.
[3] See "Hudson To Become Part of Macon System," *Highlander*, March 6, 1980.

This latter action meant that the library, after ninety-six years of existence as a privately owned and operated institution, was now public property—at least in part. The county budget currently funded its operating costs, the county leased its building for a dollar per year, but the local board of trustees retained control of the library operation, and this was important.

The arrangement for the Highlands corporation stood as unique among public libraries. The Hudson Library became public in that the county paid the salaries, taxes, and fringe benefits of the librarian and her staff and the operating costs of maintaining the building. However, the library itself remained private in that it paid for its own independent book purchases—including those that it bought through the county's acquisition program—and owned its own land and building. This meant that though the county would include the Highlands library in its budget, the Highlands library would continue to raise funds in the community for new books and magazines, a gallery director's salary, and equipment and other items not covered by the funds from the county.[4]

In the midst of the turmoil of growth, of overcrowding and of searching for every available inch of space to accommodate books, magazines, people (large and small), supplies, and volunteers, the library sent a request to the Satulah Club to find somewhere else to store its white elephants for the Hospital Bazaar and to use the annex only for their regular meetings. This would allow the

---

[4]See board of trustees, Hudson Library, memorandum to Mr. Bob Moore, chairman of Macon County Public Library board of trustees; Mrs. Cynthia Modlin, Macon County librarian; Mrs. Gertrude McIntosh, Hudson Branch librarian; and Mrs. Jacquelyn Leebrick, Louise Bascom Barratt Gallery [sic] director, September 19, 1985. See also board of trustees, "Letter of Intent, Macon County, North Carolina, Hudson Library of Highlands, N.C., Inc." and "Lease Agreement," both dated March 3, 1980.

library to convert the Satulah Room into a reading area for its patrons.

The proposal incensed the Satulah Club, which sent a letter to the library, requesting that planned improvements to the room not be made and advising that the club would continue to store white elephants there for the Hospital Bazaar.[5] Incensed in turn, the library responded that in 1939, when it added the room to the building, the agreement clearly stated that the space would serve as a meeting place for Satulah Club members so long as they needed it but would bear the name Hudson Library Annex and, in the event they no longer needed it, would belong exclusively to the library.[6] The trustees thus advised the Satulah Club that they could continue to use the room for their regular meetings but must locate another place to work on white elephants.

Subsequent records mention nothing more about the dispute, except at the very next meeting of the library's trustees, even as the Soviet Union was invading Afghanistan, a request by a woman from Atlanta to use the Satulah Room for German classes was flatly and resolutely denied.[7]

In the year that Ronald Reagan became the fortieth president of the United States and proposed the greatest-ever tax and spending cuts in his first budget, the Hudson Library juggled funds like a circus clown trying to make a dream come true. Mountain Findings donated $10,000 to the proposal for a new building. The grant for which the library had applied from the Appalachian Regional Council dried up as the organization ceased to exist. However, the State of North Carolina, through the

---

[5] Minutes of trustees meeting, April 16, 1980.
[6] See Resolution of September 29, 1939, in Secretary's Book, Hudson Library Association.
[7] Minutes of trustees meeting, May 21, 1980.

assistance of Representative Jeff Enloe[8] and Senators Joe Palmer and Bo Thomas, offered a grant of $30,000 for library construction.[9]

Attorney Richard Melvin, on whom the trustees relied heavily for legal advice—and in each case gratis—informed the board that, with the death of Helen Augur who had lived in the Bascom-Barratt house on Satulah, the library had received a very large bequest from the estate. The bequest called for a gallery to feature local artists in a wing of the library.[10] The proceeds for this wing were to come from an auction of the estate, encompassing a house and twenty acres from Satulah Ridge to the Walhalla Road.[11] The estate was appraised at between $265,000 and $425,000.[12]

Before the trustees could quiet their excitement over such unexpected good fortune, Mayor Harry Wright announced in 1981 that the State of North Carolina was sending a second check of $30,000 for library construction.

London and Highlands now had something in common. With the surprise success of the T. S. Eliot musical *Cats* in that major British metropolis, this little American community in 1981 was simultaneously and equally

---

[8]Representative Jeff Enloe was particularly helpful to Highlands not only in securing the library construction grants but also regarding the ABC store, town annexation, and the power plant and water system.
[9]Minutes of trustees meeting, March 12, 1981.
[10]The paragraph in the will of May 29, 1958, reads as follows: "The amount distributed hereunder to the Hudson Library of Highlands, North Carolina, shall be used to establish a fund to provide and maintain a room for a gallery to be known as The Bascom-Louise Gallery in memory of Mr. and Mrs. Henry M. Bascom and Louise Bascom Barratt, to be used as a repository for a permanent art collection for the display of works of art pertaining to Highlands and its surrounding areas or created by artists resident of said areas."
[11]Minutes of trustees meeting, July 15, 1981.
[12]Ibid., August 19, 1981.

astounded at the mercurial finances of its tiny but ambitious library. Concurrent with the county's 1982 budget, which allotted $20,000 to the Highlands library, the state had determined that its grants totaling $60,000 could not be used by a library on privately owned property, so the funds must be returned to the state.

Back in 1926, fifty-five years earlier, the trustees and membership of the Hudson Library had met a total of two times to carry out the affairs of the association. Now during the spring of 1981 board meetings were once a week, as the trustees struggled to acquire property for the new library, choose an architectural firm, sell the current library building and property to the Episcopal Church, auction the personal possessions of the Bascom-Barratt estate, refine the wording of legal documents, negotiate final settlement and distribution out of New York, and amend the library's charter to include a gallery.

Offers and counter-offers passed between the library and the Episcopal Church for the sale of the building and property. In the end the agreement stated that the church would buy both land and building for $85,000—that is, $65,000 down at closure and the balance plus thirteen-percent interest the following year.[13] The library fared very well considering what had originally cost just over six hundred dollars. Nevertheless, with the ebb and flood of cash, depending on what was acceptable and what was not or what might contain unwanted strings, the library suddenly found itself at low tide, owing the state $60,000.

So it made a unique proposal to the Episcopal Church. The library would "borrow the $65,000 cash" that the church would owe in a year as down payment on the library property. This amount along with the thirteen-percent interest on the balance due the library would

---

[13]Minutes of trustees meeting, May 5, 1982.

then deduct from the purchase price.[14] Might it be a comment on such an arrangement that in this year John Updike published his *Rabbit Is Rich*, which won the Pulitzer Prize for fiction, and John Cheever issued *O, What a Paradise It Seems*?

Complications mounted. By 1983, the year that Miss Gert published her history of the town, *Highlands, North Carolina . . . a walk into the past*, and received the Rotary Club Vocational Service Award in recognition of her outstanding service to the community, fund balances had reached $203,000. This presented a problem wholly new for the library, approaching its hundredth birthday. The library had on deposit at First Union Bank $175,000, only $100,000 of which the bank could insure. It had in effect too much money in the bank. The situation required finding a second bank for the excess. The trustees settled on Brevard Federal.[15] By the middle of the year the library had received at last the proceeds from the Barratt Trust amounting to $312,000,[16] and the search began for land.

The trustees considered Steve Potts's property across Main Street but eventually chose the Sidney W. Farnsworth acre next to the library itself. The negotiated purchase price was $100,000.[17]

As the campaign to raise funds for a new 6,200-square-foot building got under way, the trustees selected Eric Townsend of Murphy, N.C., as its architect and Mountain Shore Construction of Arden to construct it. With a bid of $407,000 (actual cost $440,000)[18] the disparity between

---

[14]Minutes of trustees meeting, June 9, 1982.
[15]Ibid., March 16, 1983.
[16]Minutes of Annual Meeting, June 15, 1993.
[17]Minutes of trustees meeting, July 20, 1983. See also minutes of April 21, 1982.
[18]Treasurer's Report of August 17, 1985: actual cost of construction $417,400, architect $37,000, land $101,000, for a total of $556,100. Furniture and equipment were an additional $58,000. But see the later Finance

the outlay for the new building and land and their price back in 1915—even allowing for larger building and lot sizes—remains amusing if not discouraging or enlightening. The 1985 building would figure at 80,000 percent of the builder's invoice in 1915! The land, 165,000 percent!

What was more important to the library, however, was that circulation was up 725 percent from the time when it was first regarded as important under Leila Marett in the mid-twenties. That represented an expansion from a count of 4,400 to 32,200 in just over fifty years. Betty Service must have smiled even at the larger figure for Highlands. Sarasota had seven times this number in book holdings alone. On the other hand, Sarasota had graduated more students in Betty Service's high school senior class alone than now populated K-12 of the entire Highlands School.[19] Apples and kumquats cannot be properly compared.

The year 1984 began with public opposition to the library's proposed clear-cutting of its new building site. One-hundred-four-year-old pine trees, according to the rationale of the trustees, had to come down for "safety and practical considerations."[20] The trustees considered these twenty-seven white pines—planted in 1880, the year that Ella Hudson had arrived and passed away in Highlands—a hazard. The library's argument was that it would be "nearly impossible to construct a new library and leave the trees undisturbed."[21]

Statement attached to the minutes of February 19, 1986, p. 7: construction cost: *$439,701*; total (exclusive of furnishings and equipment): $576,185.
[19] In 1983 Highlands School, K - 12, had four hundred students.
[20] Minutes of trustees meeting, January 25, 1984.
[21] The trustees, as paraphrased by Bob Scott, "Tree-Cutting in Highlands Draws Opposition," *Asheville Citizen*, January 19, 1984.

Heirs to the Farnsworth estate, which had sold the library the lot, joined with members of the Highlands Township Taxpayer's Association at a public meeting and retorted that they could not comprehend "the imagined necessity to destroy trees older than anyone" at this meeting—trees that would not "interfere with the construction, but only increase the beauty of Highlands."[22]

Then followed meetings, letters to the editor, attacks on "slash and burn methods of development,"[23] responses that white pines were "shallow-rooted" and could easily "topple over in a high wind,"[24] counter-attacks that these pines "should grow well and remain healthy for at least another hundred years,"[25] circulations of petitions, even suggestions of a compromise involving "a two-tiered parking arrangement,"[26] and in the end public despair over a general trend in commercial ventures that over many years had degraded Highlands from its original pristine state to the point that "the Library issue"[27] was only one more wound among the scars of change and development that were generally "obscene"![28] Apparently quite a number of Highlanders threw their hats into the ring and fought the issue from January through April.

---

[22] Michael Cavender, representing the Farnsworth estate, as quoted in "Plans for New Library Draw Fire: Too Many Trees to Be Downed Say Farnsworth Heirs," *Highlander*, January 26, 1984.
[23] Regina Ress, "Reconsider Tree Destruction," *Highlander*, March 29, 1984.
[24] Norma T. Pierson, chairman of the trustees, "Library Story Clarified," *Highlander*, February 9, 1984.
[25] Robert Zahner, professor of forestry at Clemson College, as quoted by Bess Hines Harkins and Sarah Hicks Hines, "Library Trees Threatened by Plans," *Highlander*, March 8, 1984.
[26] Howard Hill, "An Alternative for Library Plan," *Highlander*, March 22, 1984.
[27] Bess Hines Harkins and Sarah Hicks Hines, "Library Trees Threatened by Plans," *Highlander*, March 8, 1984.
[28] Jonathan Marion, "Missing the Forest for the Trees," *Highlander*, April, 19, 1984.

Ultimately the trees came down, just as the altitude oak, too, in the face of even more widespread opposition forty or fifty years earlier had succumbed to the ax, and there are Highlanders who still mourn that loss today.[29]

There may have been a difference between the cuttings of the town's altitude oak and the library's white pines. The most unlikely candidate to draw the distinction was Professor Harbison. In an article he published in 1930 he extolled the wisdom and generosity of H. H. Richardson for buying three hundred acres of the primeval forest north of Highlands to save it for future generations. As an aside, he made a significant distinction regarding the relative merits of certain trees for planting in Highlands.

He cited the J. Blanc Monroe estate (formerly Ravenel) as where the student of landscape gardening could appreciate the superiority of our North Carolina hemlock, for there were some fine specimens on the Monroe's lawn. On the other hand, Harbison added, here one could also learn "the lack of merit in our white pine for street and avenue planting." Years earlier, he concluded, Mr. Ravenel had "expressed his regret for not knowing the relative merits of white pine and our common hemlock for avenue planting."[30]

In the midst of the storm that broke over the tree issue, the trustees learned that the state had graciously agreed to restore to the library the $60,000 grant, which the library had returned, on condition that the town be

---

[29]Interviews with Dolly Harbison, September 22, 1993; Louise Edwards Meisel and Virginia Edwards Fleming, September 29, 1993; Harriet Zahner van Houten, September 30, 1993; Harry Wright, October 29, 1993; Marion Day Arnold, October 29, 1993, June Thompson Medlin, November 9, 1993, Margaret Gilbert Hall, November 11, 1993, and others.

[30]T. G. Harbison, "Highlands Site of Beautiful Estates: Ravenel Home One of Oldest: Tops Blue Ridge Crest and Overlooks Magnificent Scenery," *Franklin Press*, Teacher Training ed., April 10, 1930.

allowed to retain ownership of the property that the money would buy.[31] This sounded reasonable to the board, considering its fund-raising needs, so it moved to direct the town to buy the library furniture and fixtures and passed the motion unanimously!

If one were to focus only on the affairs of the trustees during this complex hundredth year in the library's otherwise plain and natural history, then the assumption would be that the library itself was being ignored, that it was standing still in anticipation of a major turning point in its career. However, with circulation at 32,400 the library remained very much alive and extremely active.

This was 1984, when Ivan Reitman's *Ghostbusters* and Michael Jackson's "Thriller" were capturing the popular interest and Donald Duck was celebrating his fiftieth birthday. Work, which had been progressing satisfactorily on the new library site, suddenly stopped. Right in the middle of Robert Rhodes's campaign to raise $178,000, there erupted contractor problems! A drainage dilemma! A bog! Right where the entry and exit drives would pass.

Surely everyone associated with the library—staff and board members alike, present and past—must have worn a knowing grin. The drainage problem, alive for seventy years, was threatening to haunt another generation! The contractor wanted to add $25,000 to the cost,[32] which the board felt was the responsibility of the architect—call it a defect conceivably in the original plan. There was nothing new in what everyone already knew, which was that probably no final solution existed.

Harvey Pierce, chairman of the building committee, whose tireless efforts on behalf of the library had already prevented building costs from escalating, addressed the

---

[31]Minutes of trustees meeting, February 15, 1984.
[32]Minutes of special trustees meeting, July 2, 1984.

work stoppage with no less fervor. An agreement emerged for a temporary access drive, which allowed construction to resume. The soil-bearing problem, however, not being at this time resolved, would "have to be dealt with at a later date."[33] A year later and several months after completion of the move, two significant nuisances would plague the new building: the heating system would "not operate properly" and the sidewalk would be "holding water."[34] As late as 1986 the heating system would still not function properly, and the drain would clog near the street, so that the library, putting new lyrics to an old refrain, would cry out—even as *Les Misérables* was raking in eight Tony awards—who is responsible? Who's to blame? The library? The town? Or the county?[35] This was the year that the *Phantom of the Opera* made its world première.

---

[33]Minutes of special trustees meeting, July 2, 1984.
[34]Minutes of trustees meeting, September 18, 1985.
[35]Ibid., February 19, 1986.

The Hudson Library and Bascom-Louise Gallery
Left: Gallery. *Right*: library. Built in 1985. Taken in February, 1994, by Gil Leebrick..

Twins: 1985–93

Walk slowly away—
don't look back
lest in looking back
your heart leads you to stay—
walk slowly away.

Leaving is too painful,
but staying is in vain
and one must go, this I know,
even though it brings pain.
Walk slowly away.

It isn't just the house we leave,
nor just the ones we love we put behind,
but a part of ourself is left—
a shedding of the past, so that
we go unladen by the things that held
and we are free—leaving home.[1]

On June 9, 1985, Mayor John Cleaveland, a trustee of the library, officially cut the ribbon honoring the new Hudson Library and Bascom-Louise Gallery. For the two weeks prior, a small army of volunteers and library staff had carted 14,000 volumes from the old 7,000-capacity building into the new facility with a projected capability of housing 24,000. Still in charge of the library proper was Miss Gert, and hired to direct the newly created gallery was Jacquelyn "Jackie" Leebrick, a photographic artist and educator who had served as

---

[1] Virginia Fleming, "On Leaving Home," *So Tender the Spirit* (Highlands, 1985), p. 13.

media specialist for two dozen schools in Durham County, N.C.

A graduate of Florida State University with degrees in art and photography education, Mrs. Leebrick had studied under Jerry Uellsmann, whose specialty was photography as an art form. His technique of multiple printing had transformed the craft of photography into an art of personal expression. Another of Mrs. Leebrick's mentors was the American photographer and educator Minor White, whose classic study *Mirrors, Messages, and Manifestations* established the discipline of photographic aesthetics, with a focus on the photograph as a symbol or metaphor. Professor White was one of the first teachers of photography as an art form.

Between graduate study and her work in Durham County, Mrs. Leebrick taught photography in Hawaii and chaired the art department at Honolulu Community College. She came to Highlands when her husband, Gil, arrived to head the Appalachian Environmental Arts Center in 1984, and the trustees selected her to direct the newly created gallery in 1985.

As much an avid reader as artist, she loved Ayn Rand in her college days, losing herself in the compelling arguments and impassioned dialogues of *The Fountainhead* and *Atlas Shrugged*. She thrived on J. D. Salinger's *Catcher in the Rye* and Jack Kerouac's *On the Road*. These writers, she recalls, "influenced us fringe people throughout the sixties and the seventies."[2] During the last half of the 1970s, however, surfing vied with reading for her spare time in Hawaii. Reading she still does, but surfing she abandoned in her move to the mountains of Highlands.

---

[2]Interview with Jackie Leebrick, December 10, 1993.

One attendant at the ceremonial opening of the new gallery and library facility was the last of the old guard of Harbisons, Miss Dolly. She found herself reflecting on a similar move into new quarters seventy long years before, when volunteers had carted one-fifth the number of volumes along a dirt road into a rustic, one-room frame structure with a low hip roof occupying a fifth the space. She had been only nine at the time.

Throughout the dedication she kept thinking, with a touch of nostalgia and genuine regret, that her sister Gertrude could not be here by her side. "If she were here," Miss Dolly said, "I'd ask her what she thought about all this, the new building and everything." Then pausing to overcome a catch in her voice, she continued, "and I know she'd say, 'I never dreamed it would come to all this.'"[3]

One could apply all this change as much to the town as to the library. Looking back over the seventy years that the library had occupied its modest quarters, Marion Day Arnold recently observed, "Highlands went from almost nothing to a tourist center."[4]

> *all the old things*
> *are gone now*
>
> *and the people are*
> *different*[5]

Indeed, between the time when John Reid first proposed the possibility of a new library building and its realization—that is, between 1980 and 1986—the town's population, which had held relatively steady for over forty

---

[3]Dolly Harbison, as quoted by Sylvia Thomas, "Love of Books: Dolly Harbison Wishes Her Sister, Gertrude, Could Have Seen Opening of New Library," *Highlander*, June 11, 1985.
[4]Telephone conversation with Marion Day Arnold, November 5, 1993.
[5]Jonathan Williams, "A Valediction For My Father, Ben Williams (1898-1974)," *Blues & Roots/Rue & Bluets* (Durham, N.C., 1985), p. 1.

years, almost doubled from 653 to 1,032.[6] The library's holdings, in reality, did double,[7] its circulation growing from 20,200 to over 38,000. What once had been a village of twenty-two businesses, when the Chamber of Commerce was first founded to promote tourism in 1931, was now a town of more than sixty shops and sixty-eight other trades.[8] The library's financial report for 1931 had totaled $77.49.[9] In 1986 it was $22,200,[10] above and beyond $38,600 spent by the county.[11]

If anything crystallizes from looking back on the Hudson Library's past, it is the one truth that old problems—problems that have existed from the beginning of time regardless of how small or how large the scale—never die! They just age! In this year that the United States was officially declared the world's largest debtor nation, with a deficit of $130 billion, the library was struggling with the problem of identifying books so as not to dispose of old volumes that might be valuable assets to its permanent collection. So it created a book committee.[12]

From a historical point of view the problem was ninety years old. In a very real sense, however, it was new, brand new. In 1896, when the first book committee, headed by Mary Chapin Smith, was created to identify valuable editions and cull out the "cheap trash" that

---

[6]See James A. Crutchfield, ed., *North Carolina Almanac and Book of Facts* (Nashville, 1988), p. 296, for the 1986 figure. Part of the reason for the population increase was annexation in July, 1980.
[7]Book holdings of 7,000 in 1980 (Minutes of the Annual Meeting, June 18, 1980), 17,900 in 1986 (Librarian's Report to the Hudson Library Board, August 20, 1986).
[8]Gert McIntosh, *Highlands, North Carolina ... a walk into the past*, rev. ed. (Highlands, 1990), p. 210.
[9]Librarian's Financial Report for the year August 25, 1930–August 31, 1931.
[10]Hudson Library Cash Flow, July 1, 1985, to June 30, 1986.
[11]"Highlands Actual 85/86," County Budget.
[12]Minutes of trustees meeting, July 16, 1986.

people were discarding by "dumping" it on the library, the intent had been to identify and remove bad books. The intent of the committee of 1986, however, was to identify and retain good books. The 1896 committee had sought to throw out the bath, while the 1986 committee sought to retain the baby. While the problem remained the same, the focus had shifted. Censorship was no longer the issue.

A second problem that challenged the trustees in their expanded quarters was also new, not just in part, but in its entirety, and in this sense uniquely new. In the hundred years of its existence as a single child the library had never experienced the dilemma of a new kid in the family. It had never known jealousy, competition, or threats to the throne. Somewhere in all the meetings to acquire property, choose an architect, sell the old building and auction an estate, refine the wording of legal documents, and amend the library's charter to include a gallery, the trustees had insufficiently defined the relationship between the old library and its newly created roommate, the gallery. Like the existence of slavery in the colonies when the Congress created its Constitution to cover all contingencies in a democracy, the founding fathers had quite simply assumed the status quo. The United States issue had taken a hundred years and a major civil war to resolve. The problems facing the library and the gallery, on the other hand, demanded much more immediate attention.

They developed gradually over the first two years. In 1986 the library continued its very successful home tours involving eighty volunteers and held poetry readings and story hours averaging fifty children per session. The gallery put on popular art exhibits and a well-represented juried show. Mountain Findings gave the combined association $3,000.

In 1987 the library again held its home tours and book sales, and the gallery scheduled a number of art shows. However, in this year the gallery put on an art auction that grossed $17,500. Deducting expenditures, the net profit was over $11,000. Jackie Leebrick reported that the result "greatly exceeded expectations."[13]

Indeed, the financial success of the gallery in the short two years since its appearance on the scene, aided by fifty volunteers and generously supported by the community at large, greatly exceeded all expectations of the library's trustees as well as members of the gallery itself, which existed as a mere committee, represented by one vote on the library board. Never had the library, in its hundred-and-three-year existence, even in its most successful home tour, netted more than $4,000. Yet it was contributing forty percent of its fund-raising receipts to the support of the gallery, whose art sales had already netted $6,000 above the $11,000 from the auction, so with individual donations to the gallery exceeding $3,000 the outcome was a net income to the new offspring of $20,000.

Listen to the heart;
listen to the mind,
but pray
that Wisdom walk between.[14]

In a parent-daughter relationship, the parent in the case at hand was earning less than the child. There were now two bank accounts, two budgets, and two fund-raising drives in desperate need of coordination lest the right hand take from the left. With the library considering air conditioning of a building that Miss Gert had said registered eighty-four degrees, who should pay for

---

[13] Minutes of trustees meeting, August 19, 1987.
[14] Bess Hines Harkins, "Balance," *Earth Songs* (San Benito, Texas, 1975), p. 14.

installing it? If the fund drives combined, how should the trustees divide the receipts? Should the gallery share its receipts from exhibitions and juried shows with the library? Should the library share its income from individual contributors with the gallery?

Furthermore, finances aside, to whom was the gallery responsible? Itself or the library? What about mailings? Under separate letterheads or a joint logo? Should the gallery have equal representation, as it felt it rightly deserved, on the library board? Board meetings frequently dragged out to two hours as issues bristled with complications.

The gallery began to smart as the library considered it a prodigal child, and the popular perception evolved that it was dependent upon the library for support. The library began to writhe as the gallery considered it a tyrannical parent, and the popular view emerged that it was feeding an insatiable parasite.

There were too many members of both organizations who loved the fine arts—both visual and verbal—not to be sensitive to the developing rift between two likely partners of the arts. Consequently, Boots Pierson appointed a select committee headed by Ted Henderson and composed of townsfolk outside both groups to review the relationship between the library and the gallery and obtain the "maximum benefit from the now unorganized members of the Corporation."[15] The committee presented its recommendations just in time, even as the gallery was celebrating the extraordinary success of its auction and pressure was coming to a head.

By the end of the year, during Gorbachev's campaign for *glasnost* or openness and *perestroika* or reconstruction in the Soviet Union, the trustees in accord with the

---

[15] Minutes of trustees meeting, December 17, 1986.

recommendations of the select committee completely reorganized as a four-part board.[16] The gallery achieved legal equality with the library, and a ways and means committee emerged to handle joint fund-raising ventures. Furthermore, these three committees found representation on an executive committee. All four committees met monthly and separately; the entire board, only quarterly.

With only seven members on any one committee, meetings lasted only an hour. The essential difference that guaranteed success of the newly structured association entailed the basic change in relationship. Separate but equal allowed for separate budgets and a new name: The Hudson Library and The Bascom-Louise Gallery.[17]

No one should infer that with restructuring all problems thereby ceased. As in any family situation involving human pairs, when the parent-child relationship gave way to a brother-sister association, debilitating conflict gave way to healthy squabbling. By 1988 a further refinement of the board's structure dissolved the ways and means committee into a single fund-raising and publicity director, who found himself in the enviable position of announcing a substantial cut in the fund-raising goal, from $31,700 the year before to only $14,200.[18] Gallery workshops, art exhibits, and a juried show and library home tours, book sales, and the county budget then supplemented local funds. In return for its contributions, the county benefited from the library, whose circulation

---

[16] See Michelle Munger, "Library Board Undergoing Re-organization," *Highlander*, November 10, 1987.
[17] There was no need to change the Articles of Incorporation, which retained the name "The Hudson Library of Highlands, North Carolina, Inc." The bylaws permitted using the names "The Hudson Library" and "The Bascom-Louise Gallery" together or separately to designate all or a part of the organization in its varied purposes.
[18] Hudson Library 1987 Budget: February 1, 1987–January 31, 1988, and executive committee minutes, January 13, 1988.

in Highlands had reached 46,000, allowing Macon County to claim its own count as "the most active in the state."[19]

Nineteen eighty-seven was the year in which the library and the town lost one of their most influential leaders, a devoted friend of both. Norma Pierson, known to her friends as Boots, died unexpectedly and reduced a whole community to tears. Having served on four separate occasions between 1965 and 1987 as president of the library board for a cumulative total of eleven years, she had also chaired the town's planning, zoning, and hospital boards and served on many other civic organizations, public and private. In all she had given her heart's lifeblood to Highlands. The pain felt by her sudden absence was extensive and real.

During her tenure as trustee president, the new library and gallery underwent construction, and those who worked with her valued her leadership, wise sense of balance, and personal warmth, but especially her candor. An editorial in the *Highlander* argued that "she was known for speaking her mind, but known as much or more for knowing what she was talking about when she did."[20] Her judgment benefited from hard work and a dedication to the organizations that she served. Indeed, she was instrumental in establishing Mountain Findings thrift shop in the 1960s, which contributed not only to the construction of facilities at the town's recreational park but also helped fund the library through generous donations ranging from $3,000 to $10,000 at a time.

She never achieved public office, having run unsuccessfully for county commissioner and sheriff, but her contributions through appointive office in local, county,

---

[19]Minutes of trustees meeting, August 17, 1988.
[20]"Commentary: Boots's Contributions Won't Soon Be Forgotten," *Highlander*, November 24, 1987.

and regional government and elected office in private civic organizations—like the school PTA, the Highlands Biological Foundation, the Macon County Democratic Women's Organization and Program for Progress, the old State of Franklin Health Council, and the Southwestern Regional Planning and Development Commission—were more extensive and more enduring than the lifetime achievements of many officials elected to public office. Since her arrival in Highlands from Georgia forty years earlier, she had devoted half of those years to town government, shaping its policies and zoning ordinances, even at one point in the late 1970s changing the zoning laws to control a wave of condominium development inside the town.

The town honored her when the Chamber of Commerce selected her as the recipient of its Robert B. DuPree Citizen of the Year Award, the first time it was ever bestowed posthumously.[21] The library trustees memorialized her name on a plaque, which they struck and hung in 1989 in the foyer of the new building. The gallery established for her a separate fund.

Besides the name of Boots Pierson, the plaque also bore the names of Watson Barratt, whose will had established the building fund; Harvey Pierce, chairman of the building committee; and John Reid, president of the trustees during part of the building's construction.

John Reid, who had resigned from the presidency of the board because of failing health, died the year after Boots Pierson, 1988. Having served in office for only four years on two occasions between 1980 and 1986, he still led the trustees through the very complex machinery of planning for the new building. It was during his tenure

---

[21]"Norma Pierson Is Honored, Is DuPree Citizen of Year," *Highlander*, November 24, 1987.

that the board met every week through one spring season to consider all aspects of financing and construction.

At the time of his death Reverend Reid, as he was known in religious circles, was rector of the St. John's Episcopal Church in Franklin, having for a number of years served as dean of the Western Deanery of North Carolina. He was also master of the Blue Ridge Masonic Lodge. Like many other presidents of the library's trustees, he functioned as a leader in a variety of Highlands community affairs. He served on the ABC board, the town planning board, and the hospital board, which he chaired while he was president of the library's trustees.

He and Boots Pierson in effect alternated leadership of the trustees during the decade from 1977 to 1987, which saw the library move from its old quarters to where it exists today. Their contributions, like those of the board members who served with them, were indispensable to the success of that move.

While acknowledging that the trustees and the staff of the library have deserved much of the credit for its growth and stability during the many years that it has served the Highlands community, the "backbone of the library"—in the words of its retiring librarian in 1987—was its body of volunteers.[22] The particular backbone, however, to which Miss Gert was referring in her statement about the library in Highlands, was Simone Kuehl. In 1988 Simone Kuehl became the first library volunteer to receive the Rotary Club Award in recognition of her contribution to the Highlands community.[23]

When viewed from the historical perspective, there were many other volunteers who had served as trustees,

---

[22]Interview with Gert McIntosh, November 2, 1993.
[23]"Arnold Keener, Simone Kuehl Are Named Rotary 1988 Award Winners," *Highlander*, October 21, 1988.

helped arrange benefits, or worked in the library and gallery and who deserved as much, if not more, recognition for their hours, days, months, and years spent promoting the association's welfare. However, on the symbolic level Mrs. Kuehl represented this type of dedication as completely as any one individual, even as she merited the honor in her own right.

For anyone who knew Simone well, it was no surprise that she would gravitate toward the library, for her whole life revolved around the joy of books. Her aunt, a sixth-grade teacher, provided the inspiration that led her to appreciate good books.[24] As a child her favorite fairy tale was "The Emperor's New Clothes," but she also loved D'Aulaires' beautifully illustrated *Greek Myths* and *Aesop's Fables*.

Like every other young girl, she thrived on *Little Women*. Unlike other girls, she read the Pulitzer-Prize-winning *Americanization of Edward Bok* about the Netherlander who founded the *Ladies' Home Journal*, for she loved biographies. It was this love that led her to get hold of a copy of *Anthony Adverse*, with the result, she adds, that "my ears were plucked back."[25]

In the thirties she discovered Hugh Walpole's just-published *Rogue Herries* chronicles, and the natural beauty of the English Lake District drew her into a family saga as romantic as anything she had ever read. John Galsworthy's trilogy, *The Forsyte Saga*, depicted for her "the seeming dignity" of the English upper middle class, especially *The Man of Property*.[26] She recognized Soames Forsyte's insensitivity and found herself sympathizing

---

[24]Interview with Simone Kuehl Sorge, November 12, 1993.
[25]Ibid.
[26]The other two novels in the *Forsyte Saga* are *In Chancery* (1920) and *To Let* (1921).

with Irene, his wife, whom he treated as just another piece of property. Margery Sharp's *Cluny Brown*, at the other extreme, gave her an appreciation of the common folk. One of her favorite books, however, was *Elizabeth and Her German Garden*.[27] "Elizabeth," says Simone, "was married to a dominant person, but she in her little English way made her life interesting. She was gentle and full of spirit and respect for herself, and was not going to be dominated."[28] Gentle, full of spirit and respect for herself are adjectives that also describe Simone.

"I've been a city girl all my life," says Simone. "I never thought I'd end up in a small town like this, but I've been very fortunate to have lived here and been a part of the community. This library is such a very, very special place. It gives so much and gets so much in return."[29]

To view Simone as representative of all the volunteers who have served the library and its new twin, the gallery, over these past hundred and ten years may prove insufficient recognition for the hundreds of people unacknowledged even by name in this condensed history. On the other hand, Simone's philosophy expresses the logic and emotion that lie behind any voluntary devotion to a civic organization. "I've always enjoyed being with people and filling their needs," explains Simone. Furthermore, seeing children use the library and gallery, a pastime she once feared was a lost art, gives her a special joy.[30]

With the birth of the world's five-billionth inhabitant in Yugoslavia, and the United States operating on its first trillion-dollar budget, the Hudson Library in Highlands established in 1989 a computer connection with the

---

[27] *Elizabeth and Her German Garden*, by Elizabeth von Arnim.
[28] Interview with Simone Kuehl Sorge, November 12, 1993.
[29] Ibid.
[30] Ibid.

county system. Notwithstanding that this was the year in which computer viruses infected networks worldwide and their proliferation in the United States was so extensive that Lloyds of London would not cover U.S. losses, the library relied heavily, and without mishap, on its newly acquired IBM-XT computer and Panasonic printer for order processing, financial planning, correspondence, and fund raising. As noted earlier, the 1980s were a time of tremendous growth for Highlands and its library, whose registered membership increased from 451 in 1979 to 6,150 in 1989—an increase that the trustees and staff could no longer address by hand.[31] The town, too, had now entered the age of the computer.

In the same year that Boots Pierson died, Miss Gert had resigned as librarian. Tracy Strain, Andrea Rudisill, and Karen Herchen filled the librarian's position until 1990. At this time the county librarian was Cynthia Modlin, whose aid during the years of the library's incorporation into the county system had been extensive and invaluable. Always one to work closely with the trustees on major decisions affecting the library, Mrs. Modlin hired Carolyn Strader of Franklin as the new librarian in Highlands.

Mrs. Strader had already served for a couple of years in Highlands as assistant librarian. She brought to the Hudson Library ten years of experience in each of the Fontana Regional System's four libraries, including Sylva, Bryson City, and Franklin. A graduate of the University of South Carolina and Emory University, she preferred the smaller library environment, where work transcended specialized tasks.[32]

---

[31]Hudson Library reports for September 19, 1979, and August 14, 1989.
[32]Michelle Munger, "Carolyn Strader Hired as New Librarian," *Highlander*, February 27, 1990.

During her tenure she would have three assistants, Linda Sullivan, Annette Herstek, and Virginia Talbot, and twelve volunteers. By 1991 the number of volunteers had increased to thirty-two, donating 2,500 hours of their time.[33] How much it would have astounded Miss Gertrude and Miss Dolly to have seen their library dependent on so many volunteers! There was no comparing the little library of Miss Gertrude and Miss Dolly, when four or five children would crowd into it in a single day, with the library of Mrs. Strader, when during one week in October "1105 persons" entered the building.[34] Indeed, "over 55,000 people" entered it during 1992,[35] the year that Bill Clinton defeated George Bush for the U.S. presidency.

Holdings had already reached 21,000 volumes in a structure whose age was only seven years and whose capacity of 24,000 was in jeopardy. The trustees decided there was no choice but to expand. They chose DeWolf & Schmitt as architects at a cost-estimate of $16,400 and Schmitt Building Contractors to construct a 2,200-square-foot addition. The bid was $123,000 (actual cost, $125,400).[36] The trustees used accumulated building funds to pay for the annex, which saw completion in 1993, the year that the "storm of the century" dumped sixteen-and-a-half inches of snow on Highlands and robbed it of electrical power for a week.[37] This annex now houses

---

[33]Minutes of executive committee, August 20, 1991.
[34]Minutes of quarterly board meeting, November 19, 1991.
[35]Minutes of Annual Meeting, June 23, 1992.
[36]"1992 Building Addition," Annual Financial Report for the Fiscal Year February 1, 1992 to January 31, 1993.
[37]The "blizzard of '93" began the night of March 12th, and by the morning of Saturday, the 13th, sixteen and a half inches covered Highlands, with drifts up to four and six feet. Power was restored to most homes and businesses by Wednesday, but many were without electricity for an entire week. Snow depth of sixteen and a half inches provided by the Highlands Biological Station, December 8, 1993.

newspapers and periodicals and provides space for the gallery's permanent collection and workshops, general educational meetings, children's weekly story hours, and an adult reading area.

Many programs, some tried but mostly new, emerged at the outset of the 1990s, which would benefit both the gallery and the library. In 1989 the art auction, as a gallery standby, netted $17,000 and featured the works of forty-two artists. In 1992 it cleared $14,000. Beginning in 1989 the gallery introduced a wholly new Words-and-Music performance, featuring the internationally acclaimed Alexander String Quartet and a show highlighting artists from China. Soon it had scheduled workshops in photography, painting, pottery, sculpture, and Japanese flower growing and arranging. It published *Kitchen Art*, a cookbook with recipes by local cooks, in 1991.

The library, meanwhile, sponsored in 1990 a Western Carolina University–Highlands lecture series that by the end of 1993 had covered eighty distinctly different topics. It initiated a very popular cooking school that by 1992 was earning $2,300 each year and, with the next year's session already sold out, would expand into a series of schools throughout the year. Meanwhile, home tours proved quite successful through the early 1990s, netting up to $5,000 each season. However, as homeowners grew reluctant to open their homes to a growing tide of visitors, the board began looking at alternative ways to raise funds to buy books, magazines, and audiovisual materials.

In the midst of a bewildering range of activities planned by both the gallery and the library to involve the entire Highlands community—despite the loss of coziness afforded by the small building from which it had moved—

the association still retained its identity as a cultural center in the town. Adults and children found the gallery to be an irreplaceable outlet for creativity. The library provided an invaluable source of information, present as well as past. Children considered it, in the words of its current librarian, a "fun place to be,"[38] especially those school and preschool children who attended the Thursday morning story hours and could check out their own books!

---

[38]Carolyn Strader, as quoted in "Past Year's Accomplishments," June 23, 1992. See Secretary's Book, Hudson Library Association.

The Harbison Home
At the southern foot of Satulah Mountain. Taken in October, 1993, by the author.

Automation: 1994

*Never lose the large
 in the little:
Be not over-anxious,
 be not brittle,
For, while at dusk
 you thread the needle's eye
Wild birds wing home
 and rose cloud flame and die....*[1]

What lies ahead for the library in 1994, as it celebrates its 110th birthday, is automation. That word rings cold to anyone who as a child relied on Miss Gertrude or Miss Dolly to give a tour of the shelves and tempt their little imaginations with just enough plot for a particular book to strike the fancy. It's not the same today as it was when one sat like a yogi and read on the library floor or carried a book barefooted along the dusty road home and then hid in a large rhododendron bush at a place where enough of the sun's rays bathed the book's pages in a golden glow to transport a reader into a world eons distant from home, until dusk or mother gave the call to supper.

To such a memory, the word *computerization* crashes like a steel ball clattering in a copper dish. On the other hand, as 1994 approaches, the four or five thousand books that long ago lined the library shelves now number 19,800.[2] Carolyn Strader, though aided by twenty-five

---

[1]Bess Hines Harkins, "Values," *Earth Songs* (San Benito, Texas, 1975), p. 14. Also in *Channels*, © April, 1975.
[2]State Library of N.C. Annual Statistical Report Fiscal Year July 1, 1992–June 30, 1993. See also Statistical Report to Library Committee,

volunteers, cannot be expected to have read them all. It's not that she would even mention to a child—no more than Miss Gertrude would have broached the subject of Stratemeyer to a girl holding a Bobbsey twins book in her hand—such terms as *electronic card catalogue, bar codes, laser pens, direct ordering,* or *networking*.

With the process of automation already under way at a projected cost of $8,000, the librarian, her staff, and her volunteers have abandoned their sluggish IBM-XT for a Myriad 386/40MHz IBM-compatible unit that in 1994 will be replaced by a check-in and check-out terminal.[3] Like those in other libraries of the region, it will tie into Franklin or Bryson City through a dedicated phone line, not digital but analog and attached to an error-correcting modem, while sporting a card and book scanner.[4]

This system will totally replace the little card, on which Miss Gertrude used to record the book that a patron took home and the fact that he brought it back. Wouldn't Miss Gertrude and Miss Dolly and even Miss Gert and all their volunteers be amazed if not thrilled that by 1995 or 1996 the infamous and cumbersome and tedious and time- and labor-consuming card catalogue will disappear?

With current circulation at 40,600[5]—almost one-third of which are children's check-outs—and another 7,000 in audios and videos, Carolyn Strader and her aids annually field 7,300 reference and directional questions posed by 68,750 patrons.[6] Only a time machine would allow Mrs.

August 10, 1993. Between 1992 and 1993 net holdings actually decreased by 1,200 due to discarding.
[3]Telephone conversation with John Norris, owner of Cullasaja Computers in Franklin and consultant for the Hudson Library, November 9, 1993.
[4]Ibid.
[5]Ibid. Adult circulation: 29,549. Juvenile circulation: 11,069. Total circulation: 40,618.
[6]Count taken during the first week in October, 1993. Minutes of trustees meeting, November 9, 1993.

Strader to serve everyone who now enters this small-town library in the same manner that Miss Gertrude or Miss Gert once were accustomed to serving.

If automation continues according to plans, library patrons in 1995 or 1996 will have access to 170,000 books through a public terminal and printer.[7] Then if Dorothy "Dot" Traylor wants the latest mystery by Dorothy Gilman, she will be able to find the book on her own. Or if she wants a Martha Grimes London pub mystery—not the *End of the Pier*, of course, which she didn't like—she can pull it up on the screen through a global search by just typing two words, *Martha* and *Grimes*, and see immediately how many copies are in the Hudson Library and if they are checked out or on the shelf. If they are all checked out, she can reserve a copy in her own name right at the terminal.

Or she can call Carolyn or Annette or Virginia or a volunteer to come show her how to work this blesséd machine and hear Carolyn say that the Hudson Library doesn't have a copy of Martha Grimes' *The Horse You Came In On*, but the library in Franklin does, and it will arrive by the next book mobile. No more must a search for Peter Mayle's *Year in Provence* be restricted to what the Hudson Library has room for on its shelves. Would it have been fortunate if the library had computerized before it abandoned its quaint and cozy quarters in its Huger Elliott-designed first home, where it could have had access to all these books without the necessity of a move?

In one sense the new is not always better than the old. For Dot Traylor enjoyed the old library much more than the new one. "It was smaller!" she says, but is quick to

---

[7]Memorandum from Steve Farlow, Director Fontana Regional Library, October 28, 1993. See Secretary's Book, Hudson Library Association.

admit, "and here I am, having gone into the Carnegie Library!" Still, she feels the new Hudson Library, "except for the wonderful staff, is too big." She doesn't like the books all arranged alphabetically (as they were originally, incidentally, some sixty years ago when Miss Gertrude and Miss Dolly followed no modern system). She would prefer that fiction be arranged by category. She can find the green-stickered mysteries, but she has to go from A to Z. They're not all together.

"I know that Fontana says you must do it this way," she says, sympathizing with Carolyn Strader's plight, "but I have to locate the D's to find Colin Dexter's Inspector Morse mysteries, like *Sudden, Fearful Death*, or the P's for Anne Perry's *Dangerous Morning*, and then go to the S's to find Dorothy Sayers. I love everything she wrote. She was a delightful theologian, you know."[8]

What saves the new from being less than ideal may be what saved the old from being the same: the personnel. Mrs. Traylor relates how "Annette called me the other day to say the library had the new *Mrs. Pollifax and the Second Thief* in by Dorothy Gilman." Moreover, when Dot arrived to pick it up, Carolyn Strader told her she just *had* to read *The Trial of Abigail Goodman* by Howard Fast, whose Immigrant series she knew Dot loved. From all this Dot concludes, "I come so often that I told the staff I was going to get a cot."[9]

Jan Chmar still loves the old library for nostalgic reasons but feels it was no longer effective. It wasn't suited to the changing times.[10] Its holdings and patrons

---

[8] Interview with Mrs. Forest (Dorothy) Traylor, November 11, 1993.
[9] Ibid.
[10] Today the old library building houses Fibber Magee's Closet in the main room and the Highlands Emergency Council in the children's and Satulah rooms. Both organizations are charities.

outgrew it. She felt the wrench of leaving it but knew it had to be. One of her favorite additions to the new building, which had the space to accommodate it, was the sixty-volume set of the *Library of America*, which was added to the collection beginning in 1987 at one volume a month, courtesy of an Andrew Mellon Foundation grant. Her favorite works in this handsome edition of classic American authors are those of Mark Twain. One could spend a lifetime steeped in the literature of this little self-contained *Library of America* and still ask at death's door for the next volume that time had not yet proven sufficient to read.

Looking back at life in the old library, Simone Sorge remembers those Tuesday nights when she volunteered to keep the library open for Miss Gertrude from six to nine. "They were deadly," she recalls. "Maybe one person came. I got a lot of reading done."[11] The library back then was run "hit and miss," she remarks without a hint of reproach. "When you got a book, you wouldn't even have to sign for it." It was more personal then. There were more friendships formed.

Yet in the new larger library, Simone can remember Jeff Rowe, Carla and Leslie Sanders, Lanette Pierson, and more of the many children who come to the library today. From time spent in both libraries, she recalls that Lois Morrow sought out medical books, that Captain Henriques was quite a historian and wanted Civil War books, while his wife, Jean, checked out reams of fiction. Ted Wilcox, Harriet Elms, and Jan Chmar cycled through whole sections, seeking out new arrivals, whether classic or new, that they had somehow missed or not yet read.

Some things never change, no matter what the venue. In the old library Miss Gertrude once walked the two and

---

[11]Interview with Simone Kuehl Sorge, November 12, 1993.

a half miles home before she received word that she had missed Sarah Thompson and locked her in. Fifty years later Simone Kuehl closed up on a Saturday and had just reached her car before she realized there was a man in the rest room. "He was rapping on the window," she recalls.[12]

Nothing, automated or not, will replace the human element that has always characterized the Hudson Library. When Charlotte Biedron was still on the staff recently, she received a phone call from Atlanta. Someone had found a Hudson Library book on Peachtree Street and offered to mail it back. Mrs. Strader reimbursed the kind man the cost of the mailing and notified the patron who had checked the book out that it had been returned. The patron in response sent a donation of fifty dollars to the library.[13] Kind deeds cascade, like trickles over Bridal Veil Falls, gathering downstream for the impressive pitch over Dry Falls,[14] and culminating at last in the thundering torrent over Cullasaja, where everyone stops to gaze at its glorious volume near the base of the gorge.

Perhaps in this 110th year of the Hudson Library's existence there are proportionately many more adults who borrow from its holdings than there were when Miss Gertrude ran the little library a half century ago. The majority of the local readers at that time, as Miss Gertrude remarked, were "school children who read for di-

---

[12]Interview with Simone Kuehl Sorge, November 12, 1993.
[13]Interview with Carolyn Strader, November 8, 1993.
[14]In 1900 Dry Falls was also called the Pitcher Falls, because "they pitch over the ledge of rock from which the water falls clear out, like the stream flowing from the mouth of a pitcher when you pour the water out." See "Highlands," *Franklin Press*, November 21, 1900. As recently as 1931, Dry Falls was called Cullasaja Falls as distinct from Lower Cullasaja Falls. See map of Thomas N. E. Greville, "Highlands and Vicinity," September 13, 1931. Lower Cullasaja Falls was also known as Sugar Fork Falls, now just Cullasaja Falls.

version and to enable themselves to make book reports in connection with their school work."[15]

Nevertheless, despite the enormous increase of adults who now frequent the library, children remain stalwart supporters. Katy Betz discovered her favorite stories by C. S. Lewis, his *Chronicles of Narnia*, and she is reading all the Nancy Drew mysteries that she can find. I asked my sons Tom and Jack what they liked about the Hudson Library, and this is what I was told: "I like getting books. There are lots of books that you've never seen, like *Curious George* and *Amelia Bedelia* and the *Berenstain Bears*, and I like seeing them put the cards in the machine," says Jack, and Tom adds, "There are lots of books you can pick out, and you don't have somebody bossing you which one to pick out, and you don't even have to pay for them. They have *Garfield* books and Peggy Parish's *Pirate Island Adventure* and a movie about Tutankhamun."[16]

As long as children love to read, the Hudson Library will continue to thrive, for it is certain that in childhood books have a deep influence on our lives, and the fires they light are never extinguished. "Our library is one of the busiest places in town," noted Ralph Morris, editor of the *Highlander,* recently. "There are book lovers coming and going in a steady stream. We're very fortunate to have the Hudson Library. It's a town treasure, a local institution, a Highlands landmark."[17]

Highlands with a current population of 970 remains a small town, to be sure.[18] To stand on Sunset Rock above

---

[15]Gertrude Harbison, "Hudson Library Notes," *Franklin Press & Highlands Maconian,* July 13, 1939.
[16]Interviews with Tom and Jack Shaffner, November 8, 1993.
[17]Ralph Morris, "Journey Begins at Hudson Library," *Highlander,* November 5, 1993.
[18]Town population is 970, township, 1,700. Interview with Sam Bass, president of the Chamber of Commerce, November 20, 1993.

the little village on the roof of the world is to realize clearly what anyone from New York or Miami or Atlanta grasps instantaneously: that Highlands still is a little village nestled in an ocean of mountain peaks blanketed with forests as far as the eye can see. Here on the rock is afforded restoration of the soul to countless residents and visitors who take the time to climb up and luxuriate in the profoundly peaceful, panoramic view.

> *The overpowering roar and rush of sound*
> *Upon the granite crest of Sunset Rock*
> *Roll onward with the surge and thundering shock*
> *Of many a rank of billows come aground;*
> *'Tis but the voice from over waving mound*
> *Of Chestnut trees below that interlock*
> *In gold and green; Satulah's clouds that mock*
> *And glower by day, at midnight flow around*
> *Her slippery crags, an ocean at her feet;*
> *And when, where wavering sky and earth-line meet,*
> *Wide seas of foothills shimmer in the light,*
> *The soul, sans care, like ship escaped from night,*
> *From storm and wrack, with shining sails and free,*
> *Sets out thereon to search infinity.*[19]

Sometimes the tourist cannot see Highlands from Sunset Rock, and it must be pointed out. The thick green foliage of spring and summer or the flaming scarlets and brilliant yellows of trees and shrubs standing in their last glory before undressing for winter hibernation obscure the town during most of the year. From this overlook, the library remains invisible.

If the complaints and regrets that prefer the Highlands of the past to the Highlands of the present hold true, then they live in the understandable nostalgia of lost youth.

---

[19] Mary Chapin Smith, "Sonnet V," *Earth Songs* (Boston, 1910), p. 124.

They dwell in far-off memories of long-gone individuals like Albertina Staub, Mary Chapin Smith, Professor Thomas Harbison, and the Misses Gertrude and Dolly. Or in scenes of Anne Altstaetter reading in her pine throne or Stephen Vincent Benét slumped over a shabby copy of *St. Nicholas* magazine, Ethel Calloway sending Miss Gertrude to the post office for the mail, or Virginia Edwards with other little savages making a teepee from feed sacks in the woods near her home.

Scenes like these, all new and different, are being lived by children in Highlands today. When the time comes for a sesquicentennial history of the library, they, too, will recall their long-ago people and scenes and tell their long-ago stories about books that became their inseparable and unforgettable friends. There's even a chance they will tell of finding one book by a very long-ago Highlands child, who had grown up in the very same library that they, too, had come to know and love. They will tell how they found *Singing of the Heart* or *Songs Out of Silence* by the very long-ago Bess Hinson Hines and were moved by the beauty and majesty of the mountains and waterfalls in her *Unknown Seas*.[20] They will tell how they found a not-so-long-ago story by Highlands' Virginia Fleming, a story about *Eddie Lee,* and learned what really mattered in life, or how they came to appreciate and cherish for the first

---

[20]Bess Hinson Hines (later Harkins) divided her time between the sea in California and the mountains of her hometown in North Carolina. She has authored books under her maiden name and co-authored collections with her husband, Butler Harkins, many of the poems illustrated by her sister Sarah Hicks Hines and her daughter Sarah Harkins Olson. Her poems have been characterized as springing "from the heart as naturally as violets from the forest floor." Almost invariably they focus on nature. Like Wordsworth, she is the "woods wanderer." Active in the California Federation of Chaparral Poets, she received First Prize awards for her poems. She was also recognized by the Poetry Council of N.C. and the Fellowship of American Poets. For a list of her books, see "Poets of Highlands" in the Bibliography.

time the stirring and beckoning moods of the lofty mountains and their people in *So Tender the Spirit* or *Wellspring*.[21]

In forty years they will remember. They will tell their stories as nostalgically as we tell them today. Because stories of books and people, of what we have loved with all our hearts in the past, will always warm the mind and heart and make a library a home.

---

[21]Virginia Edwards Fleming writes primarily for children, having reared three of her own and taught nursery school for ten years, and even those poems that are not for children are about them or her childhood home, with the sole exception of those that express an adult's heartrending loss. She divides her time between her native Highlands and New Jersey schools, where she assists children with creative writing and entertains with readings of her poetry. She is widely published in books, magazines, and newspapers and an active member of poetry societies in North Carolina, New Jersey, and Pennsylvania. For a list of her books, see "Poets of Highlands" in the Bibliography.

Highlands from Biscuit Rock
Foreground: Lindenwood Lake. Taken ca. 1893 by R. Henry Scadin.
Courtesy of the Highlands Historical Preservation Society, Inc.

Highlands from Sunset Rock
Taken in October, 1993, by the author.

Not a poet's world, you say?
Ah, Friend, you're not a poet—
For he who travels the glory road
Will deeply, dearly know it.

And whether he struggle and whether
  he strive
He never would trade his wine
Of the shining, white immortal grapes
For any brew of thine;

And whether he tremble and whether
  he freeze
He never would forego
His ragged cloak of a wind-blown cloud
For the warm, wool coat you know.

O pity him not, whose eyes have seen
Above the clouds at dawn
A white-winged horse that soars and fades
With the stars, but is not gone.[1]

---

[1]Bess Hines Harkins, "Answer From the Poet (And his kind)," *Unknown Seas* (Los Angeles, 1958), p. 60.

Appendix I

Librarians of the Hudson Library

1.	1883	Mrs. Laura G. "Kittie" Kibbee
2.	1884–85	Miss Mary L. Sheldon
3.	1885	Miss Ellison
4.	1887	Professor Thomas G. Harbison
5.	1889–95	Miss Jessie E. White
6.	1895–1911	Miss Albertina Staub
	1912–15	Mrs. J. Jay (Mary Chapin) Smith [*Acting Librarian*]
7.	1916–17	Miss Lucy P. Elliott
8.	1917–21	Miss Charlotte B. Elliott
9.	1921–23	Mrs. Luther W. (Christina Anderson) Rice, Sr.
10.	1923–26	Mrs. S. T. (Leila Lewis) Marett
11.	1926–74	Miss Gertrude Harbison
	1974–75	Miss Dorothea "Dolly" Harbison [*Acting Librarian*]
12.	1975–77	Mrs. Steven (Anne) Ham
13.	1977	Miss Melinda Russell
14.	1977–78	Mrs. Grant (Martha Hedden) Keener
15.	1978–87	Mrs. Harold ("Gert") McIntosh
16.	1987	Miss Tracy E. Strain
	1987–88	Mrs. Andrea Rudisill [*Acting Librarian*]
17.	1988–90	Ms. Karen Herchen
18.	1990–	Mrs. Harold (Carolyn) Strader

Appendix II

Presidents of the Board of Trustees

1884–89	Mr. Samuel Truman Kelsey, Sr.
1889–1910	Mr. T. Baxter White
1911–14	Mrs. J. Jay (Mary Chapin) Smith
1914–20	Mrs. Hampton (Florence) Perry
1920–35	Mrs. J. Jay (Mary Chapin) Smith
1935–38	Miss Mary J. Crosby
1938–42	Miss Marguerite Ravenel
1942–45	Miss Rebecca C. Nall
1945–48	Mrs. Ralph M. (Louise) Sargent
1948–50	Mrs. J. A. (Bessie Hinson) Hines
1950–52	Miss Rebecca C. Nall
1952–55	Mrs. J. A. (Bessie Hinson) Hines
1955–56	Miss Helen Augur
1956–58	Mrs. Tudor N. (Margaret) Hall
1958–60	Mrs. Thomas H. (Elizabeth) Tyson
1960–61	Mrs. Overton S. (Helen) Chambers
1961–63	Miss Helen Augur
1963–65	Mrs. Harold N. (Rebecca) Cooledge
1965–67	Mrs. Val (Norma T. "Boots") Pierson
1967–69	Mrs. C. B. (Jean) Henriques
1969–71	Mrs. Ernest C. (Lillian) Stevens
1971–73	Mrs. James S. (Bess W.) Blair
1973–75	Mrs. Worth C. (Delores "Dee") Sherrill
1975–77	Mrs. Theodore (Terry) Hoffman
1977–80	Mrs. Val (Norma T. "Boots") Pierson
1980–83	Mr. John Reid
1983–85	Mrs. Val (Norma T. "Boots") Pierson
1985–86	Mr. John Reid
1986–87	Mrs. Val (Norma T. "Boots") Pierson

1987–90	Professor Randolph P. Shaffner
1990–91	Mr. Ernest O. Wood
1991–92	Mrs. Milton (Jean W.) Prevost
1992–	Colonel Allen L. "Buck" Trott

Appendix III

Mayors of the Town of Highlands

1883	Mr. Stanhope W. Hill
1884–85	Mr. Henry M. Bascom
1885	Mr. Stanhope W. Hill
1885–86	Mr. Henry M. Bascom
1886–87	Mr. Ebenezer Selleck
1887–88	Dr. H. T. O'Farrell
1888–89	Mr. J. Jay Smith
1889–90	Mr. Charles L. Boynton
1890–91	Dr. H. T. O'Farrell
1891–92	Mr. Ebenezer Selleck
1892–93	Professor Thomas G. Harbison
1893–94	Mr. Theron D. Walden
1894–1900	Dr. H. T. O'Farrell
1900–	Mr. Henry M. Bascom

Records are missing for the years 1901–08.

–1909	Professor Thomas G. Harbison
1909–11	Mr. Henry M. Bascom [*Acting Mayor*]
1911–13	Mr. Charles N. Wright
1913–25	Mr. Henry M. Bascom
1925–27	Mr. J. Jay Smith
1927–29	Mr. William S. Davis
1929–30	Mr. George W. Marett
1930–31	Mr. William S. Davis
1931–33	Mr. James A. Hines
1933–35	Mr. S. Porter Pierson
1935–36	Mr. S. Eugene "Gene" Potts
1936–37	Mr. William W. Edwards [*Acting Mayor*]
1937–39	Mr. William S. Davis
1939–41	Mr. William W. Edwards

1941–47	Mr. Wilton H. Cobb
1947–49	Mr. James O. Beale
1949–55	Mr. Wilton H. Cobb
1955–59	Mr. V. William McCall
1959–61	Mr. Charles C. Potts
1961–62	Mr. Wilton H. Cobb
1962–65	Mr. A. Claude "Pat" Patterson
1965–66	Mr. Ted Crunkleton
1966–68	Mr. Otto F. Summer
1968–75	Mr. A. Claude "Pat" Patterson
1975–81	Mr. Harry R. Wright
1981–83	Mr. J. Steve Potts
1983–	Mr. John W. Cleaveland

Appendix IV

Members of the Board of Trustees

Aaron, Mr. William F.
Aaron, Mrs. Anna M.
Adkins, Mrs. W. H.
Allen, Mrs. Red (Georgia)
Allen, Mrs. John
Anderson, Mrs. T. Peden
Arnold, Mrs. Wayne (Elizabeth)
Augur, Miss Helen
Barnett, Mr. Wren
Bascom, Miss Louise
Bascom, Mr. H. M.
Bauknight, Mrs. John E. (Susan)
Baumrucker, Mrs. John (Joanna)
Benjamin, Mr. Allan H.
Benson-Zahner, Ms. Jody
Betz, Mr. Richard
Billstein, Mrs. Nathan (Louise)
Blair, Mrs. James S. (Bess W.)
Bliss, Mrs. Arthur L.
Bohling, Mr. Ed
Boyd, Mrs. John (Patricia T.)
Boynton, Mr. Charles A.
Boynton, Mr. Charles L.
Brown, Mrs. John (Harriet C.)
Brundage, Mrs. Helen S.
Bunn, Mrs. Roy
Burbridge, Mrs. Clinton
Burt, Mrs. Ed
Cabler, Mrs. James A. (Pat)
Callaway, Mrs. Cason J., Jr. (Nancy)

Carter, Miss Ruth
Chambers, Mrs. Overton S. (Helen)
Child, Mrs. William
Chmar, Mrs. Paul (Jan)
Clarke, Mrs. S. Dilworth (Polly)
Cleaveland, Mr. John W.
Clifton, Mrs. C. C. (Betty)
Coker, Mrs. W. C.
Cole, Miss Betty
Cook, Miss Mary Bascom
Cooledge, Mrs. Harold N. (Rebecca)
Copple, Mr. Lee B.
Crane, Mrs. Baker (Susan)
Crosby, Mrs. Ralph (Dorothy S.)
Crosby, Mrs. Mary J.
Dayton, Mrs. Gertrude
De Ville, Mrs. Ralph W. (Marilyn S.)
DeWolf, Mrs. Dennis K. (Jane)
Dunning, Mrs. Priscilla
Edwards, Mrs. Donald W. (Linda)
Emmons, Mrs. Elizabeth H.
Esty, Mr. A. S.
Eubanks, Mrs. George M. (Carol M.)
Evans, Mrs. Lloyd F. (Thryza)
Ewing, Mrs. Upton C.
Ferry, Mr. Alan
Fifer, Mrs. Paul
Fitz Patrick, Mr. Kevin W.
Fogartie, Reverend James E.
Freese, Mrs. John B. (Nancy)
Frost, Dr. Charles L.
Gardner, Mrs. F. T. (Margaret)
Gary, Mr. M. Wistar
Gilbert, Mrs. E. R.

Gorham, Mrs. H. W.
Guthrie, Mrs. M. H.
Hall, Mrs. John T. (Judy)
Hall, Mrs. Tudor N. (Margaret G.)
Ham, Mrs. Steven (Anne)
Harbison, Miss Gertrude
Harbison, Miss Dorothea
Harcombe, Mrs. Lyda W.
Hardie, Mrs. Newton
Harper, Mr. Hugh P.
Harris, Mrs. Walter F. (Lorrayne R.)
Harris, Mr. Lucien
Heard, Mrs. Earl, Jr. (Terese)
Heinlein, Mrs. Blair (Margaret)
Henriques, Mrs. Charles B. (Jean)
Hiden, Mrs. Robert
Hines, Mrs. J. A. (Bessie Hinson)
Hodges, Madeline
Hoffman, Mrs. Theodore (Terry)
Howe, Colonel James H.
Howie, Mr. Vic
Huger, Miss Marie
Humphries, Carol
Joel, Mr. Richard
Jones, Mr. V. Barry
Kelsey, Mr. Samuel T., Sr.
Kelsey, Mr. S. T., Jr.
Kibbee, Mrs. George W.
Kibbee, Mr. Augustus
Kibbee, Mr. Horace G.
Lamb, Mrs. Theodore
LeBus, Mr. John
Lewis, Dorothy
Lounsbury, Mrs. Ralph R.

Lucas, Mrs. Stephen L. (Carol D.)
Magner, Mr. Glenn
Many, Miss Anna
Many, Mrs. Peter W. (Madeleine)
Marett, Mrs. S. T. (Leila Lewis)
Marett, Mrs. George W.
Marett, Dr. William C.
Martin, Mrs. Robert I. (Katherine M.)
Martin, Mrs. M. M.
Matthews, Mrs. William A.
Mayeron, Mrs. Donald (Thelma W. "Sam")
McCarty, Mrs. Sidney
McConnell, Mrs. O. W. (Yrene)
McDowell, Mrs. Charlie (Gladys)
McMechan, Mr. Jervis B.
Meltzer, Mrs. Curtis (Enid)
Melvin, Mr. Richard F.
Melvin, Mrs. Richard F. (Margie E.)
Miltimore, Miss Cora
Mitchell, Mrs. Duncan F. (Jane)
Morgan, Mr. Dane D.
Morrow, Mrs. Charles D.
Mullen, Mr. James M.
Nall, Miss Rebecca C.
O'Brien, Mrs. F. X. James (Estelle)
O'Farrell, Dr. H. T.
Oglesby, Mrs. William H.
Olive, Mrs. Lindsay S. (A. Jeanne)
Painter, Mrs. E. S. (Cindy)
Palmer, Mrs. Beulah H.
Partridge, Mr. William
Partridge, Mrs. William
Pearson, Mrs. L. S. (Lillian L.)
Perry, Mrs. J. Lamb (Agnes B.)

Perry, Mrs. Hampton (Florence)
Peterson, Mrs. E. C. (Helen)
Pierce, Mr. Harvey F.
Pierson, Mrs. Val (Norma T. "Boots")
Pierson, Mrs. Annie
Porterfield, Mrs. Herbert D. (Florence V.)
Potts, Mrs. Frank H.
Prevost, Mrs. Milton (Jean W.)
Quinn, Mrs. Edythe K.
Rankin, Mrs.
Ravenel, Miss Marguerite A.
Reese, Mrs. Laura Kibbee
Reid, Mr. John
Reitt, Mrs. J. Peter (Dr. Barbara B.)
Rice, Mrs. Lewis C. (Ruth C.)
Richmond, Mr. Bert O.
Rideout, Mr. James
Rogers, Mrs. Richard (Nancy P.)
Rymer, Mrs. John (Beverly S.)
Salinas, Mrs. Anthony J.
Sanford, Mrs. John T. (Aletha)
Sargent, Mrs. Ralph M. (Louise A.)
Sargent, Dr. Ralph M.
Saussy, Mrs. George (Florence)
Schenck, Mrs. Jay E. (Page)
Schmitt, Mrs. George (Marie)
Scott, Ms. Ann W.
Scott, Mrs. James (Louise)
Selleck, Mr. Ebenezer
Selleck, Mrs. H. P.
Sewell, Mrs. Grover (Mary)
Shaffner, Professor Randolph P.
Shaffner, Mrs. Randolph P. (Margaret R.)
Sheldon, Mr. Frank S.

Sherrill, Mrs. Worth C. (Delores "Dee")
Shuler, Mrs. Glenn A.
Smith, Mrs. J. Jay (Mary Chapin)
Sorge, Mrs. George (Simone Kuehl)
Squier, Mrs. T. L. (Priscilla)
Staub, Miss Albertina
Stevens, Mr. Ernest C.
Stevens, Mrs. Ernest C. (Lillian)
Tannahill, Mrs. Sam (Claire)
Taylor, Mr. Walter J.
Taylor, Mrs. R. J.
Thompson, Mrs. H. P. P. (Helen M.)
Trively, Mrs. I. A. (Maxine)
Trott, Colonel Allen L. "Buck"
Trotter, Mrs. James P. (Kitsy)
Trowbridge, Mr. W. C.
Tyson, Mrs. Thomas H. (Elizabeth)
Valentine, Mrs. Elizabeth P.
Vaughn, Miss
Wadewitz, Miss Martina
Walker, Mrs. Burton (Betty)
Walker, Mr. Burton
Warren, Miss Minnie D.
Watson, Mr. Richard B.
Wax, Mrs. Ben W. (Polly)
Webbe, Reverend Gale D.
Wells, Mrs. Louise E.
Wheeler, Dr. Guy F.
Whitby, Mrs. Edmund P. (Jean S.)
White, Mr. T. Baxter
Wightman, Mrs. Frank (Alice G.)
Wilcox, Mrs. Jack (Virginia "Ted")
Wilson, Mrs. Dennis F. (Sandy V.)
Wilson, Mrs. C. A. (Mildred)

Appendix IV: Trustees

Wood, Mr. Ernest O.
Wotton, Mrs. Jamie A.

Appendix V

First Books of the Hudson Library

This is an annotated list of seventy books from the boxes in which the Hudson Library was born. They are currently shelved in 2 Globe-Wernicke sectional bookcases.[1]

19 Books of Fiction

Anonymous. *An Ernest Trifler*. Boston, 1880. A romance set in late nineteenth-century Massachusetts.

Beecher, Henry Ward. *Norwood; or, Village Life in New England.* New York, 1868. A novel by an intensely emotional American clergyman and brother of Harriet Beecher Stowe. [Gift from E. H. Bullock, Worcester, Mass.]

Bremer, Fredrika. *Homes of the New World; Impressions of America*. Vol. 1. Trans. from Swedish by Mary Howitt. New York, 1853. A series of romances by a Swedish advocate of equal rights for women.

Brontë, Charlotte. *Jane Eyre*. In *Home Library of Entertaining Books*. Boston, 1848. A new type of hero and heroine by the English Romantic novelist.

Hawthorne, Nathaniel. *The Marble Faun; or, The Romance of Monte Beni*. Two vols. in one. Boston, 1880. A novel of the fortunate fall by the American Romantic.

---

[1] These two bookcases were given to the library in 1946 by Mrs. Ralph M. (Louise) Sargent. They came from Red Wing, Minnesota, as part of the library of her father, Dr. Alexander P. Anderson, whose discovery of puffed wheat and puffed rice made him world famous. "Museum Given Bookcases By Mrs. Sargent," *Franklin Press & Highlands Maconian*, January 24, 1946.

Howells, William Dean. *Sketch of the Life and Character of Rutherford B. Hayes.* Boston, 1876. A biography of the president by an American critic and author of realistic novels.

James, Henry, Jr. *Confidence.* Boston, 1880. A weak novel by the English master realist.

Juncker, E. *Margarethe or Life Problems: A Romance.* Trans. from German by Mrs. A. L. Wister. Philadelphia, 1878. A tragedy of infidelity and reconciliation whereby suffering perfects morality and produces a purer, stronger love.

Ker, David. *From the Hudson to the Neva.* Boston, 1849. A novel that takes the reader from New York to Russia.

Littell, Eliakim. *Living Age.* Vol. 30 (July–September). Boston, 1851. A series begun in 1844 and primarily containing reprints of articles from British sources, especially book reviews, scientific essays, fictional works, etc.

O'Reilly, John Boyle. *Moondyne: A Story from the Under-World.* Boston, 1879. A novel by a British convict, who, sentenced to death for inciting a revolt, escaped from Australia, the setting for the novel, to the United States to become a poet and editor. The novel is dedicated to "all who are in prison for whatever cause."

Raimund, Galo. *A New Race: A Romance.* Trans. from German by Mrs. A. L. Wister. Philadelphia, 1880. A Cinderella story of an orphan girl's recovery of lost wealth and rank and discovery of love as the foundation of a new breed of aristocracy.

Reuter, Fritz. *Seed-Time and Harvest: A Novel.* Trans. from Platt-Deutsch (German dialect). Philadelphia, 1878. An autobiographical story about German village life.

Ropes, Hannah Anderson. *Cranston House: A Novel.* Boston, 1859. A family saga set in England.

Stowe, Harriet Beecher. *The May Flower and Miscellaneous Writings.* Boston, 1879. A series of New England sketches.

Tenney, E. P. *Agamenticus.* Boston, 1878. A romance of early New England life in the shadow of Mount Agamenticus in Maine.

Thackeray, William Makepeace. *Confessions of Fritz-Boodle; and Some Passages in the Life of Major Gahagan.* New York, 1852. Satiric and moralistic sketches of upper- and middle-class English life by the popular author of *Vanity Fair.* Known as the Fritz Boodle Papers.

Thackeray, William Makepeace. *Mr. Brown's Letters to a Young Man About Town; with the Proser and Other Papers.* New York, 1853. Lesser-known satiric sketches of English life.

Vicar of Wakefield, Rasselas, Paul and Virginia. Complete in 1 vol. New York, n.d. The well-known pastoral novel by Oliver Goldsmith, philosophical romance by Samuel Johnson, and idyllic, highly successful French romance by Bernardin de Saint-Pierre.

44 Books of Nonfiction

Abbott, John S. C. *History of Madame Roland.* New York, 1850. An account embracing the most interesting events of the French Revolution.

Adams, Nehemiah, D. D. *Agnes and the Little Key; or, Bereaved Parents Instructed and Comforted.* Boston, 1869. A self-help book dealing with the issue of heartrending grief.

Appendix V: First Books

Brassy, Anna. *Around the World in the Yacht 'Sunbeam.' Our Home on the Ocean for Eleven Months.* New York, 1880. A narration by the wife of an English railway contractor and mother of the secretary to the admiralty.

Brown, John, M. D. *Spare Hours.* Boston, 1866. Essays by a Scottish physician on the practice of medicine and literature. [Gift from Wyll Gannett, Boston]

Child, Lydia Maria. *Letters from New York.* 2nd ser. Boston, 1847. Arguments of an American abolitionist.

Collection of Psalms and Hymns for Social and Private Worship. 2nd ed. New York, 1822. A collection of sacred poetry aimed at no sectarian distinctions.

Colman, Henry. *European Life and Manners; in Familiar Letters to Friends.* 2 vols. Boston, 1849. A personal narrative of the author's residence abroad, depicting first impressions of scenes, objects, persons, and places in private and domestic life.

Cook, Reverend Thomas. *New Universal Letter Writer, Containing Letters on Friendship, Love, Courtship, Marriage, Duty, Religion, Trade, Amusement, etc.* Vol. 1 of 2. Hallowell, Maine, 1812. Samples of model letters.

Cunningham, Allan. *The Lives of the Most Eminent British Painters and Sculptors.* Vols. 4 and 5 of 6 vols. New York, 1838. Biographies of eighteenth- and nineteenth-century European and American lesser-known painters by a Scottish poet and man of letters. [Gift from H. B. Goodwin]

De Quincey, Thomas. *Biographical and Historical Sketches.* Boston, 1880. Essays on Shakespeare, Goethe, Schiller, Milton, Charlemagne, Joan of Arc, Shelley, Keats, etc., by the English Romantic.

Elder of the Free Church of Scotland. *The Assembly's Shorter Catechism Catechetically Illustrated and Practically Explained, Adapted for Public and Private Instruction.* 2nd ed. Edinburgh, 1846. Questions and answers concerning belief in God and Christ and the duties required of man, with appropriate scriptural support. Published three years after the Evangelicals declared their independence from the state-run Church of Scotland.

Gilfillan, George. *Sketches of Modern Literature and Eminent Literary Men, (Being a Gallery of Literary Portraits).* Vol. 1. New York, 1846. A Scottish Presbyterian clergyman's biographies of Shelley, Carlyle, Coleridge, Emerson, Wordsworth, Keats, Macaulay, etc.

Gosse, Philip Henry. *Wonders of The Great Deep; or The Physical, Animal, Geological, and Vegetable Curiosities of the Ocean.* Philadelphia, n.d. A scientific study by an English naturalist.

Greenwood, F. W. P., D.D. *Miscellaneous Writings.* Boston, 1846. Includes journal kept in England and essays on Milton, eternity of God, female literature, moral education, Niagara Falls, the study of natural history, etc.

Headley, Reverend Joel Tyler. *Rambles and Sketches.* New York, 1852. An American historian's travels to Paris, London, the English countryside, Waterloo, and Rome.

Hillard, George Stillman. *Six Months in Italy.* Vol. 1 of 2. Boston, 1853. [Presented by the First Parish Library, Cambridge, Mass.] An account of the author's visit in 1847–48 filled with astute and memorable impressions of Italy's historical, cultural, and natural beauty.

Appendix V: First Books 219

Jamieson, John, D.D. *A Vindication of the Doctrine of the Scripture, and of the Primitive Faith; concerning The Deity of Christ: in Reply to Dr. Priestley's History of Early Opinions, etc.* Vol. 2. Edinburgh, 1794. A defense by a Scottish clergyman, antiquarian, and lexicographer of the Scottish language.

Judd, Sylvester. *Margaret: A Tale of the Real and the Ideal, Blight and Bloom; including Sketches of a Place Not Before Described, called Mons Christi.* Rev. ed. 2 vols. Boston, 1851. Another ed. in 1 vol. Boston, 1871. America's religious and social views emerging from the Revolution, by an American Unitarian clergyman.

Mitchell, S. Augustus. *Mitchell's Ancient Atlas, Classical and Sacred, Containing Maps Illustrating the Geography of the Ancient World, as Described by the Writers of Antiquity; etc., etc.* Philadelphia, 1867. Atlas by an American geographer.

Morgan, Lewis H. *Ancient Society or Researches in the Lines of Human Progress from Savagery through Barbarism to Civilization.* New York, 1878. A focus by an American ethnologist on the American Indian culture.

Motley, John Lothrop. *Merry-Mount: A Romance of the Massachusetts Colony.* Vol. 1. Boston, 1849. A chronicle by an American historian, scholar, and diplomat.

Parkman, Francis. *Parkman's Works.* 8 vols. Boston, 1880. The last volume of the set by this American historian is *The Oregon Trail*.

Scott, Thomas. *The Force of Truth; An Authentic Narrative.* New York, 1825. An account of an English preacher's religious conversion, God's defeat of Satan in his heart, and his proposal of three doctrines as the leading truths of Christianity.

Smith, William. *History of Greece, with Supplementary Chapters on the History of Literature and Art.* New York, 1869. A history by an English classical and biblical lexicographer.

Taine, Hippolyte A. *History of English Literature.* Trans. from French by H. van Laun. New York, 1873. A deterministic interpretation of literature and its creation.

Thalheimer, M. E. *Manual of Ancient History.* New York, 1872. A history of Ancient Asia, Africa, the Persian Empire, Greece and the Macedonian Empire, and Rome.

Tupper, Martin Farquhar. *Proverbial Philosophy: A Book of Thoughts and Arguments.* New York, 1838. A world-famous series of didactic and moralizing commonplaces, seemingly in verse but without rhyme or meter, by an English versifier.

Ware, John, M. D. *Memoir of the Life of Henry Ware, Jr.* New ed. 2 vols. Boston, 1863. Autobiography of the Unitarian son of the American clergyman whose courses at Harvard evolved into the Harvard Divinity School. As an interesting aside, Emma Hudson's father, a Unitarian minister also from Boston, was named Henry Ware Emmons.

Waring, George Edwin. *Village Improvements and Farm Villages.* Boston, 1877. A treatise by an American sanitary engineer who later made his reputation for efficiency as street-cleaning commissioner of New York City.

Watson, John T., M. D. *Dictionary of Poetical Quotations; or, Elegant Extracts on Every Subject.* Philadelphia, 1847. [Gift from Matchett] A collection culled from English and American poetry and arranged topically to illustrate a great number of subjects.

White, Reverend James. *The Eighteen Christian Centuries*. New York, 1871. A chronology from the birth of Christ through the French Revolution.

7 Children's Books

Butler, E. H. & Co. *New American Pronouncing Speller*. Philadelphia, 1872. [Presented by Mrs. Louise Gwynn]

Gellibrand, Emma. *J. Cole*. New York, n.d. A story about a poor, disarmingly honest pageboy serving a wealthy family.

Higginson, Thomas Wentworth. *A Book of American Explorers*. In *Young Folks Series*. Boston, 1877. Stories of discoverers and explorers of North America.

Hughes, Thomas. *Tom Brown at Oxford*. A book for boys, portraying life in an English university by an English jurist. New York, 1861.

Phippen, A. R., ed. *The Schoolmate Monthly Reader for School and Home Instruction*. Vol. 1. New York, 1852.

Whitney, Adeline Dutton. *Patience Strong's Outings*. Boston, 1869. A book for girls by a Boston writer. [Gift from A. Ginger Bullock, Worcester]

———. *Real Folks*. A second book for girls. Boston, 1872.

Appendix VI

Works by Louise Bascom Barratt

Manuscripts, tear sheets, and published copies held by the Hudson Library among the "Louise Bascom Barratt Papers," which also include personal documents and memorabilia.

Adult Fiction

Some of Louise Bascom Barratt's many stories and articles that were published in over forty magazines under her maiden name, Louise Rand Bascom (listed chronologically) are "Empress Eugenier," *Wellesley Magazine* (March, 1906), pp. 254–60; "Modern Fairy Godmother," *Youth's Companion* (August 17, 1911), pp. 413–14; "Adventure in High Finance: James Martin Realizes on An Investment in Brains," *American Boy* (March, 1912), pp. 10, 20; "Havana Theatres," *New York Dramatic Mirror* (March 27, 1912), p. 5; "Land of Make-Believe," *Housewife* (February, 1913), pp. 3–4, 30; "Aunt Sarah and the Policeman: How He Helped Her to Have Her Fling," *Ladies' Home Journal* (July, 1913), pp. 7, 41; "Gatherer of Tributes," *Housewife* (September, 1913), pp. 3–4, 15, 21; and "Aigretta's Handicap," *Smith's Magazine* (May, 1914), pp. 257–66.

She published romantic serials, such as "Story Time in Prose and Rhyme," *Today's Housewife,* April, 1919–October, 1920, and "Peacock Robe: A Story of Mystery and Love," *Today's Housewife,* May–October, 1921.

Regional Fiction

She wrote several dialect mountain stories, such as "White Shoes" (November, 1914), pp. 462–72, and "The Better Man," (February, 1916), pp. 913–20, in *Harper's Magazine* and "Corilla's Corn" in *McBride's Magazine* (January, 1916), pp. 137–45. An illustrated article, "Uncle Sam in the Appalachia," appeared in *Outlook* (October 27, 1915), pp. 483–89.

Nonfiction

On the practical side, she contributed household articles to *Table Talk, Good Housekeeping, Delineator, Designer, The Housekeeper*, and similar magazines.

She wrote critical articles for *Editor* magazine, including "Logical Plot Building," September, 1910; "Touchstone of Literary Achievement," December, 1910; "Economy in Writing," January, 1911; "Strained Figures," February, 1911; "Eternal Vigilance," April, 1911; "Three Secrets of Literary Success," September, 1911; "Bolstering the Memory," February, 1912; "Vivid Verb Pitfalls," April, 1912; "Happy Thoughts," June, 1912; "A Hint on Series Writing," September 10, 1913; "Point of View," February 10, 1914; "Contrast," June 5, 1915; "Possibilities of the Special Article," October 9, 1915; "Rejections," November 20, 1915; and "Literary Miser," June 17, 1916.

Juvenile Fiction and Drama

Her one book for children was *Bugaboo Men* (New York, 1914) along with seven plays for juveniles: *Masonic Ring* (1910), *Golden Goblet* (1911), *Vera's Vacation* (1912), *Bachelor Club's Baby* (1912), *Catching Clara* (1914), *Molly's Aunt* (1916), and *Posey Pot's Mission* (1917), all published by March Bros. in Ohio. She composed several dozen children's stories and dialogues for use in the public schools. *Today's Housewife* carried twenty-seven of her original stories for children, twenty-seven original poems, and many of her drawings. And there were children's stories in *American Motherhood*, such as "Mr. Mossybank" (July, 1911), "Higglety Pigglety Town" (January, 1913), "Little Billy Robin" (June, 1913), "The Nicest Part of Christmas" (July, 1915), "How Dicky Lost His Fear of the Wind" (September & October, 1918), "How Dicky Learned to Listen" (November, 1918), and others.

Guide Books

Under her married name, Louise Bascom Barratt, she authored the *Book of Entertainments and Theatricals*, with Helena Smith Dayton (New York, 1923); *New York in Seven Days* (New York, 1925); and *New York Visitor* (New York, 1937).

Appendix VII

Permanent Collection of the Bascom-Louise Gallery
(dated according to when the works were acquired)

Photograph of the Bascom-Louise Hotel. Taken ca. 1953. Bequeathed by Watson Barratt.

Anderson, Linda. *Winter Scene*. Primitive oil, 1988.
Daugette, Julia. *Winter in Highlands*. Oil, 1989, acquired through a donation by Dorothy and Richard Wertzler.
Dodd, Elsa. Two views of the old dry cleaners building on North Fourth Street in Highlands. Sepia conte crayon drawings, 1993.
Dresch, Elsie. *Ravenel Lake II*. Pastel, 1991, acquired by the Allen Ferry Memorial Fund.
Harris, Lucien. *Hummingbirds in Rhododendron*. Acrylic, 1987.
Hill, Polly Knipp. Nine hand-painted original etchings of Appalachian Mountain scenes, 1991.
Hunt, Walter. *The Chellah*. Pencil drawing, 1993.
James, Amelia. *Sun Worshippers*. Oil, 1993.
Leebrick, Gil. *Mesa Verde: Cliff Palace*. Platinum photograph, 1993.
Owle, Lloyd Carl. *The Bird Clan*. Stone carving, 1988.
Shaddick, W. Thomas. *Queen Anne's Lace*. Watercolor, 1987.

Bibliography

Library/Gallery Records

Barratt, G. Watson. "Last Will and Testament," signed May 29, 1958. Copies available in library files.

Barratt, Louise Bascom. Manuscripts. Include a journal recording submissions, acceptances and rejections, and payments from publishers. Also, a list of her published works.

———. Memorabilia and family letters. Include a scrapbook of Wellesley College mementos, ledgers and financial papers including tax receipts from the town of Highlands and a partially used checkbook for a Highlands business, illustration boards for her children's book *The Bugaboo Men,* and correspondence from well-known people.

———. Photos. Include both framed and unframed items.

———. Published works. Include issues of magazines containing her articles or stories, books, plays, and periodicals she edited.

Highlands scrapbook. Thirty newspaper clippings on the founding and growth of Highlands from 1885 to 1932.

Hudson Library Board of Trustees. Memorandum to Mr. Bob Moore, chairman of Macon County Public Library Board of Trustees; Mrs. Cynthia Modlin, Macon County librarian; Mrs. Gertrude McIntosh, Hudson Branch librarian; and Mrs. Jacquelyn Leebrick, Louise Bascom Barratt [sic] Gallery director, September 19, 1985.

———. Letter of Intent, Macon County, North Carolina, Hudson Library of Highlands, N.C., March 3, 1980.

———. Lease Agreement, March 3, 1980.

Hudson Library Board of Trustees. Records. Include minutes, treasurer's reports, special reports, pamphlets, and clippings.

Hudson Library Board of Trustees. Scrapbook. Includes clippings and photos.

———. Secretary's Book, Hudson Library Association. 6 vols. Annual and Trustee Meetings: August 30, 1926–September 21, 1954, including two meetings of 1955 and one of 1956; August 31, 1970–June 22, 1993. Minutes for the years prior to 1926 and from 1955 through the first half of 1970 are missing.

Lyle, Mrs. David (Nancy Jussely). Letter to Randolph P. Shaffner, November 4, 1993. In author's possession.

Photographs. Circa 1880–1995.

"Record of First Sunday school, Highlands, N.C., March 12, 1876." Original document.

Sloan estate scrapbook. Includes photos of the exterior, particularly of the formal Cheeononda gardens, currently the George Heery home.

Maps

Architectural plans and drawings. Hudson Library building and addition.

Kerr, W. C. "Physiological Map of North Carolina." 1883.

"North Carolina, South Carolina, and Georgia." Reproduction of 1835 Bradford map.

Pamphlets

"Above the Clouds." A pamphlet about Highlands, published by *The Star*. Highlands, May, 1890.

Blue Ridge Highlands in Western North Carolina, The. Greenville, S.C., 1876.

Carnegie Hero Fund Commission. Pittsburgh, Pa., 1914.

Catalogue of the Hudson Library. Highlands, Macon County, North Carolina. Highlands, 1906.

Deal, J. A. *The American Mountaineer.* N.d.

"Dr. Thomas Grant Harbison." Reprinted from *Journal of Elisha Mitchell Scientific Society*, vol. 52 (1936): 140–45.

Highlands, North Carolina: The Greatest Health and Pleasure Resort in the United States. The Most Perfect Climatic Sanitarium in the World. Rising Sun, Md., 1887. A promotional pamphlet distributed by Samuel T. Kelsey.

Howell, Thelma. *Highlands Museum and Biological Laboratory: A Preliminary Check-List of the Birds of the Highlands Region.* Highlands, 1945.

"In the Heart of the Mountains" Lies Highlands, Western North Carolina. Clinton, S.C., 1890. A promotional pamphlet distributed by Samuel T. Kelsey and including photographs and a fold-out panoramic view of Highlands from Sunset Rock.

Johnston, David W. *Birds of Highlands, North Carolina, With a Preliminary List from Cashiers and Nearby Gorges.* Reprinted from *Journal of Elisha Mitchell Scientific Society*, vol. 80, no. 1 (May, 1964).

Kerr, W. C. *Physiological Description of North Carolina.* N.C. Dept. of Agriculture *Monthly Bulletin*, July, 1883.

Macon Review, vol. II, nos. 15 (January, 1935) and 16 (February–Mar., 1935).

Perrin, Carol Carré. *Highlands Historic Inventory: Project Completion Report.* Highlands, March, 1982.

Quarterman, Elsie, and Catherine Keever. *Highlands Museum and Biological Laboratory: A Summer Check List of the Vascular Plants of the Highlands Region.* Highlands, 1947.

Smith, Mary Chapin. *History of the Hudson Library Association.* Highlands, 1931. 12 pp.

Town Records

Greville, Thomas N. E. "Highlands and Vicinity." Map dated September 13, 1931.

Highlands. Minutes, Board of Supervisors for the Blue Ridge Township. First Monday of May, 1879–April 5, 1905. Town Hall.

———. Minutes, Board of Commissioners. 23 vols. May 31, 1883–March 2, 1994. Minutes covering January, 1899–May, 1909, August, 1920–August, 1921, and March, 1923–March, 1925, are missing. Town Hall.

Highlands Cemetery Company. Minutes. In the possession of Louis "Bud" Potts.

Interviews

Unless otherwise indicated, all were conducted with the author in Highlands in 1993.

Arnold, Mrs. Marion Day. Telephone conversations, October 29, November 5, and December 9.

Bass, Mr. Sam. November 20 and December 17.

Bruce, Mrs. Richard (Elizabeth). December 14.

Calloway, Miss Ethel. November 8.

Chalker, Mrs. Albert L. (Marna Cobb). November 17.

Chmar, Mrs. Paul (Jan Chambers). September 24, 1993, and February 23, 1994.

Coward, Mrs. Nancy Potts. Telephone conversation, November 27.

Christian, Mrs. Elaine. Telephone conversations, February 24 and 25, 1994.

Cranston, Mr. Craig. October 18.

Edwards, Mr. Louis. September 30.

Fleming, Virginia Edwards. September 29.

Hall, Mrs. Tudor N. (Margaret Gilbert). November 11.

Harbison, Miss Dorothea "Dolly". September 22 and 30, December 6.
Hertzberg, Mrs. Rudolph (Winnie). October 30
Holt, Mr. Richard "Bill." October 14.
Leebrick, Mrs. Gilbert (Jacquelyn "Jackie"). December 10.
Marett, Dr. William C. January 28, 1994.
Matthews, Mrs. George (Mary Pugh). September 28.
McDowell, Mr. Charlie. October 30.
McIntosh, Mrs. Harold (Gertrude). November 2.
McNamee, Mrs. Sarah Thompson. Black Mountain, N.C., October 27.
Medlin, Mrs. W. T. (June Thompson). November 9.
Meisel, Mrs. Louise Edwards. September 29.
Norris, Mr. John. Telephone conversation, November 9.
Pell, Mrs. Simon (Emma Potts). February 9, 1994.
Potts, Mr. Louis "Bud." October 17.
Quin, Mrs. Hillrie (Beverly Cook). November 25.
Reese, Mr. Harold. November 2.
Reese, Mr. Joseph W. December 1.
Reese, Mrs. Joseph W. (Lucile Pierson). November 27 and December 1.
Rice, Mr. W. Herbert. January 10, 1994
Rhodes, Mrs. Robert L. (Anne Altstaetter). October 31.
Shay, Mrs. Robert P. (Esther Cunningham). Telephone conversations, December 6 and 7.
Sherrill, Mrs. Worth (Delores "Dee"). October 25.
Smith, Mr. Victor. November 1.
Sorge, Mrs. George J. (Simone Kuehl). November 12.
Strader, Mrs. R. Harold (Carolyn). November 8.
Traylor, Mrs. Forest (Dorothy "Dot"). November 11.
Van Houten, Mrs. Harriet Zahner. September 30.
Wilcox, Ms. Jeremy. December 4.
Wilson, Mr. Everette. September 28.
Wright, Mr. Harry R. October 29 and December 1.

Articles

"Arnold Keener, Simone Kuehl Are Named Rotary 1988 Award Winners." *Highlander*, October 21, 1988.

"Bascom—Town Builder and Merchant Prince of Highlands, Retires." *New York Tribune*, October 21, 1920.

Baty, A. J. "Helen's Gamble." *North Carolina State* (September, 1982), pp. 12–14.

"Box of Books Became the Hudson Library." *Highlander*, April 17, 1964.

"Brief History of Highlands, Highest Town East of Rockies." *Franklin Press*, July 5, 1928.

"Carolina Mountain Towns: Highlands." *Asheville Carolina Mountains*, June, 1893.

"Charm of Highlands Mountains Lured Professor Harbison, Botanist: Region Escaped Sweep of Glaciers—Consequently Contains Plant Life Not Found Elsewhere." *Franklin Press*, Highlands ed., July 5, 1928.

"Commentary: Boots's Contributions Won't Soon Be Forgotten." *Highlander*, November 24, 1987.

"Commentary: Library Patrons Are Losing Special Friend [Gert McIntosh]." *Highlander*, February 3, 1987.

Copple, Lee. "One Man's Highlands [Betty Service]." *Highlander*, June 28, 1979.

———. "One Man's Highlands [Hudson Library]." *Highlander*, August 22, 1974.

———. "Professor Anderson's Windmill." *One Man's Highlands* (Highlands, 1975), pp. 92–95.

"Death Claims J. H. Durgin, 95." *Franklin Press & Highlands Maconian*, February 23, 1939.

"Deepest Snow: In Highlands History Last Week; 18 to 20 Inches." *Franklin Press & Highlands Maconian*, March 12, 1942.

"Development of Highlands As Resort Dates from 1872: Dream of Hutchinson and Kelsey Now Being Fulfilled." *Franklin Press & Highlands Maconian*, September 12, 1935.

"Dr. Anderson: Scientist, Compiles New Reader." *Franklin Press & Highlands Maconian*, August 21, 1941. Repr. as "Alexander P. Anderson's 'Seventh Reader' Among New Library Books." *Mountain Trail*, August 22, 1941.

"Dr. Thomas Grant Harbison." *Journal of the Elisha Mitchell Scientific Society*, vol. 52 (1936), pp. 141–45.

Editor of *New Orleans Times*. "In the Mountains." *Franklin Western Reporter*, April 2, 1880. A graphic and poetic description of the trip from New Orleans to Horse Cove in 1880.

"Educational Records Date from 1885." *Franklin Press*, Teacher Training ed., April 10, 1930.

"'80 Census: Results Are In, County Population Up 25%." *Highlander*, July 24, 1980.

Flinn, Kathleen. "Librarian, Storyteller Betty Service Dies at 82." *Sarasota Times*, August 22, 1991.

"Gem Benefit Big Success." *Highlander*, September 13, 1963.

"Gray Cottage Has Interesting History, The." *Highlander*, May 26, 1966.

Harbison, Dorothea. "T. G. Harbison, Botanist." *Highlander*, January 25, 1973.

Harbison, Gertrude. "A Brief History—The Hudson Library." *Highlander*, August 14, 1964.

———. "A 75th Anniversary." *Highlander*, June 18, 1959.

———. "An 85th Anniversary." *Highlander*, August 7, 1969.

Harbison, Gertrude. "Hudson Library Notes." *Franklin Press & Highlands Maconian*, July 13, 1939. Repr. as "The Hudson Library," *Mountain Trail*, July 14, 1939.

Harbison, Mrs. T. C. "Highlands Attracts Noted Visitors: Town Is Haven for Notables." *Franklin Press & Highlands Maconian*, September 5, 1935.

———. "Many New Homes Built at Highlands: Town Enjoys Building Boom." *Franklin Press & Highlands Maconian*, August 29, 1935.

Harbison, T. G. "Highlands Site of Beautiful Estates: Ravenel Home One of Oldest." *Franklin Press*, Teacher Training ed., April 10, 1930.

Harkins, Bess Hines, and Sarah Hicks Hines. "Library Trees Threatened by Plans." *Highlander*, March 8, 1984.

"Heavy Rains Wreak Havoc at Highlands." In Mrs. H. G. Story, "Highlands Highlights." *Franklin Press & Highlands Maconian*, September 5, 1940.

"Highlands Current Prices." *Blue Ridge Enterprise*, January 22, 1885.

"Highlands is Enjoying New Power Supply." *Asheville Times*, April 17, 1927.

"Highlands Locals [First Movies]." *Franklin Press*, July 2, 1920.

"Highlands Man, 95, Has Had Dangerous, Colorful Career." *Franklin Press & Highlands Maconian*, September 22, 1938. An account of the life of John H. Durgin.

"Highlands to Unveil Monument to Founder: Three Events Will Be Celebrated There on August 10." *Asheville Citizen*, August 1, 1929.

"Highlands Writer's Poem To Be Reproduced For Blind Children." *Highlands Maconian*, December 3, 1930.

Hill, Howard. "An Alternative for Library Plan." *Highlander*, March 22, 1984.

Hines, Sarah Hicks. "Farnsworths Study Science and Arts at Highlands Home." *Franklin Press*, May 15, 1930.

———. "Highlands Has Unique History: Two Interesting Stories Related of Town's Establishment." *Franklin Press & Highlands Maconian*, June 30, 1932.

———. "Mountain Paradise Found in Garden of Cheeononda." *Franklin Press & Highlands Maconian*, June 30, 1932.

———. "Sequoyah Name Given to New Highland Lake." *Franklin Press*, June 26, 1930.

———. "Town Growing in Popularity: Mountain Resort Offers Many Attractions for Tourists." *Franklin Press & Highlands Maconian*, June 30, 1932.

"History Buffs, Family Mourn Loss of Russell House." *Highlander*, May 20, 1988.

"H. M. Bascom Final Rites: Prominent Highlands Resident Dies at Home of Daughter in N.Y." *Franklin Press & Highlands Maconian*, March 5, 1942.

Hopper, Helen. "Library Greatly Pleased with $10,000 Allocation." *Highlander*, February 7, 1974.

"Hudson Librarian Gert McIntosh Is Calling It Quits After Eight Years." *Highlander*, February 3, 1987.

"Hudson Library Has Grown Over Its 96 Year History." *Highlander*, September 25, 1980.

"Hudson Library Is 95 This Year." *Highlander*, August 30, 1979.

"Hudson Library Marks Its 85th Anniversary." *Highlander*, June 26, 1969.

"Hudson To Become Part of Macon System." *Highlander*, March 6, 1980.

Hughey, Elizabeth House. "Public Libraries in North Carolina." In *North Carolina Libraries*, vol. 13 (November, 1954), pp. 11–16.

"J. J. Smith's Life Sketched: Served Town as Mayor; Road Builder; Artist and Craftsman." *Franklin Press & Highlands Maconian*, September 11, 1941.

Jenks, Colonel C. W. "The Climatic Conditions at the Highlands, Macon County, N.C." *Highlander*, February 19, 1886. An account of the "unique atmospheric and climatic conditions of the elevated plateau" upon which Highlands is located.

———. "More About Highlands." *Highlander*, March 5, 1886. A continuation of the above article.

J., M. P. "My Friends at Highlands: An Appreciation." *Franklin Press & Highlands Maconian*, July 20, 1939.

"Journey Begins at Hudson Library." *Highlander*, November 5, 1993.

"Lee's Inn Celebrates 10th Anniversary." *Highlander*, May 5, 1966.

"Librarian Closes Book On 50 Years of Work." *Asheville Citizen*, August 23, 1974.

"Library Awaiting Word on Grants for New Building." *Highlander*, September 25, 1980.

"Library Benefits from Bascom-Barratt Bequest." *Highlander*, August 20, 1981.

"Library Fund Increased $500: Sum from Bobby Jones' Exhibition Match to Prove Useful." *Highlands Maconian*, August 19, 1931.

"Library Observing 90th Anniversary." *Highlander*, August 15, 1974.

"Library Patrons Are Losing Special Friend." *Highlander*, February 3, 1987. A farewell editorial to Gert McIntosh.

"Library Will Issue History." *Highlands Maconian*, September 16, 1931.

"Library Reception Is Well Attended [Harbison sisters' retirement]." *Highlander*, August 29, 1974.

"Macon Pioneer Passes Away: T. Baxter White, for Many Years a Resident of Highlands, Died on July 14, at La Verne, California." *Franklin Press*, August 4, 1922.

Marion, Jonathan. "Missing the Forest for the Trees." *Highlander*, April, 19, 1984.

Messer, Stephanie. "Dolly Harbison Recalls Vivid History of Library." *Highlander*, June 15, 1993.

"Miss Harbison Gets Weather Bureau's Award." *Franklin Press*, August 10, 1978.

"Miss Harbison Given Awards." *Highlander*, August 31, 1978.

"Miss Harbison Recognized." *Highlander*, September 27, 1973. Reprint of John Parris, "Roaming the Mountains [Gertrude Harbision]." *Asheville Citizen*, September 20, 1973.

"Miss Harbison To Be Ordained as Presbyterian Ruling Elder." *Highlander*, February 12, 1965.

"Miss Rebecca Nall Dies At Age of 89." *Highlander*, February 23, 1967.

"Miss Staub Passes; Funeral Monday Morning." *Franklin Press & Highlands Maconian*, July 2, 1942.

"Miss White, Daughter of Highlands Founder, Succumbs in California." *Franklin Press & Highlands Maconian*, April 12, 1956.

Moore, Bill. "From a Case of Books a Modern Library Grew." *Asheville Citizen-Times*, February 13, 1992.

Morris, Ralph. "Journey Begins at Hudson Library." *Highlander*, November 5, 1993.

"Mr. and Mrs. A. W. Hudson Visit Highlands." *Franklin Press & Highlands Maconian*, April 20, 1939.

"Mrs. Barratt's Funeral Held in Highlands." *Franklin Press & Highlands Maconian*, September 8, 1949.

"Mrs. Elliott Dies Thursday." *Highlands Maconian*, October 7, 1931.

"Mrs. J. J. Smith Dies Tuesday: Highlands Pioneer Was Poet, Artist and Botanist." *Franklin Press & Highlands Maconian*, April 4, 1940.

"Mrs. J. M. Cobb Dies at Age of 91." In Mrs. T. C. Harbison, "Highlands Highlights," *Franklin Press & Highlands Maconian*, November 29, 1934.

"Mrs. Kibbee, Ex-Highlands Resident, Dies." *Franklin Press & Highlands Maconian*, February 20, 1947.

Munger, Michelle. "Carolyn Strader Hired as New Librarian." *Highlander*, February 27, 1990.

———. "Library Board Undergoing Re-organization." *Highlander*, November 10, 1987.

"Museum Given Bookcases By Mrs. Sargent." *Franklin Press & Highlands Maconian*, January 24, 1946.

Nall, Mrs. A. R. "North Carolina Home." *Franklin Press & Highlands Maconian*, July 15, 1943.

"New Books in Hudson Library." *Highlander*, August 17, 1937.

"New Highway Being Built." *Franklin Press & Highlands Maconian*, March 18, 1937.

"New Photo Book by Valentine Now on Sale." *Highlander*, November 15, 1979.

"Norma Pierson Is Honored, Is DuPree Citizen of Year." *Highlander*, November 24, 1987.

Norris, Helen Hill. "First Sunday school 1876." *Looking Backward* (Highlands, ca. 1960), pp. 46–47.

———. "Looking Backward [The Hudson Library]." *Highlander*, July 13, 1962.

"Notice [Petition for an act of incorporation]." *Blue Ridge Enterprise*, January 22, 1885.

"Obituary [Reverend and Mrs. Henry Emmons]." *Franklin Press*, November 29, 1899. The deaths of Ella Hudson's parents.

"Old Map Of Highlands Presented Museum By Former Local Resident." *Franklin Press & Highlands Maconian*, January 27, 1949.

"133 Members Join Library in Campaign." *Franklin Press & Highlands Maconian*, September 19, 1946.

Parris, John. "Roaming the Mountains [Gertrude Harbison]." *Asheville Citizen*, September 20, 1973.

———. "She Watched the Skies for More Than 50 Years." *Asheville Citizen*, September 3, 1978.

Paul, Guy. "The Assets of Highlands." *Highlander*, September 4, 1937.

Phay, Robert E. "The Origins of the Public Library in North Carolina." In *The Public Library: A Guidebook for North Carolina Library Trustees*, 2nd ed. (Chapel Hill, N.C., 1984), pp. 1–2.

Pierson, Norma T. "Library Story Clarified." *Highlander*, February 9, 1984.

"Plans for New Library Draw Fire." *Highlander*, January 26, 1984.

"Poet, Publisher Jonathan Williams Unknown to Many Highlanders." *Highlander*, May 18, 1978.

"Reopening of Library Urged: Mrs. Margaret Ordway Asks for Volunteers to Aid in Task." *Franklin Press & Highlands Maconian*, January 19, 1933.

"Resolutions of Sympathy on the Death of Mr. Huger Elliott and Sister, Miss Charlotte Barnwell Elliott." *Franklin Press & Highlands Maconian*, December 9, 1948.

Ress, Regina. "Reconsider Tree Destruction." *Highlander*, March 29, 1984.

"Romance of Highlands." *Greenwood (S.C.) Index-Journal*, August 24, 1929.

Scott, Bob. "Tree-Cutting in Highlands Draws Opposition." *Asheville Citizen*, January 19, 1984.

Scott, Louise. "Hudson Library Celebrates 91st Year This Summer." *Highlander: Centennial Edition*, July 19, 1975.

"Site of Highlands Purchased in 1872: Mountain Trail Was Only Path." *Franklin Press*, Teacher Training ed., April 10, 1930.

"Site of Highlands Was Carved From Mountain Wilderness." *Highlands Maconian*, June 24, 1931 and July 29, 1931.

Smith, Mary Chapin. "Center of Beauty's Realm Lies In Highlands' Country: Wonderland Is Described." *Highlands Maconian*, November 5, 1930.

———. "Library Active at Highlands." *Franklin Press*, July 5, 1928.

———. "Women Do Much for Highlands." *Franklin Press*, July 5, 1928.

Story, Mrs. H. G. "Children's Room Planned at Library." *Franklin Press & Highlands Maconian*, July 24, 1941.

———. "Highlands Has Much to Offer: Town's Origin Dates Back to Days of 1872." *Asheville Citizen-Times*, August 11, 1940.

———. "Highlands: The Place and Its People." *Franklin Press & Highlands Maconian*, July 20, 1939.

"Story Hour Big Success," *Highlander*, November 11, 1960.

Taylor, Skip. "On the Move: Library Volunteers, Staff Move Into the New 6,200 Square Foot Facility." *Highlander*, May 31, 1985.

"This Winter At Highlands Mild, Old Paper Suggests." *Franklin Press & Highlands Maconian*, February 7, 1946.

Thomas, Sylvia. "Highlands Integral Part of Shuptrine's Art." *Highlander*, December 1, 1987.

Thomas, Sylvia. "Love of Books: Dolly Harbison Wishes Her Sister, Gertrude, Could Have Seen Opening of New Library." *Highlander,* June 11, 1985.

———. "New Library Is Opened: Ceremonial Ribbon Cut Sunday on New Hudson Library, Art Gallery." *Highlander,* June 11, 1985.

Turley, Caroline. "Library Continues to Grow and Expand to Meet Changing Needs of Highlands." *Highlander,* December 17, 1991.

Turner, Nancy, and Jim Horton. "Diapensia Family: *Shortia galacifolia* Torrey & Gray." *The Summer Times* (Tampa, 1979), p. 94.

"28th U.S. President Once Visited Here." *Franklin Press & Highlands Maconian,* September 6, 1956.

"Ty Cobb and Jones Golf Together: Bobby meets Diamond King." *Highlands Maconian,* September 10, 1930.

"Watson Barratt, Designer, 78, Dies." *New York Times,* July 8, 1962.

"Watson Barratt Dies in New York Hospital: Highlands Summer Resident Was Famous Theatrical Designer." *Highlander,* July 13, 1962.

White, Elias D. "Early Highlands Days, An Historical Sketch." *Franklin Press & Highlands Maconian,* June 5, 1941. An early history of education in Highlands.

Wood, Lawrence E. "Mountain Memories: A Tribute to Miss Gertrude." *Highlander,* August 22, 1974.

Wuntz, Bud. In the *Raleigh Post,* as quoted in "Highlands." *Franklin Press,* November 21, 1900. A brief history of the growth of Highlands.

Yarborough, Margaretta J. "Library Service to the Strands: North Carolina's Lighthouse Libraries." In *North Carolina Libraries,* vol. 50, no. 1, pp. 27–30.

Newspapers

There follows a list of local newspapers listed chronologically. Original issues that are held by the Hudson Library are starred. Most issues are accessible on microfilm in N.C. public or academic libraries, such as Macon County and Western Carolina University.

*Blue Ridge Enterprise.**
January 1, 1883–1885. First newspaper in Highlands, a four-page format, actually begun in 1881 and devoted to village chatter and politics, editorials, and advertisements. Edited by E. E. Ewing, former publisher of the *Kansas Farmer*.

*Highlander.**
August 7, 1885–February 25, 1887. Edited by Mrs. A. F. Clark.

Highlands Star.
May 1, 1890–June 3, 1891. Edited by Richard Goldie.

Mountain Eagle [March 31, 1892*]
September 9, 1891–1892, 1893. Ed. by T. G. Harbison.

*Carolina Mountains.**
June, 1893. Asheville, N.C.

[For 37 years—1893 to 1930—Highlands was without a newspaper.]

Franklin Press [January 12, 1916,* and July 5, 1928 (Highlands ed.)*]
July 11, 1889–December 24, 1902. T. Baxter White, "Highlands."

1903–1919. Copies of issues for these years were destroyed in the great fire that swept the Franklin Press on December 20, 1922.

January 23, 1920–1928. "News of Week of Highlands: Brief Items of Interest from Macon's Pretty Mountain City as Told by Correspondent of The Press."

Franklin Press (cont.)
>1929–February, 1931. Sarah Hicks Hines, "Highlands Flings," in "Highlands—The Roof Garden of the Southeast."
>1931–April 28, 1932. "Social and Personal News from Highlands."

Highlands Maconian.* September, 1930–1932. Edited by Charles A. Coe.

Franklin Press & Highlands Maconian [1932* and special eds.: July 20, 1939, and July 5, 1947*]
>May 5, 1932–July, 1937. Mrs. T. C. Harbison, "Highlands Highlights."
>1936. Issues missing, never microfilmed.
>July, 1937–June, 1938. Mrs. Frank Bloxham, "Highlands Highlights."
>June 1938–September, 1938. Mrs. E. A. Burt, Jr., "Highlands Highlights."
>September, 1938–1953. Mrs. H. G. Story, "Highlands Highlights."
>1954. James Blakley, "Highlands People."
>1955. Jan Burnette, "Highlands People." In December, Mrs. Wayne E. Crowe, columnist.
>1956–December 24, 1958. No Highlands column.

Highlander.* August 6–September 4, 1937. Edited by S. J. Fulwood. A local newspaper that ran for only five issues.

Mountain Trail.* November 24, 1938–1952. A mimeographed weekly published by the Highlands School Theatre.

Galax News.* 1951–1970. A mimeographed weekly published during the summer season by the Galax Theatre.

Highlander.* May, 1958–.

Franklin Press. January 1, 1969–.

Books and Manuscripts

American Library Directory, 1993–94. 46th ed. 2 vols. New Providence, N.J., 1993.

Crumpler, Thomas B. "History of Highlands." Unpublished manuscript, c. 1975. In possession of the author.

Crutchfield, James A., ed. *North Carolina Almanac and Book of Facts.* Nashville, 1988.

Davis, Evangeline McLennan. *The Lure of Highlands.* Highlands, 1981.

Holt, Betty. *History of the First Presbyterian Church: Highlands, North Carolina, 1885–1985.* Highlands, 1985.

Lombard, Frances Baumgarner. *From the Hills of Home.* Whiteside Cove, N.C., 1972. Repr. 1993.

Macon County Historical Society. *Heritage of Macon County.* Franklin, N.C., 1987. Summaries of Macon County families.

McIntosh, Gert. *Highlands, North Carolina . . . a walk into the past.* Rev. ed. Birmingham, Ala., 1990.

Marett, Bill. *Courage at Fool's Rock.* Highlands, 1975.

Morley, Margaret W. *The Carolina Mountains.* Boston, 1913.

Norris, Helen Hill. *Looking Backward.* Highlands, ca. 1960.

Reynolds, T. W. *Born of the Mountains.* Highlands, 1964.

———. *High Lands.* Highlands, 1964.

———. *The Southern Appalachian Region.* 2 vols. Highlands, 1966.

Sharpe, Bill. *A New Geography of North Carolina.* Raleigh, 1961. Vol. 3.

Siler, Margaret R. *Cherokee Indian Lore & Smoky Mountain Stories.* Franklin, N.C., 1938. Reissued 1993.

Turner, Nancy, and Jim Horton. *The Summer Times.* Tampa, Fla., 1979.

Poets of Highlands

The poet is the one who puts things together.
—*Buckminster Fuller*

Christman, Will.
In T. W. Reynolds, *Born of the Mountains* (Highlands, 1964), p. 35.
Farnsworth, Mrs. Patrick T. (Dorothy McPherson) [Robert Emmet Ward, Ann F. Barr, pseud.].
Fleming, Virginia.
Be Good to Eddie Lee. New York, 1993.
So Tender the Spirit. Highlands, 1985.
Wellspring. Highlands, 1986.
Harkins, Bess Hines.
Dream Blue Altitudes. Highlands, n.d.
Earth Songs. San Benito, Texas, 1975.
"Our Mountains" (a series of prose reflections on early life in Highlands), *Highlander*, February 10–June 23, 1966, October 29, 1966–.
Sequoia Bound. N.p., 1978. With Butler S. Harkins.
Songs Out of Silence. Oxnard, Calif., 1964.
Unknown Seas. Los Angeles, 1958.
Harkins, Butler Sterling.
Sequoia Bound. With Bess Hines Harkins.
Sing Down, Sandman. N.p., 1986.
Hawkins, Laura.
In Frances Baumgarner Lombard, *From the Hills of Home in Western North Carolina* (Whiteside Cove, N.C., 1972, repr. 1993), pp. 20–24.
In T. W. Reynolds, *Born of the Mountains*, pp. 34–35, 78.
In T. W. Reynolds, *High Lands* (Highlands, 1964), pp. 23–25, 51–55.

Hawkins, Laura (cont.)
   In T. W. Reynolds, *The Southern Appalachian Region* (Highlands, 1966), vol. 1, pp. 30–33, 37.
Hines, Bess Hinson (see also Bess Hines Harkins).
   Singing of the Heart. Atlanta, 1943.
McCollum, Dee.
   Poems for Women. N.p., 1993.
   The Summer Mountain: Poems of the Hills. N.p., 1986.
Rice, Christina Anderson.
   "Clouds," "Love," and other poems. In the possession of her son, W. Herbert Rice.
Smith, Mary Chapin.
   Earth Songs. Boston, 1910.
Williams, Jonathan.
   Blues & Roots/Rue & Bluets: A Garland for the Southern Appalachians. Durham, N.C. 1985.
   Ear in Bartram's Tree: Selected Poems 1957–1967, An. Chapel Hill, N.C., 1969.
   Elite/Elate Poems. Highlands, N.C., 1979.
   Get Hot or Get Out. Metuchen, N.J., 1982.
   In the Azure Over the Squalor: Ransackings and Shorings. Frankfort, Ky., 1985.
   Magpie's Bagpipe: Selected Essays, The. San Francisco, 1982.

Index

—A—

Altadona, 23
Altitude oak, *see* Trees
Altstaetter, Anne, *see* Rhodes
Altstaetter, Raoul, 84
Anderson, Anne, *see* Sellers
Anderson, Dr. Alexander P., 94, 108, 115-17
   puffed rice and wheat, 115
   seventh McGuffey *Reader*, 116
Appalachian Environmental Arts Center, 173
Appalachian Regional Council, 160, 162
Armor, Mrs. G. Maxwell, 44
Arnold, Marion Day, 76, 92, 98, 101, 103, 113, 174
Augur, Helen, 137, 163
   as trustee president, 203

—B—

Baptist Church, 130
Barratt, G. Watson, 119, 129, 131, **136-38**
   as art director, 137
   as benefactor of gallery, 137, 181
   as scene designer, 129
   as student of Whistler & Pyle, 136
   Barratt Trust, 165
   Chetolah, 127, 137, 163
   courtship, 129
   death of, 136
Barratt, Louise Bascom, 37, 79, 119, **127-29**, 137
   as biographer, 128
   as dramatist, 128
   as library trustee, 127
   as popular writer, 127
   courtship, 129
   death of, 127
   instructional articles by, 128
   works by, **222-24**
Bascom, Florence Coffin, 12
Bascom, H. M., 10, 12, 21, 37, 59, 111, **117-19**, 129, 137
   as mayor, 118, 205
   as owner of Davis House, 118
   as owner of general store, 118
   as realtor and insurance agent, 118
   as road commissioner, 118
   death of, 117
   first wife, 127
   on first library board, 19
   second wife, 12
Bascom, Ida Crockett, 127
Bascom, Louise, *see* Barratt, Louise Bascom
Bascom-Barratt house (Chetolah), *see* Barratt, G. Watson
Bascom-Louise Gallery, 129, 164
   archives of, 226-28
   created by bequest, 163
   first director of, 161, 172
   permanent collection, 187, 225
   relations with library, 176-79
Bascom-Louise Hotel, *see* Lee's Inn
Baty, Gus, 43
Baty, James, 111
Baty, Roliver, 98
Beale, Callie, 44
Benefits for gallery, 176, 177, 179, 187

Index

Benefits for library, 89, 90, 135, 149
Benét, Laura, 143
Benét, Stephen Vincent, **55-56**, 75, 143
   John Brown's Body, 55, 75
   The Devil and Daniel Webster, 55
Benét, William Rose, 143
Betz, Katy, 196
Biedron, Charlotte, 195
Blair, Bess W., 146
   as trustee president, 203
Bookcase, first, *see* Hudson Library
Boynton, Charles A., Jr., 23
Boynton, Charles A., Sr., 25
   on first library board, 19
Boynton, Frank E., 23
Brevard Federal, 165
Brown, Harriet, 135, 144
Bryant Funeral Home, 97
Burke, Judge Leo, 96

—C—

Calloway, Betts, 157
Calloway, Ethel, 100, 101
Catholic Church, 130
Central House, 31, 63, 111
Chalker, Marna Cobb, 120
Chamber music, 40, 150
   Alexander String Quartet, 187
Chamber of Commerce, 175
Chambers, Helen, 144
   as trustee president, 203
Chambers, Jan, *see* Chmar
Channing, Dr. William E., 35
Cheeononda Garden, 60
Chestnut blight, 73

Chestnut Burr Cottage, 14, *see also* Hines, James A.
Chestnut Lodge, 96
Chetolah, *see* Barratt, G. Watson
Chmar, Jan Chambers, 70, 193, 194
Christman, Will, poetry of, 38, 244
Civic Center, 51
Clark, Sumner, Sr., 43
Cleaveland, John W., mayor, 172, 206
Cleaveland, W. M., 74
Cobb, Gertrude, *see* Holt
Cobb, Jessie M., *see* Harbison, Jessie Cobb
Cobb, Judson M., 22
   Altadona, 23
Cobb, Lucy, 22
Cobb, Marna, *see* Chalker
Cobb, Ty, 89
Condiment Shop, 58
Connemara, 65
Cook, Beverly, *see* Quin
Cook, Mary Bascom, 121
Coward, Nancy Potts, 121
Cranston, Craig, 118
Crisp, Willard, 43
Crumpler, Thomas B., 45, 51, 55
Cullasaja River, 69

—D—

Davis House, *see* Lee's Inn
Day, Marion, *see* Arnold
De Ville, Marilyn "Lynn", 141
De Ville, Ralph, 148
DeWolf & Schmitt, architects, 186
DeWolf, Wendy, 157
Dillard Road (Smith's Road), 114
Duane, Margaretta, *see* Wood

Dugout, 101
Dunning, Priscilla, 145
Durgin, J. H. "Papa", 78
Durgin, Mrs. John, 44

—E—
Edwards, Fred A., 98
Edwards, Louise, *see* Meisel
Edwards, Virginia, *see* Fleming
Electricity, 69, 109
Elliott, Charlotte B., 56, **57-60**, 61, 64
   as eighth librarian, 57, 202
Elliott, Dr. J. B., 56
Elliott, Elizabeth, 125
Elliott, Huger, 125
   as library architect, 51
   as museum director, 51
   radio program of, 60
Elliott, Lucy Huger, 56
Elliott, Lucy P., 49, **56-57**
   as seventh librarian, 56, 202
Ellison, Miss
   as third librarian, 20, 202
Elms, Harriet, 194
Emmons, Reverend Henry, 35-36
Enloe, Representative Jeff, 163
Episcopal Church, 25, 43, 125, 164
Esty, A. S, on first library board, 19

—F—
Farnsworth, P. T., 65
Farnsworth, Sidney W., 165
Fibber Magee's Closet, 193
First motorcar, 46
First movies, 60
First Union Bank, 165
Fleming, Virginia Edwards, 76, 77, 79, 95
   poetry of, 198, 244
Fogartie, Reverend James E., on first library board, 19
Ford, Gerald R., Jr., 124
Franklin, 127
Franklin Library, 93, 122
   Macon Co. Library, 94
Franklin Road, 75, 82, 84
Fund raising, *see* Benefits for gallery, library

—G—
Galax Theatre, 130
Gilbert, Margaret, *see* Hall
Greville, Thomas, 89

—H—
Hale, Edward Everett, 4, 9
Hall House, *see* Satulah House
Hall, Margaret Gilbert, 63, 65, 66
   as trustee president, 203
Hall, Sarah, *see* Paxton
Halleck, Joseph, 3
Ham, Anne, 151
   as twelfth librarian, 151, 202
Harbison home, 95, 189
Harbison, Dorothea "Dolly", 58, 67, 68, 70, 71, 82, 84, **92**, 94, **95**, **97**, **100**, 101, 102, 103, 106, 110, 120, 121, 123, 126, 151, 174, 186, 190, 191
   as acting librarian, 148, 202
   as assistant librarian, 69
   as Girl Scout leader, 130
   as ruling elder, 136
   as Sunday school teacher, 121
   Order of Eastern Star, 136
   reception, fiftieth-year, 146
   starting salary, 85

Index 249

Harbison, Gertrude, 67, 68, **70**, **71**, 73, **75**, 82, 83, 84, **95**, 96, **97**, 98, 99, **100**, 101, 103, 105, 110, 120, 121, 123, 124, 133, 136, 140, 142, 143, 144, 145, 174, 186, 190, 191, 194, 195
   as eleventh librarian, 69, 202
   as longest-serving librarian, **69**
   as treasurer of Biological Station, 159
   as weather observer, 74
   chief interests, **120**
   death of, 158-59
   National Weather Award, 151
   reception, fiftieth-year, 146
   starting salary, 85
Harbison, Jessie Cobb, 21, 22, 23, 26, 159
Harbison, Margaret, 95, 159
Harbison, Professor T. G., 17, 21, **23-28**, 65, 66, 70, 74, 119, 159
   arrival in Highlands, 23
   as founder of Highlands Academy, 24
   as fourth librarian, 26, 202
   as mayor, 205
   as newspaper editor, 24
   as president of Scientific Society, 26
   death of, 111
   education of, 26
   personal library, 27
   personality, 27
   views on pine vs. hemlock, 168
Harbison, Tom C., 105
Harkins, Bess Hines, 73
   poetry of, 8, 36, 79, 198, 201, 244, 245
Harkins, Butler S., 198
   poetry of, 244
Hawkins, Laura, poetry of, 30, 50, 244, 245
Helen's Barn, 43-44
   first annual square dance, 135
Henderson, Ted, 178
Henriques, Captain C. B., 194
Henriques, Jean, 194
   as trustee president, 203
Henry, Joe, 114
Henry, Miller, 114
Henry, Wallace, 44
Herchen, Karen, seventeenth librarian, 185, 202
Herstek, Annette, 186, 192
Highlands
   number of businesses, 175
   overview, 200
Highlands Academy, 24
Highlands Bank, 64
Highlands Cemetery, 36, 40, 120
   Mount Hope Cemetery, 8
Highlands Community Club, 113
Highlands Community Theatre, 135, 136
Highlands Emergency Council, 193
Highlands Garden Club, 133
Highlands Gem Shop, 64
Highlands Improvement Society, 104, 113
Highlands Inn, 3, 111
   Highlands House, 3, 31, 87
   Smith House, 3, 20, 37, 112
Highlands map, 126
Highlands Museum, 74, 113, 119, 123

Botanical Garden, 133
  move into library, 74
  move out of library, 94
Highlands population
  in 1884, 20
  in 1904, 39
  in 1926, 154
  in 1931, 91
  in 1960, 134
  in 1974, 154
  in 1980, 157, 175
  in 1986, 174, 175
  in 1993, 196
Highlands roads
  asphalt paving, 110
  crushed stone paving, 92
  Fourth Street, 108
  Main Street, xii, 19, 43, 52, 65, 84, 125, 130, 133, 134, 165
  parking problem, 133
Highlands School, 130
Highlands Scientific Society, 26
Highlands Taxpayer's Association, 167
Highlands water fountain, 87
Highlands weather
  rain, 46, 74
  snow, 21-22, 101, 110, 186
Highlands, overview
  Sunset Rock, 200
Hildegard's Restaurant, 114
  Smith Cottage, 37, 112
Hill House, 22
Hill, Stanhope W., 22
Hines, Bess, *see* Harkins
Hines, Bessie Hinson, 73, 83
  as trustee president, 203
Hines, James A., 119
  Chestnut Burr Cottage, 14
Hines, Sarah Hicks., 73

  as artist, 79
Holt, A. C. "Gus", 22, 28
Holt, Gertrude Cobb, 22
Holt, Richard "Bill", 28, 70, 72, 79
Horse Cove, 6, 22, 45, 53, 83, 92
Horticultural Society, 39
Hospital Bazaar, 162
Hudson Library
  and Highlands Museum
    move into library, 74
    move out of library, 94
  and Satulah Club, 103-4, 105, 161-62
  and town council, 106, 122, 150
  animals, resident in, 151
  annex for 1993, 186-87
  archives of, 226-28
  audio and video tapes, 156
  birth date, 18
  book cards, 44, 103, 144, 154, 155, 191, 196
  book committee, 32-33, 175-76
  book culling, 32, 33, 143, 154, 155, 175-76
  book purchasing, 33, 39, 71, 103, 124, 133, 144, 150, 154, 155-56, 157, 161, 185, 187, 191
  books catalogued, 39, 142
  building, 47, 139, 171
  children's reading program, 150
  children's room, **94**, 95, 103, 130, 141, 158
  circulation, 65, 69, 91, 123, 151, 156, 157-58, 166, 169, 175, 179, 191
  compass, pocket, 65

Index

computerization, 184-85, 190-92
Dewey Decimal System, **103**, 155
drainage problem, 104-7, 169
financial state of, 39, 85, 86, 88, 89, 90, 165
first bookcase (cupboard), 13, 18, 25, 33, **94-95**, 116, 143, **214-21**
first books, 9, 11, 52, 95, 116, 123, **214-21**
founder of, 9
Franklin usage, 93, 122
holdings, 13, 39, 50, 65, 124, 130, 134, 142, 143, 156, 175, 186, 193
in the schoolhouse, 13, 14, 15, 18, 25, 52, 55
incorporation, 30
incorporation into county system, 160
incorporation into regional system, 140
large-type books, 156
lecture series, 148, 187
membership in N.C. Library Association, 123
myth of single box, 11
name changes, 132, 179
name origin, 9
negotiations for new building, 164-65
new building dedications, 52, 172
new building plaque, 181
official recognition, 18
oldest association, 18
oldest public library, 11
open all week, 150
open all winter, 142

overdue books, 65, 75, 83, 124
paperbacks, 150
patrons, numbers of, 139, 157, 191, 193
public but private, 161
reorganization, 179
Satulah Room, 104, 140, 142, 145, 148, 158, 161-62
select committee, 178
state grant, 163, 164, 168
tree issue, 166-68
trustee presidents, 203
trustees, 207-13
Hudson Library Annex, *see* Satulah Club
Hudson, A. W., 102, 141
Hudson, Ella Emmons, **3-9**, 34, 40, 102, 119, 166
as library's namesake, 9
Hudson, Scott, 89
Hutchinson, C. H., 65
Connemara, 65

—I—

Islington House, *see* King's Inn
Ivins, Colonel Charles, 148

—J—

Jacobs, Mrs. G. A., 7
Jargon Society, *see* Williams
Jewell, Mrs. William (Mary), 138
John Martin, *see* Magazines in library
Jones, Bobby, 43, 84, 89, 90
Jussely, Nancy, *see* Lyle

—K—

Kanonah Lodge, 65
Keener, Martha Hedden, fourteenth librarian, 152, 202
Kelsey, Dr. Harry, 65

Kelsey, Mrs. Samuel, 7
Kelsey, Samuel Truman, Sr., 16, 20, 23, 24, 65, 118
 as first trustee president, 18, 203
 death of, 61
 Kanonah Lodge, 65
 on first library board, 19
Kibbee (Dr. George W.) house, 14
Kibbee, Dr. George W., 14
Kibbee, Laura G. "Kittie", **13-15**
 as first librarian, 13, 202
 as pantomimist, 14
King's Inn, 13
Kuehl, Simone, *see* Sorge

—L—

Ladies' Industrial and Floral Society, 38, 39, 85, 113
Lake Sequoyah, 69, 110
Lamb, Floyd, 43
Lapham, Dr. Mary, 41, 51
Lee's Inn, 12, 130
 Bascom-Louise Hotel, 129, 131, 225
 Davis House, 10, 12, 19, 118
 King's Inn II, 12
 Martin House, 12
 Tricemont Terrace, 118, 129
Lee, Richard, 12, 130
Leebrick, Gil, 173
Leebrick, Jacquelyn "Jackie", 177
 as artist, 172
 as first gallery director, 161, 172
 as teacher of photography, 173
Lend-a-Hand Society, 4, 9, 12
 binding principle, 9

Lovingood, Joey, 12
Lyle, Nancy Jussely, 73
Lyon, Elizabeth, 73

—M—

Macon County Board of Commissioners, 141
Macon County Book Fair, 142
Magazines in library
 John Martin, 76, 98, 99
 St. Nicholas, 34-35, 41, 55, 79, 80, 198
Marett, Leila Lewis, **64-65**, 66, 68, 88, 89, 153, 166
 as tenth librarian, 64, 202
Marett, S. T., 64
Martin House, *see* Lee's Inn
Mashburn, Joel, 150
Masonic Lodge, 46, 60, 66
Matthews, Dr. W. A., 127
Matthews, Mary Pugh, 96-97
Mayors of Highlands, 205-6
McCollum, Dee
 poetry of, 68, 148, 160, 245
McDowell, Charlie, 114
McDowell, Gladys, 141
McGuffey *Readers*, 115
McIntosh, Gertrude "Gert", 152, 154, 177, 182, 191
 as fifteenth librarian, 152, 202
 as historian, 165
 as story lady, 147, 156
 Rotary Award, 165
McNamee, Sarah Thompson, 71, 97-99, 100, 102, 195
Medlin, June Thompson, 97, 99, 101
Meisel, Louise Edwards, 79, 83
Melvin, Richard, 143, 163
Michaux, André, 23

Index

Moccasin War, 20
Modlin, Cynthia, 161, 185
Monroe, J. Blanc, 168
Moore, Bob, 161
Morris, Ralph, 196
Morrow, Lois, 194
Mount Hope Cemetery, *see* Highlands Cemetery
Mountain Findings, 150, 162, 176, 180
Mountain Shore Construction, 165
Mountain, The (Unitarian Center), 35, 85
Murphy, Gene, 44

—N—

Nall, Rebecca C., 89
    as acting librarian, 64
    as teacher and principal of Highlands School, 64
    as trustee president, 64, 203
Nature Center, *see* Highlands Museum
Nick's Calico Cottage, 14
Norris, Helen Hill, 11, 12, 13, 14, 53

—O—

O'Brien, Estelle, 144
Ordway, Allen, 82
Ordway, Margaret, 93
Owens, Jessie Potts, 121

—P—

Palmer, Senator Joe, 163
Parry, Judge H. L., 86
Parry, Mrs. H. L., 85
Passmore Trail, 83
Paxton, Sarah Hall, 121
Pierce, Harvey, 169, 181

Pierson, J. Quincy, 119
Pierson, Lanette, 194
Pierson, Lucile, *see* Reese
Pierson, Norma T. "Boots", 111, 155, 178, **180-81**, 182
    as hospital chairman, 180
    as Mountain Findings facilitator, 180
    as planning chairman, 180
    as trustee president, 180, 203
    as zoning chairman, 180
    death of, 180
    DuPree Award, 181
Pierson, Val, 111
Potts, Arthur B. "Shine", 27
Potts, David, 43
Potts, Jessie, *see* Owens
Potts, Nancy, *see* Coward
Potts, Steve, 136, 142, 165, 206
Presbyterian Church, 19, 120, 121
Pugh Memorial Fund, 97
Pugh, Franklin, 97
Pugh, Lea, 97
Pugh, Mary, *see* Matthews

—Q—

Quin, Beverly Cook, 130
Quinnett, Marita, 143

—R—

Ravenel, Margaretta A., 19, 51
Ravenel, Marguerite, 122
    as trustee president, 203
    Wolf Ridge, 90
Ravenel, S. P., Sr., 19, 39, 54, 168
Recreation Bridge, 150
Reese, Harold, 124
Reese, J. Walter, 51, 52

Reese, Joseph W., 28, 45, 53, 114, 126
Reese, Lucile Pierson, 70, 126
Reese, Robert W., 51
Reese, Thomas C., 14
Reid, John, 174, **181-82**
   as Episcopal dean and rector, 182
   as hospital chairman, 182
   as master of Masonic Lodge, 182
   as trustee president, 160, 181, 203
   death of, 181
   honored as trustee president, 181
Reinke, Dr. E. E., 123
Rhodes, Anne Altstaetter, 72, 77, 101
Rhodes, Robert L., 169
Rice, Christina Anderson, 49, **61-64**
   as ninth librarian, 61, 202
   poetry of, 62-63
Rice, Elizabeth, 63
Rice, Eloise, 63
Rice, Luther W., 63
Rice, W. Herbert, 72
Richardson, H. H., 168
Rideout, James, 21, 43, 130
Rogers, Albert, 111
Rowe, Jeff, 194
Rudisill, Andrea, acting librarian, 185
Russell House, 5, 6, 22
Russell, Melinda, thirteenth librarian, 152, 202

—S—

St. Nicholas, *see* Magazines in library

Salinas, Mrs. A. J., 83
Sanatorium, 41
Sanders, Carla, 194
Sanders, Leslie, 194
Sargent, Dr. Charles S., 23, 70
Sargent, Dr. Ralph M., 78, 117
Sargent, Louise A., 78, 117
   as trustee president, 203
Satulah Club, 113
   formation of, 104
   Highlands Community Club, 113
   Highlands Improvement Society, 104
   move into library, 103
Satulah House, 130
Schmitt Building Contractors, 186
Schoolhouse, 13, 14, 15, 18, 25, 48, 52, 55, 73
Selleck, H. P., 25
Selleck, Mrs. H. P., 32
Sellers, Anne Anderson, 121
Service, Betty, 147, **153-54**, 156, 166
   as mentor of Gert McIntosh, 153, 155
   as Sarasota librarian, 153
   as storyteller, 154
Shay, Esther Cunningham, 56
Sheldon, Frank S., 19, 42
Sheldon, Mary L., 20
   as second librarian, 19, 202
Sheldon, Olive White, 42
Sherrill, Delores "Dee", 141
   as trustee president, 203
Shortia galacifolia, 23
Shortoff community, 7, 40, 53, 83
Shortoff Mountain, 2
Shuptrine, Hubert, 144
Slagle, Charles, 65

Index

Sloan's Gap, 87, 95
Sloan, Henry W., 60, 73, 105, 137
   Cheeononda Garden, 60
Smith's Road, *see* Dillard Road
Smith House, *see* Highlands Inn
Smith, J. Jay, 25, 29, 37, 111, 112, **113-15**
   as mayor, 114, 205
   as owner of first sawmill, 114
   as postmaster, 114
   as surveyor of Dillard Road, 114
   as wood carver, 114
   death of, 113
Smith, Mary Chapin, 29, 31-35, 37, 40, 42, 50, 51, 52, 62, 68, 83-85, 89, 92, 111, **112-13**
   as acting librarian, 45, 55
   as book committee chairman, 32
   as historian, 25, 53, 90, 113
   as illustrator for Asa Gray, 113
   as organizer of Highlands Improvement Society, 113
   as student of botany, 112
   as trustee president, 44, 112, 203
   death of, 112
   poetry of, 21, 112, 113, 143, 245
Smith, Victor, 100
Sorge, Simone Kuehl, 144, **182-84**, 194, 195
   as library volunteer, 182
   Rotary Award, 182
State of North Carolina, 162, 163
Staub House, *see* Hill House

Staub, Albertina, 29, 32, 33, 38, 39, 44, 45, 103, 111, **119-20**
   as a founder of Biological Station, 119
   as realtor and insurance agent, 119
   as sixth librarian, 30, 119, 202
   as Sunday school teacher, 120
   death of, 119
   starting salary, 38
Staub, Professor Albert, 119
Stock market crash, 85
Strader, Carolyn, 185-86, 190, 191, 192
   as eighteenth librarian, 185, 202
Strain, Tracy E., sixteenth librarian, 185, 202
Sullivan, Linda, 186
Sullivan, William W., 116
Summer, Otto F., 100, 206
Sunset Rock, 54, 196, 200

—T—

Talbot, Virginia, 186, 192
Talley, Bobby, 43
Terhune, Sooky, 124
Thomas, Senator Bo, 163
Thompson, Dr. Percy, 97
Thompson, June, *see* Medlin
Thompson, Mrs. H. P. P. (Helen M.), 97
Thompson, Peggy, 97, 98
Thompson, Sarah, *see* McNamee
Town House Motel, 19
Town Square, 19
Townsend, Eric, 165
Traylor, Dorothy "Dot", 192-93
Trees

altitude oak, 111, 133, 134, 168
Carolina hemlock, 168
dogwoods on Main, 133
library's white pines, 166-68
red maples on Main, 134
Tricemont Terrace, *see* Lee's Inn
Trowbridge, W. C., first trustee treasurer, 19

—U—

University of North Carolina, 143

—V—

Valentine, James, 156

—W—

Warren, Minnie, 52
Water fountain, Main and Fourth, 92
Wells, Louise Emmons, 3, **40-41**, 34, 35
  as Hudson Library's founder, **9**
  death of, 40-41
Wheeler, Guy F.
  first trustee secretary, 19
White, Becky, 80, 81, 82
White, Eleanor C., 16
White, Elias D., 127
White, Jessie E., 126
  as fifth librarian, 28, 126, 202
  death of, 127
White, Olive M., *see* Sheldon
White, Robb, **80-82**
White, T. Baxter, xii, 16, 18, 25, 28, 36, 44, **61**, 127
  as first settler, 18
  as first trustee vice president, 18
  as insurance agent, 19, 42
  as Justice of the Peace, 61
  as longest-serving trustee president, 42, 203
  as news correspondent, 36, 61
  as superintendent of Christian Endeavor, 19
  death of, 61
  departure for California, 42
  first postmaster, 19
Whiteside Mountain, 2, 130
Wilcox, Collin, 135
Wilcox, Jeremy, 71
Wilcox, Virginia "Ted", 194
  as story lady, 135
Williams, Jonathan, **148-49**
  as founder of Jargon Society, 149
  poetry of, 148, 149, 174, 245
Wilson, Bill, 43
Wilson, Everette, 70
Wilson, Woodrow, 45, 46, 61
Wilson, Zella, 59
Wit's End, 63
Wolf Ridge, 90
Woman's Club, 150
Wood, Margaretta Duane, 84
Wright, Charles N., 43
Wright, Harry R., 72, 79, 96
  as mayor, 163, 206
Wright, Helen, 43

—Z—

Zahner, Dr. Robert, 167
Zahner, Kenyon B., 114
Zoellner, Henry, 111